For kim and Puenktchen

Acknowledgements

I have my wonderful publisher Kim Maya Sutton from Safkhet Publishing to thank for the idea for *Grumpies on Board*.

Last year we were on a trip to complete some crazy challenges for my previous novel, *Three Little Birds*. As we raced from challenge to challenge, she regaled me with hilarious anecdotes (and some hair-raising ones) about her holidays and voyages with her grouchy father. We swapped "grumpy stories" as I too have spent decades dragging my own grump about the world on numerous trips. She suggested I write a book for those, who would like to do something different on holiday—a "Book it" list of ideas for those of us, who are older but are not ready to give up on what life has to offer. And so, *Grumpies on Board* came to be.

Grumpies on Board attempts to cajole you, the reader, into booking life-enhancing trips and will, I hope, encourage you to grab life by the horns. We are, after all, here for a good time, not a long time.

I would also like to thank the team at Kuoni Travel in Solihull, especially Mary Janiec, Polly Waterhouse and Matt Barley for their input and recommendations, putting up with my endless demands, changes to plans and bookings, frantic emails and organising some fantastic trips for us. Special thanks also go to Kirker Travel.

Thank you for the memories.

13/8

HEM

Please renew or return items by the date shown on your receipt

www.hertsdirect.org/libraries

Renewals and enquiries:

0300 123 4049

Textphone for hearing or speech impaired

0300 123 4041

Hertfordshire

Safkhet
Publishing

522 269 97 7

First published in 2015 by Safkhet Select, Wilhelmshaven, Germany
Safkhet Select is an imprint of Safkhet Publishing GbR
www.safkhetpublishing.com

Text Copyright 2015 by Carol E Wyer
Design Copyright 2015 Safkhet Publishing GbR

ISBN 978-3-945651-05-6

Printed and bound by Lightning Source International

Typeset in Crimson, Ale and Wenches, and DK Butterfly Ball with Adobe InDesign

Find out more about Carol on www.carolewyer.co.uk
and www.facing50withhumour.com
and meet her on Facebook at
www.facebook.com/pages/Carol-E-Wyer/221149241263847

Carol E Wyer   *author*

Kim Maya Sutton   *managing editor and cover artist*

Sally Neuhaus   *cover designer*

Walter Richardson   *proofreader*

William Banks Sutton *copy editor*

 The colophon of Safkhet is a representation of the ancient Egyptian goddess of wisdom
and knowledge, who is credited with inventing writing.
Safkhet Publishing is named after her because the founders met in Egypt.

INTRODUCTION

Are you a grumpy guts, who hates going on holiday and sharing your space with noisy families? Are you looking for somewhere different where you can try out new activities, or just somewhere away from the madding crowds where you and your other half can relax? Look no further. I have the answers here along with many suggestions— some rather surprising—to ensure you both, however grumpy you may be, cherish your time away.

We "older folk" are becoming more demanding about our holiday destinations. No longer satisfied with the usual haunts, we are roaming further afield. We are following in the footsteps of our children, who took off on gap years in their late teens to exotic destinations we had never before considered visiting.

So, what sort of holidays are there out there? Far more than you might have considered. Pack your bags and get ready for some Extreme Active Ageing? Then keep reading, after all, YOLO.

Mr. Grumpy has decided to rate some of the trips for you. They are only his opinion so do not be completely swayed by them. He is after all, a very grumpy grump.

Rating Scores:

😠😠😠😠😠 – no way would he go on this holiday.

😠😠😠😠 – not keen to go on this holiday.

😠😠😠 – might go at a push.

😠😠 – this is a possible.

😠 – he would give it a go.

😠 – good trip

😠 – recommended.

**AS SOON AS the STEWARDESS SERVES
the COFFEE, the AIRLINER encounters
turBuLence.
davis's expLanation of ROGER'S Law:
SERVING COFFEE On aircraft causes
turBuLence.**

A is for airports, abseiling, adults-only, adventure holidays, airplanes, alternative holidays, arctic boot camp, art, and ayurvedic holidays.

A large number of journeys begin at the **airport**, but it is a place hated by most grumble-guts. My other half becomes even grumpier than usual the second we enter an airport. I put this down to one of several factors: the long queues at check in; the fact that almost every flight we take departs at some silly hour requiring us to be there, baggy-eyed, at three o'clock in the morning; the drag through security where one of us will inevitably set off the alarm bells on the metal detector even when dressed in only pants and socks; or the prospect of being confined in an area where all there is to do is shop, eat, drink, and spend. Whatever the reason, we both sink into a gloom before we even board the aircraft.

To make matters worse, there is the prospect of the flight ahead to add to your woes. Regardless of what time you check in, you will discover that the person checking you and your grumpy onto the flight has assigned the seats in front or behind yours to a family with young children. At best, you will get a toddler, who kicks your seat all the way to your destination, or at worst, you will get the screaming baby, who howls down your ear until the flight begins to descend, when the child will finally fall into a deep sleep.

Whatever happens, do not catch the eye of the child, who peers at you from the seat in front. Last month, my husband made that mistake. The child insisted on standing on his seat and staring at us. Children have a sixth sense when it comes to grumpy old people like me and my husband. They are like cats, who know you are allergic to them, yet insist on purring around your feet or launching themselves into your lap while you sneeze uncontrollably.

This child was no exception. I tried to warn my husband: You should never engage in face-pulling or chat with them. They will find you even more intriguing. Husband made the mistake of snarling. The child loved that. The toddler then insisted on popping up and pulling faces at us throughout the flight—all four hours and thirty-seven minutes of it.

Do not get me wrong; I like children. I am just less tolerant of them than I used to be, especially when I want some quiet time. My advice is to ignore them and whatever you do, do not smile or growl at them.

Be prepared for the flight. Take earplugs to drown out noise or earbuds so you can listen to music. Buy your other half two miniature bottles of whisky as soon as the trolley appears to ensure they fall into a slumber or grit your teeth tightly and distract him or her with the following trivia facts:

- You can fit 45 mid-size cars on only one wing of a Boeing 747-400.
- There are approximately 200,000 flights every day around the world.
- You can fit six million golf balls inside a Boeing 757 freighter.
- One windscreen or window frame of the Boeing 747-400s cockpit, costs as much as a BMW. (Not sure, which model of BMW they mean. I expect they don't mean the second-hand one for sale near our house. It has done 100,000 miles, is several shades of faded red and is a bargain at £700.)
- When Concorde used to fly over the Middle East on the early Bahrain routes, there were complaints that the sonic booms upset the camels and ruined their sex lives. (I am curious as to how the locals discovered this fact.)
- Your tea on an airplane will taste funny because proper

tea is made with water that has been heated to 100 degrees centigrade — the temperature at, which it boils on the ground. Unfortunately, in the reduced-pressure environment of an aircraft cabin, the boiling point of water is lowered to around 90 degrees centigrade, which means that the brewing process is unsatisfactory. Good reason to have a bottle of wine instead.

- The world's oldest airline is KLM, established in 1919. Its first flight between Amsterdam and London took place on 17th May, 1920.
- A man once wore seventy items of clothing in a Chinese airport to avoid the baggage charge. No, it was not a Ryanair flight.
- British Airways lost the luggage of an average nine passengers on every jumbo jet flight in the first half of 2008, according to a study by the Association of European Airlines.
- The wingspan of the A380 is longer than the aircraft itself. Wingspan: 79.75 metres. Length: 72.72 metres.
- British Airways was once the world's largest purchaser of champagne, with passengers drinking a minimum of 90,000 cases every year. (I wonder if they purchased all this champagne by selling the contents of the suitcases they lost in 2008.)
- It took him two years, but Michael Lotito, a French entertainer, ate a Cessna 150. Lotito deliberately ate indigestible objects, such as bicycles, beds, shopping carts, chandeliers, a coffin, and the aforementioned Cessna 150, among other things. He said these things were not a problem, but bananas and hard-boiled eggs gave him indigestion.

Have you buckled up? Time to head off to your chosen destination.

"as you exit the plane, please make sure to gather all of your belongings. anything left behind will be distributed evenly among the flight attendants. please do not leave children or spouses."

I am not sure how adventurous you are but **abseiling** courses and holidays are readily available worldwide from Kangaroo Point in Brisbane, Australia to the Peak District in the United Kingdom.

The word "abseil" comes from the German word for rope "seil" and "ab", which means to go down. I believe the German word for "Aaargh!" is similar to ours. Listen out for it as you hurtle from the top of a tall structure.

Abseiling is suitable for people of all ages and fitness levels and no special gear is needed. Being over fifty does not preclude you from this activity. The Northamptonshire Fifty Plus Club with over one hundred and eighty members, even has a few eighty-year-olds, who are up for all sorts of challenges, and abseiling is one of the activities they have tried.

It is not just members of such clubs, who are experiencing thrills later in life. Approximately thirty-five percent of all trips made abroad are made by people over fifty years old, and they are not merely going to hotels and flopping by the pool. Research from the Foreign and Commonwealth Office's Travel Advice Unit reveals that *nearly seventy percent* of the over-fifties say that they are more adventurous with their trips now than they were ten years ago. Over a third have visited more than twenty countries and almost a fifth have taken part in adventure activities like bungee jumping or abseiling on recent holidays.

I suspect it depends on how adventurous you are feeling as to how far you are willing to go and what activities you are willing to take up, but I recommend you just go for it!

In May 2014, Doris Long celebrated her 100th birthday and confirmed her status as the World Oldest Abseiler with a record breaking descent from the Spinnaker Tower in Portsmouth with ITV News Meridian presenter, Fred Dinenage.

Doris has abseiled several times over the years for charity with various celebrities, who were willing to accompany her.

😑😑😑😑😑: Mr. Grumpy said, "Not a chance of me going on an abseiling holiday. You'll have to find another way to bump me off."

Mr. G and I have spent many years tracking down hotels that have child-free zones, child-free areas, or no children at all. Following an episode (related below) that involved Mr. G, a small child, and a swimming pool, I deemed it wise to book into hotels that ensure we are separated from children.

Some travel companies offer holidays for couples or **adults-only** holidays. Make sure you do your research because although the company may offer a couples-only retreat or "exclusive for adults", often the hotel allows children under the age of sixteen years.

Club Med offers a large choice of club holidays, with adults-only villages available throughout the summer in Italy, the Maldives, Mexico, Tunisia, Turkey, and Turks & Caicos.

H10 hotels are specifically for adults with hotels in Spain, the Canary Islands, Italy, Germany, UK, Portugal, Cuba, and the Dominican Republic. Join their loyalty programme to get rewards or upgrade to their Privilege service for some added bonuses such as sea view rooms, slippers, Nespresso Coffee Machine, and other treats. (My bathroom cabinet is full of such goodies including some small candles, lush creamy body lotion, Clarins body oil and a strangely shaped loofah.)

Luxury Resort Plus have all-inclusive adult only resorts in luxurious locations such as Barbados, the Bahamas, Mexico, Jamaica, and Tahiti, as well as some European destinations. Perfect for romance, luxury, and a blissfully peaceful holiday.

Spoil Yourself holidays offer boutique accommodation in Turkey, Greece, Italy, Mallorca, St Lucia, Thailand, and Bali.

There are other hotels world-wide that offer "adult only" facilities or are "adult only" hotels. The model is most widely available at beach destinations, where hoteliers are focussed on travelling couples, who would prefer a more romantic atmosphere.

Once such hotel is The Glenmere Mansion to be found in New

York's Hudson Valley. It sits in one hundred and fifty acres and was voted the number one Romantic Hideaway Hotel in 2011.

In Mexico, you will find El Dorado Casitas Royale. Those of you, who book a private casita on the beach will be able to delight in having your own Jacuzzi, private beach beds, a butler service, and access to the amenities next door at the Karisma Hotel's El Dorado Royale.

Ponta dos Ganchos, Santa Catarina in Southern Brazil is situated on a peninsula and has twenty-five villas each with private verandas and hammocks. This really is a retreat away from the world.

Be prepared for the ultimate in relaxation. Cambridge Beaches and Resort and Spa on Bermuda, not only features a spectacular spa but has an acclaimed restaurant, fabulous landscaped gardens, and a lap pool.

Imagine our delight when we discovered a hotel that offered an "adults only" area. The Hotel Volcán on Lanzarote, one of the Canary Islands, is the flagship hotel for The Total Hotel Experience Group. The hotel is delightful, resembling a Lanzarote village at the foot of a volcano, situated behind the exclusive Marina Rubicón yachting harbour.

You cannot fail but be impressed by the magnificent entrance to reception, itself housed in the "volcano". The entrance is a copy of the famous Tequise church of "Nostra Senora de Guadalupe" and you would be forgiven for thinking you had made an error and were not in fact, at a hotel.

Sunbathing terraces are equally impressive. Some surround a meandering pool while others are adjacent to smaller pools or the large main pool where black rocks appear to tumble down to the water and exotic plants sit proudly by the water's edge.

Nestled within the "village" are romantic courtyards where you can read a book and appreciate some shade.

Inside the volcano, you will be astounded by the waterfall that gently cascades to a seating area. But for grumpy old people, best of all is an area purely for adults.

Also known as THe Club, this area is tucked away from the main areas. Within THe Club is a private dining room where breakfast and complimentary afternoon tea are served and, each evening, a courtesy bar is set up for all residents of THe club.

On the terrace, you will find a private sunbathing area overlooking El Castillo de las Coloradas and the island of Fuerteventura. There is a swimming pool purely for THe Club residents as well as open-air Jacuzzis and large Balinese beds on which to lounge upon.

In brief, it is an ideal place to spend your holiday should you desire peace, with no children attempting to jump on you as you swim up and down the pool, or shrieking beside you at breakfast.

Imagine sipping sundowners on your private terrace overlooking the sea in perfect peace.

The Hotel Volcán is one of several hotels in the Spanish-owned Total Hotel Experience chain; you can find more of them throughout the Canary Islands.

Although the hotel accepts children, you will not find any in this part of it. Book early. Rooms and suites here get booked very quickly. It goes to prove there are lots of us grumps, who prefer child-free time away.

There is no doubt in my mind that a child-free holiday can be the most relaxing, especially if you tend to be a little cranky some days. Have a look about and see what is on offer for your budget. Hope to see you at the cocktail bar!

The last time I booked into a hotel that accepted children, we found ourselves in a room overlooking two small swimming pools. The room had a splendid balcony and my overworked, highly stressed curmudgeon, who was ready for some serious *R and R*, plonked himself outside on the reclining bed. A few minutes later, he dozed off. Soon after that, a small child arrived at one of the pools. The child was moderately noisy and woke my husband, who huffed and pulled out a book to read. We accepted that children do not have volume knobs and expected a little noise. What we did not expect was for the child to suddenly transform into an uncontrollable shrieking banshee. He decided to yell, scream, and make more noise than one child should humanly be able to create. He did not stop. His mother must have been deaf or so used to her offspring's vociferous noises that she did nothing to placate or quieten him. He marched up and down the pool screaming, "Captain Scambut" over and over again. By now, other guests were looking over at the child and tutting but no one asked the woman to silence her child.

My poor husband tried to cover his ears with his hands. He glowered politely over the balcony at the mother. He coughed to attract attention and was ignored. He picked up a book to read but the noise was too much for anyone to concentrate.

Mr. Grumpy huffed again and said in a loud voice, "You would think some people would be able to control their children." The child, aware he had attracted an audience, became noisier.

Mr. Even-Grumpier-Than-Normal picked up his book once more, at which point the child let out an ear-piercing scream that chilled everyone to the bone. My husband threw his book down with an almighty thud, leapt to his feet and hanging over the balcony, yelled, "That's it! Shut up you little…!"

Every sunbather sat up in astonishment. Heads appeared from behind books like a mob of meerkats popping up from behind a hill. The mother finally realized her child was annoying people and gave him a bag of sweets to chomp on. I tried to hide behind my iPad.

I am not sure how news got back to reception but shortly afterwards we received a call from the manager. He invited us to move to another room—one not overlooking the children's pool. It turned out to be a much larger room with a lounge, a private balcony and a view over the harbour. Maybe it pays to yell at children.

I have recently discovered that there are to be some changes for travellers commencing next year, including the introduction of more child-free sections on long-haul planes, with state-of-the-art soundproofing. Excuse me for a second while I let out a small cheer. What an old grumpy pants I am.

🧓: Mr. Grumpy says: "I am too old and too grumpy to put up with other people's children. If it isn't quiet and child-free, I'm not going. So there."

Abseiling might not be your choice of activity or adventure holiday, but **adventure holidays** can be found almost anywhere. My recommendation for a great adventure holiday is to go on safari in South Africa. This is not necessarily as unaffordable as you might think because accommodation can be very reasonably priced. Finding deals and bargains just requires research, innovation, expert advice, and—in some cases—the ability to step out of your comfort zone and hit the road on your own.

Thanks to the internet and Smart phones, information is at our fingertips. On our travels through South Africa, we met several middle-aged and elderly couples, who were travelling with laptops and mobiles and were making reservations as they went along. It gave them freedom to stay longer in one region, and the flexibility to change their travel itineraries or negotiate rates at local lodges.

Travel off-season, and lodge rates drop by up to forty percent. Camps in South Africa are open year round, so why not take advantage of the quieter May-July winter months when the weather is cooler, animal sightings are better, and prices are lower? Another option is to stay in a small, owner-operated lodge that doesn't have the high overheads of the big chains and therefore can be more flexible. Finally, choose lesser known lodges and resorts to ensure you keep costs down. We discovered lodges that boasted excellent facilities and food, and were much friendlier than some of the larger ones.

Going on safari is a "must-do." We relished every moment of it, even when we were caught in a torrential rainstorm one night while trying to track down a lion.

My other half appreciated the cartoon-like moment when having accidentally sat on a humongous ant nest while photographing hippos, I was forced to drop my trousers in haste and let several biting ants escape, all the while attempting to hold on in the back of a speeding jeep.

Of all the holidays we have taken, this one was right up there as the best.

: Mr. Grumpy said: "Loved it from start to finish. Top holiday. I'd recommend it to anyone."

A BIG~GAME HUNTER WENT ON SAFARI WITH HIS WIFE AND MOTHER~IN~LAW. ONE EVENING, WHILE STILL DEEP IN THE JUNGLE, THE WIFE AWOKE TO FIND HER MOTHER GONE. RUSHING TO HER HUSBAND, SHE INSISTED ON THEM BOTH TRYING TO FIND HER MOTHER. THE HUNTER PICKED UP HIS RIFLE, PUT ON HIS HAT, AND STARTED TO LOOK FOR HER. IN A CLEARING NOT FAR FROM THE CAMP, THEY CAME UPON A CHILLING SIGHT: THE MOTHER~IN~LAW WAS BACKED UP AGAINST A THICK, IMPENETRABLE BUSH, AND A LARGE MALE LION STOOD FACING HER. THE WIFE CRIED, "WHAT ARE WE GOING TO DO?"

"NOTHING," SAID THE HUNTER HUSBAND. "THE LION GOT HIMSELF INTO THIS MESS, LET HIM GET HIMSELF OUT OF IT."

Although I began this book discussing airplanes, I would like to put in a short section about them here and mention **air shows**. If your partner, like mine, is aircraft mad then there are some exceptionally good air shows that might thrill and entertain. Combine a trip away with a day at an air show for an added dimension to your trip.

The Bournemouth Air Festival in Dorset, UK, is the largest free annual air show in Europe and combines two great things: airplanes and the beach. The four-day festival draws over a million spectators for its aerial shows, hot air balloon rides and fun in the sun.

Canada's largest air show, the Abbotsford Airshow attracts more than 125,000 spectators each August and has some of the most exciting performers including the Canadian Snowbirds, SkyHawks (parachuting team), Thunderbirds and Blue Angels, all of, whom will keep you oohing and aahing.

My favourite, the Paris Airshow, is the world's oldest and largest. Established in 1909, it is currently held every other year at Le Bourgeot Airport in Paris, France.

🙂: Mr. Grumpy says, "Better than Euro Disney," but he did not like all the crowds.

Serious plane enthusiasts with pilot's licences might fancy a flying holiday for licenced pilots. Pilots Paradise, who are Florida based, offer you fly-in accommodation, PA28 aircraft, and the opportunity to explore the USA and Bahamas. Fly yourselves to the Bahamas, the Keys, New York and beyond with a light aircraft that is exclusively yours without all the added costs.

Included—at no additional cost—is use of their one-bedroom studio accommodation based on a fly-in community home. You will be staying here as private guests in their family home.

For those without a pilot's licence but a passion for planes, send them on a plane spotting break or book a hotel near an airport where they can watch the planes take off and land all day while you sunbathe. Or, thumb through this book to take a quick peek at what you can find in the section about unique places to stay.

Airboarding, which consists of throwing yourself headfirst downhill on what looks like an inflatable sled or sledge, is the latest craze on the winter slopes. It is a high-tech twist on traditional winter sledding.

It was invented in the 1990s by Joe Steiner from Switzerland, who injured his leg while snowboarding and wanted a safer way to get the thrill of the hill. It was introduced to the United States in 2004 at the Hoodoo Ski Area in Oregon and now is offered at about a half dozen resorts across the country. It is extremely popular in Europe with children and parents and is generally perceived as being suitable for any age group interested in hitting the slopes.

Airboards are inflated raft-like sledges with underside grooves and side handles that allow you to turn using forearm pressure and shifting body weight. You grab the board, take a few running steps, plop down on your stomach headfirst, and you are off.

One of the appeals of this sport is the cost. Unlike skiing, you do not need to invest in expensive attire. Your main purchase should only be a helmet, which is compulsory. Now that fact alone should please a grumpy guts.

Beginners are welcome. You attend classes and will be using airboard trails as you head down the slopes, consequently you should have no fear of speeding into skiers.

Unfortunately, I could not find any holiday companies offering this as a holiday, but research the subject and you will find slopes where it is offered.

Go on, book a trip and throw someone you love down a hill on an airboard.

Snow is not white. Snow is actually clear and colourless.

😠😠😠😠: Mr. Grumpy says, "After you, my dear."

For those, who prefer less adventure, consider an **alternative holiday**. Choose from locations worldwide, pursue new ideas and unearth talents you did not even suspect you possessed. Take the opportunity to reassess your life, redefine your needs and re-set your priorities.

Attempt courses that ordinarily you would not think of—circle dancing, laughter yoga, meditation, Tai Chi, tree planting, poetry, or singing. You may be pleasantly surprised, that is once you stop your other half from sniggering at the idea.

😠😠😠😠😠: Mr. Grumpy says, "I do not need to reassess my life or re-set my priorities. I am very content being a miserable old grumble-guts, thank you."

The masochist in me thinks it would be amusing to send my other half on **a boot camp in the Arctic**. I would go with him. For motivational purposes, of course. That way we could both shape up and take on a challenge of a lifetime.

Book a well-being break with Discover the World and you too could be jogging on winter trails, learning the art of cross-country skiing, ingesting pure Arctic air and staying at the jaw-dropping beautiful Icehotel in Lapland.

The contrast of crisp clean air blowing out all the pollution accumulated in my lungs over the decades, drinking pure water from rivers and then basking in the warmth of a sauna appeals to my ageing brain.

I am no exercise fiend but I believe a trip here would be the kickstart I require to begin to look after myself and gain a true sense of well-being.

Imagine jogging (slowly, very slowly) past herds of reindeer and snow-covered trees and over a beautiful winter wonderland with only the sound of your breath as you wheeze along. You can do all this with a guide, who will also take you cross-country skiing.

A few days here, running, skiing and recovering in the saunas will reinvigorate you and put a smile—albeit a frozen one—on your face.

There are many other optional winter activities to enhance your stay at the Icehotel, from husky sledging and reindeer safaris to snowmobiling and ice sculpting so if you slope off the running you will find another activity to work those muscles.

Art holidays are very popular, in truth almost too popular. I spent fifty minutes queuing to get into the Louvre in Paris and a further four hours shuffling about from room to room, squashed among crowds of Chinese people, who waved cameras at everything there in spite of signs forbidding photographs. I did not see Da Vinci's *Mona Lisa* due to the fact it is actually quite a small portrait and there were about sixty people between it and me. It is one of the most popular exhibits so be prepared to jump up and down to get a view of it, or wait patiently until you reach the front of the crowd.

With 652,300 square feet of exhibition space, five floors and seventeen wings, the grand Louvre is one of the most famous museums in the world. The Louvre contains over 380,000 objects and displays 35,000 works of art. It is said that if one were to walk through the Louvre and spend only four seconds gazing at each object, it would take you three months to get through the, whole museum.

Grumpy Tip: Arrive early, wear comfortable shoes and don't forget to grab a map. You will need it to navigate the many corridors, rooms, and throngs of people.

Mr. Grumpy and I gave up trying to get into the State Hermitage Museum founded by Catherine the Great and housing huge collections of art and antiquities. It might be one of the most famous attractions in St Petersburg but one glance at the enormous queue of people curling around the building sent him scurrying for an early lunch instead.

In Florence, I dragged him to the Uffizi gallery but only after it had closed and the masses that had been blocking every route to it during in the day had finally departed. He admired the exterior and took a couple of photographs, then claimed he couldn't understand all the fuss about Michelangelo's art—the Philistine! It was just as well, because we sat and scoffed ice creams by the Ponte Vecchio instead. When I returned home, I discovered you can watch a virtual tour of the gallery online by clicking on the official Uffizi site. That certainly saves you getting trampled by crowds and missing out on some of the sights.

I love art, and do not let my words put you off booking a holiday where you can spend time taking pleasure in some of the greatest masterpieces, but you might want to adopt some of the following strategies:

- Try to go out of season. Obviously, summer months are going to be the busiest.
- Be mindful of cruise ships that also deposit people at popular destinations like St Petersburg, so get a ticket for first thing in the morning or last thing in the afternoon and avoid those crowds.
- Gen up on what you want to see, and regardless of the "route" around the gallery, head to the pictures or works that interest you.
- Never plan to visit the, whole gallery. You will not manage it.
- The Louvre is open late some evenings until nine-thirty, so go then. It is much quieter and you will avoid all the queues.
- Try visiting smaller, lesser-known galleries rather than the usual famous ones. You can find some with excellent pieces of art and no jostling crowds.

There are more masterpieces of art per square mile in Italy than any other country in the world.

For a serious art fix, sign up for one of the Royal Academy of Arts worldwide tours in conjunction with Cox and Kings. The lecturers, who accompany the tours often concentrate on specific themes or topics, but tours are suitable for enthusiasts or experts.

Tours include access to artworks not open to the wider public, or talks by the curators of local exhibitions, and there is time for individuals to explore further, independently of the group

The focus is on the art, architecture, archaeology and culture of some of the world's most fascinating destinations including Jerusalem, Tuscany, Uzbekistan, Oman, Jordan, China, and Mexico among many others.

For those, who are passionate about art or would like to learn about cultures and art around the world, you can get no better than taking one of these tours. Be prepared to be enthused and inspired.

Kirker Holidays are specialists in organising city breaks and cultural tours. They offer tours to a variety of destinations including Lisbon, Portugal, Madrid, Spain to see "Greco and Modern Painting" at the Prado, and to Amsterdam and The Hague where visits to the recently re-opened Rijksmuseum, Stedelijk Museum and Van Gogh Museum are on the agenda.

You might prefer a trip to Nice or a seven-night tour to galleries and gardens in the Cote d'Azur in France, a magnet for artists including Henri Matisse, and Pablo Picasso, who, inspired by the scenery and light, spent time living in Cannes, Aix en Provence and Mougins and painted scenes from across the Riviera.

Kirker also offer tours to Italy—Ravenna, Modina, Rome, Umbria, and Florence.

Florence is known as the "art capital of Italy" due to its long association with great painters and sculptors.

Should you fancy dabbling in watercolours, charcoal, or oils yourself, then why not book onto an **art course holiday**? Many courses accept novices and some even combine art with other activities such as photography.

There is a huge variety of courses in countries all over the world including Portugal, Morocco, Italy, and France, or you can travel further afield to Cambodia, or even do a residential course in Old Blighty. (You will find some more ideas in the section on painting.)

In 2012, Condé Nast Traveller website recommended The Watermill at Posara—a restored seventeenth-century grain and olive mill in Tuscany, as a place that held the best art holidays. The mill is owned by run by Lois and Bill Breckon, who offer courses in watercolours, oils, pastels, acrylics and other media. You will also be able to take part in excursions to the medieval walls of Fivizzano and the castle and village of Verrucola. There is also a visit to the walled city of Lucca or the fishing villages of the Cinque Terre.

Painting courses here are run by leading artists from all over the world from May through to October. Tutors are inspirational and, with their varied backgrounds and areas of expertise, bring a variety of mediums and styles to suit everyone.

The Watermill is an ideal retreat with its superb scenery and location. Be inspired by the light and landscapes, like many, who have come to Tuscany, and let your creative juices flow.

Type "art course" into your search engine and you will be spoiled for choice. Try to choose a course and location that best suits your requirements and read testimonials.

what do you get if you cross a painter
with a boxer?
mohammed dali

: Mr. Grumpy said, "The only painting I seem to do involves emulsion and a roller. This ought to be more therapeutic. I suppose I could cover the lounge wall with all my efforts. It would save me having to decorate it."

Ayurveda, "the science of life," began in India about three thousand years. It aims to prevent and heal diseases and their symptoms, strengthen the immune system, increase the body's general well-being and vitality, and delay the ageing process. In Ayurvedic philosophy, the body comprises of three life energies, or doshas - Vata, Pitta and Kapha. These constitutions shape the physical and mental characteristics of each person. Diseases result from the body's imbalance of these three doshas. Imbalances result from everyday living, include problems such as unhealthy eating, stress, negative feelings, and lack of exercise, tension, air and noise pollution. Some of the symptoms of dosha imbalances are tension, insomnia, pain, and depression. The Ayurveda treatment and diet

16

brings the three doshas together on an equal level, thus bringing about harmonious balance within the person.

This sounds exactly what a querulous fifty-year-old needs. Certainly, that is the case in our house. I suffer from insomnia and am always tired, whereas Mr. G suffers from tension and general depression brought on by living on a windy cold island with an irritating wife, who keeps testing out experiences on him.

There was a time when you had to go to India or Sri Lanka for serious Ayurvedic treatment. These days it is possible to have such treatments much closer to home, or indeed at home. Well-being breaks take place throughout Europe, including Spain, Italy, Slovakia, and Germany or at resorts throughout the UK. A search engine will produce many results for you. Type in "Ayurvedic" followed by the country you want to visit to get suggestions.

I could not convince my cranky other half to come and join me at a spa. He shuddered at the thought of sitting with groups of women all dressed in fluffy white towelling robes. As a consequence, he missed out on a superb Ayurvedic Indian head.

Indian head massage can provide welcome relief from the symptoms of stress, anxiety, depression, tension, fatigue, insomnia, headaches, some migraine, sinusitis, temporal-mandibular joint tension, eyestrain, and muscle tension in the neck and shoulders. It leaves clients feeling energised, revitalised, stimulated and able to concentrate better. "The treatment is energising and revitalising, and is an excellent way to relieve stress, tension, fatigue, and even insomnia." So read the blurb on my leaflet. That sold it. My neck was a mass of knots and I hadn't slept for five days in a row. My eyes sported the largest black bags known to man and I was grouchy. Before you could say *dosha* I was booked in to try it out.

The massage is carried out whilst you sit in a massage chair, fully clothed. The therapist uses a range of movements to release the knots and muscle tension. I have had sports massages before but they can be quite brutal depending on your injury, so the thought of fragrant massage that would leave me relaxed and energised appealed.

My therapist was a small girl, who looked remarkably like comedienne Sarah Millican.

"Just pop yourself on the chair," she said in a Brummy accent, sounding nothing like Miss Millican.

"I'm going to use almond oil on your head today. It'll help with aches and pains and help relax you. But first, I'm going to work on your shoulders and back to loosen you up. You are tense, aren't you?"

She pressed on my shoulder blades and worked the knots gently yet firmly, each gradually surrendering to her persistent kneading. Then she worked around the base of my neck. I became aware of a feeling of immediate release. Next, she worked upwards to my scalp. She pressed on a magic spot somewhere up there and that was it. I felt calm, relaxed and drowsy and promptly slunk into a delicious slumber, missing the rest of the treatment and surfacing only slightly as she worked my sinus area gently squeezing pressure points. Sarah look-alike had to wake me up at the end of the session.

"My, you look a lot better than when you came in," she announced with confidence. I wiped a drool stain away from my chin and noted with a certain amount of satisfaction that I did indeed look less stressed and my face had lost several of its frown lines. My hair however, looked like I had been out in a whirlwind. I attempted to smooth it down to no avail, so I gave up.

"It seemed a shame to wake you up," she continued. "You were quite sweet, especially when you made that purring noise while I massaged your head."

I thanked her and left feeling lighter and more relaxed. My knots were gone but I am afraid I cannot tell you a lot about the actual treatment.

Should you be able to convince your other half to wear a fluffy white gown then take him away to one of many resorts—watch a fatigued man enter the treatment room and see a rejuvenated man re-emerge. If, like me, you struggle to get him in a treatment room, book a trip where you can benefit from an Ayurvedic treatment and he can do something he fancies.

😁😁😁😁😁: Mr. Grumpy says, "This is suitable for very grumpy old women. It might make them easier to live with." I have to add he looked pointedly at me when he said it, so I immediately booked myself into the spa at the hotel we are visiting next month and signed up to the full range of treatments. One of us will be returning with a smile on our face.

B

air travel: breakfast in London, dinner in New York, luggage in Brazil

B is for backpacking, bananas, base jumping, beaches, bees, beers, birdwatching, boats, bobsleigh, bowls, Buddhist holidays, bullfighting, bungee jumping, butterfly spotting.

Backpacking is usually considered to be the domain of the young, but do not sniff at this suggestion. There is a growing trend for over-sixties, who are retiring to pull out the backpacks, book a round-the-world ticket and embark on the adventure of a lifetime.

If you would like to watch the sun set over an alpine lake, wash in snow melt, and feel forest bracken under your feet instead of bits of chewing gum and uneven pavements then consider backpacking. Backpacking can provide respite from frantic routine and electronic demands. It allows us to get in touch with nature and dispose of the clutter that fills our lives.

Stride out in Morocco, beginning your trip with a night or two in a riad in Marrakesh. I recommend Riad Ambre—one of the three riads that come under the umbrella of Riads Lotus. This is a small riad with three well-appointed rooms and two suites, situated behind the main square of Jemaa-El-Fna.

From the exterior, you may be forgiven for thinking you had stumbled into someone's old house. However, once you enter the cool dark entrance, this riad transforms into a stunning hotel with a courtyard, dining area and hammam (steam room) downstairs and above, a terrace filled with lavish banquettes, plush cushions and a small Jacuzzi. Dine al fresco under the brightly-lit heavens with the intoxicating perfume of flowers and aroma of incense.

After embracing all that Marrakesh has to offer, head off into the Middle Atlas for exceptional walking and outstanding vistas, then make your way to the desert, stopping at walled towns of Ouzazarte and Zagora—the gateway to the desert.

Visit Casablanca, Essouira, Fez or Rabat and try to stop off in the Rif Mountains. You could always catch the *Marrakesh Express* to sample more of what is on offer in this wonderful country.

Try an epic, ninety-six day adventure on the Silk Road. Sleep in tents, hotels, guesthouses and yurts as you travel from Istanbul to Beijing. Book with dragoman.com where transport and accommodation will be taken care of, leaving you to work out what essentials you need to pack.

A female backpacker once told me that backpacking had changed her life. She had walked the pilgrim route to Castello di Campanello and waxed lyrical about the benefits of it. Having survived for several weeks on only what was in her backpack, she realised she no longer needed all the material items she harboured at home. She returned to the UK, refreshed and renewed to dispose of all her clutter and "junk." It is tempting to drag Mr. G away on a backpacking holiday because on his return he might dispose of all the accumulated garbage in his shed that falls out every time I open the door. Mind you, he might take it very seriously and dispose of more than the material possessions.

Backpacking is an affordable and simple way for us "older" folk to travel. You do not need to drag or carry an over-sized suitcase around. You can carry everything that you need on your back, but you can make the weight light enough that you will barely notice it. The fact that you can carry your travel possessions on your back; means you can easily get around small towns and villages. So, take your time to learn more about each culture. See how people live, work, and play. Use buses and trains to be closer to local people and, thus, appreciate a more meaningful trip.

Hostels have come a long way over the years and these days, many are clean, bright, and airy with a range of modern facilities including Wi-Fi internet access, bars, breakfast included, and sometimes even a swimming pool and a games room. Many hostels have private rooms similar to no-frills hotel rooms so you will not have to share a dorm with other backpackers. These private rooms often get booked up so it is wise to book rooms in popular hostels in advance.

For the first-time backpacker, head for a destination that is easy to get around. Europe is very backpacker friendly, but should you be up for adventure further afield, you could even backpack in South Africa. Hop on (and off) the Baz Bus between Cape Town and Johannesburg. A week's unlimited travel only costs eighty-six pounds per person and the bus takes you to great very affordable hostels (some just nine pounds per person a night).

Useful backpack facts:

- The lightest objects in your pack should be located at the bottom.
- All packs should be worn on the lower half of the back to minimize the effect on posture.
- Many injuries result from improper lifting or carrying a backpack with one strap instead of both.
- Some backpacks are three feet or taller.
- Backpacks have many different names, including rucksacks and knapsacks.
- Packs are far better for you than suitcases.
- Packs are the best way to carry multiple objects around when used correctly.

Reading that list, I really should get a backpack and leave my handbag at home.

☹☹: Mr. Grumpy says, "After a lifetime of travelling on public transport smelling other people's armpits, they will have to smell yours now if you backpack. I was tempted to give it three frowning faces, but settled on two and a half as it has more appeal than travelling in a motorhome."

It might seem bizarre for me to suggest you go **bananas** on holiday. Or, you may think I am suggesting you go bouncing on the waves on a large inflatable banana such as you see in the Canary Islands. Hold that thought for a moment—two grumpy old fools trying to remain balanced on a large bouncy banana while grimacing furiously and no doubt complaining—no, it is not likely, is it? Amusing, but not viable. In truth, I was thinking more of a vacation at a banana plantation in the Canary Islands such as the Hotel Patio near Garichico on Tenerife.

Hotel Patio, a manor house owned by the de Ponte family, has sublime views and is surrounded by their banana plantation.

Signposted footpaths guide you through it and down to the wild coastline, where volcanic black sand contrasts sharply to the white blue waves that crash onto the shore.

The hotel has twenty-six rooms spread throughout the estate, some in the manor house, others in the stable or winery, a swimming pool, tennis court, and a croquet pitch. It is a total escape from your normal hotel. The de Ponte family have resided here since 1507. They built their own church in 1565, then ruled the island from 1608.

By day, you can stroll through the banana plantation marvelling at how the yellow fruit develops and is harvested or you can languish on cushioned wicker chairs in the shade of the century-old palms that soar in the ancient courtyard, where you can soak up the beauty of the gardens rich with lemon trees, hanging ferns, and purple bougainvillea. Marvel at the four-hundred-year-old dragon tree that stands in the courtyard, or head to the swimming pool where you will be bowled over by mountain views as you swim.

By night, head to the local town for a meal, stroll by the sea, or sit on your balcony and sample the tranquillity and a romantic starry night.

Absolute bliss for stressed-out curmudgeons.

There are a few banana plantations that accept guests on Tenerife and in other locations in the world, so get Googling and find your perfect retreat.

🐌: Mr. Grumpy says, "A definite "yes" for this holiday, although be advised to bring sensible walking shoes as paths can be steep. I'll give it a smiley face. It's worth it. Besides, I like bananas."

time flies like an arrow, but fruit flies like a banana.

The 'base' in **base jumping** is an acronym that stands for buildings, aerials, spans, earthen objects. Base jumpers climb to the top of one of these structures and hurl themselves off the top, hoping that they have enough time for their parachute to deploy and arrest their descent before they hit the ground, and that they do not smash into the structure on the way down.

I really cannot imagine a queue of over-fifties wanting to go on a base jumping holiday but some of you might. Base jumping is not an extreme sport. It should be categorized, instead, as a "very extreme sport." Or maybe as a "commonly lethal sport." Unlike skydiving and bungee jumping, it is not uncommon for people to be killed. I rest my case. Why would you want to do it?

Anyway, if you still harbour a desire to launch yourself off a mountain in Norway or Thailand wearing a flying suit and a small parachute, then ensure you have insurance!

Age is not a barrier to this activity, after all Donald Cripps from the USA, parachuted off the 267-metre-high New River Gorge Bridge near Fayetteville in West Virginia, USA, on 19th October 2013, when he was eighty-four years and thirty-seven days.[1]

According to Teletext holidays, five great base jumping sites include the tallest waterfall in the world, Angel Falls in Venezuela, the Petronas Towers in Kuala Lumpur, the Troy Wall in Norway (the tallest vertical rock face in Europe and is in fact the place where the first Guinness World Record for the highest jump was set in 1984), the 829m Burj Khalifa in United Arab Emirates and the Perrine Bridge, Twin Falls, Idaho.

☺☺☺☺☺: Mr. Grumpy says, "You must be out of your mind to try this. It's safer to fly a helicopter with your eyes shut!"

what washes up on tiny beaches?
microwaves.

If you don't want to throw yourself from a mountain dressed in a wing suit, and not many of us really want to do that, then you might like to consider a more sensible option—**the beach**. The problem is that beaches are also usually filled with other holiday-makers, children screeching, the stench of suntan oil and worse still—sand. What grumpy guts likes having sand in their bits? I certainly don't. However, I made an exception when I discovered a splendid hideaway-from-it-all beach on the island of Benguerra, off Mozambique.

This little-known beach on one side of the island can only be

---

1   www.guinnessworldrecords.com/records-2000/oldest-base-jumper

reached by boat and the hotel will drop you off from their boat, along with a luxury hamper, beach chairs, tables, sunshade, and everything else imaginable to make your stay comfortable. You can, for a while at least, pretend you are the only people on the planet, yet slump back against plump cushions under a large parasol that has been erected for you, scoffing tasty food and quaffing champagne. The beach is made up of pure white sand with odd pieces of interesting driftwood sticking out of it. The background is vegetation and there is not a soul to be seen. This was definitely an idyllic setting. "Paradise" just about covers the description.

Sitting on a beach with a sundowner and staring at the vibrant orange, red and pink sky, while white-tipped waves lap up to shore is quite possibly one of the most pleasant moments a cranky person can have. Peace, serenity, and inner calm. You even forget about the sand in between your toes and in your ears. For a magical escape, seek out lesser known beaches. Here are three that may enchant rather than exasperate:

If you really want to make a dent in the kids' inheritance, head to Cousine, one of the one hundred and fifty-five islands that make up the Seychelles Islands in the Indian Ocean. It costs a, whopping 6,500 Euros per night but that is a small price to pay for absolute isolation, right?

Reached only by helicopter, Cousine Island accommodates up to eight people per day in one of their four exclusive island villas. You don't have to find six others to share your villa but if you have space, my grumpy old man and I will happily join you. We promise to be quiet.

Whale Island in Vietnam is (unsurprisingly) famous for its whale-spotting as well as coral-reef-snorkelling. It boasts translucent waters and diverse coral reefs that spurred Jacques Cousteau's underwater obsession. The only building on this almost deserted island is Whale Island Resort and it promises its guests complete isolation. Likey, likey!

Be unconventional and head towards the west coast of Harris in Scotland. The sparsely inhabited Luskentyre, is home to a few farms and holiday homes and excellent beach views. Visit the pebbled beach that curves into the vast sand dunes where the North Harris

Mountains tower in the distance. You might need woollies for this trip but at least you will not grumble about the sand.

Finally, purchase your own beach. In fact, purchase an entire island. Orivaru, a fourteen-hectare island in the northern part of the Maldives has come up for sale with an estimated price tag of fourteen million US dollars. Don't worry, you can claw some of that money back because planning permission to build a luxury island resort has been approved by the Maldivian Ministry of Tourism, allowing for one hundred five-star rooms, water villas and additional space for restaurant and spa facilities. One hundred miles north from the Maldivian capital Male, Orivaru is part of the Noonu Atoll, a collection of seventy-one islands of, which only thirteen are currently inhabited.

Buy this and you would certainly be guaranteed a peaceful holiday retreat and you would get the beach to yourself.

A search on the internet will produce some interesting results so, do your homework and you could be playing Robinson Crusoe with your other half as your personal Man Friday.

The longest natural beach in the world is Cox's Bazar beach in Bangladesh. It stretches for seventy-six miles along the south-eastern tip of Bangladesh.

☺: Mr. Grumpy says, "As long as I don't have to sit behind a windbreaker or on one of those impossible-to-erect deckchairs, I'll plod about on a deserted beach for a while."

Television presenter Kate Humble and her husband have opened their Monmouthshire farm up to the public for a string of rural skills courses, including hedge laying, truffle-making and "Get the Buzz" sustainable **bee keeping**.

Once suited and booted, guests meet the honey bee colonies, learn basic bee biology and ecology and find out how to harvest honey; as well as gaining a broader understanding of the sustainable relationship between bees, people and the environment.

The course is run by Bees for Development, whose main work is assisting beekeepers living in poor and remote areas of the world, lifting them out of poverty through beekeeping. They are a charity, who work with community groups and associations, raising the profile of apiculture.

Prefer bee products to the buzzing insects themselves? Book the Beeswax Soap and Balm course and learn to make natural beeswax lip balms and lotion bars. You will also learn the art of making cold pressed soap and produce your own one-hundred percent natural beeswax lip balms and beautifully scented lotion bars, which you will label and take home.

Stay in the Piggery, The Hayloft, or in the romantic Humble Hideaway for a holiday that gets you back to nature and inspires you to start a smallholding of your own. Grumpy Utopia!

🐷: Mr. Grumpy says, "More Kate Bumble than Kate Humble."

why do beer companies bother with an expiration date... it's never going to make it anywhere near that.

How about taking off on a **beer trip**? Before your other half says it would be cheaper to head to the pub, flag up the idea of heading to Munich, home to the Oktoberfest. The beer festival in October is swamped with visitors from all over the world filling up tents, swigging large beers from buxom maidens in Bavarian dress and making merry, so consider going ahead of the pack or after they have vacated the city.

Munich is a picture-perfect Bavarian city, jam-packed with charm, history, sights, museums, and superb shopping. It also has some of the finest beer gardens you can visit. In earlier times, when brewers were desperate to keep their beer cool during the summer, they stored their barrels in cellars and planted chestnut trees above them, since their wide branches and large leaves keep the place nice and shady. King Maximilian I Joseph of Bavaria granted the brewers the right to sell their beer on the spot—but not food. Since then, the people of Munich have flocked to these gardens to drink fresh beer straight from the barrel, bringing along their own food.

Nowadays, food is also served there but you can still bring your own if you prefer. Beer gardens have both tables with tablecloths, where you are served by a waitress, and long tables and benches without tablecloths where you consume what you have brought along.

Gardens seat thousands of people and one of our favourites is in the "Englische Garten" (The English Garden) one of the largest urban parks in the world. Choose one of the spots out of the seven thousand available next to the Chinese Tower, drink beer, listen to concerts and soak up the convivial atmosphere.

There are six main beers in Munich—all of them very good—so try them all while you are there. I am not a big beer or lager drinker and I found them refreshing. If you are not a huge fan of beer, try a Radler—a shandy.

No trip would be complete without heading to the famous Hofbräuhaus (one of Munich's oldest breweries) where you can join a table of strangers as is the custom here, drink beer from a litre glass and listen to an oompah band. The atmosphere is superb with hundreds of locals and tourists sitting and chatting on long benches quaffing some of Munich's finest beers. A little different to the local pub.

If you like stronger beers, travel to Belgium and discover hundreds of Belgian beers. Belgium has a history of brewing that dates back to the Middle Ages when it was only brewed by monks.

Google "Belgium breweries" today and you will be astounded at the number there are to visit. The Belgians take their beer seriously and it is an important part of their culture. There is even a driving tour through the countryside called the Beer Route.

With the huge variety of beers available, including fruit beers, this is a top destination for beer lovers or those, who might soon become beer connoisseurs. There are trips galore for you to consider.

I wonder if the Manneken Pis—the little statue of a peeing boy in Brussels is anything to do with having drunk too much beer.

Pop to Prague for a chilled pils at one of the cafes and then check out (oh dear, sorry about the pun) the five microbreweries, all within easy stumbling distance of Prague's main attractions. It is worth making reservations before you go, though, as these pubs are just as popular with the locals as with visitors.

Prague is a truly delightful city, but it is crammed with tourists, so do your main sightseeing in the morning before the organised tours really get going and then nip off to the brewery.

Our favourite brewery was at the Strahov Monastry, a stunning

Baroque complex near Prague Castle. They have been brewing here since the fourteenth century. The grounds are beautiful and the view of Prague itself on the walk back down the hill is breathtaking and necessary after lunch and a couple of beers.

Should you merely fancy a fun night out—unlikely if you are a true grumpy guts—visit The Beer Factory. Located in the centre of Prague in Wenceslas Square, The Beer Factory is a bar/restaurant offering good food, music and, of course, beer. Each table has four beer taps and a beer monitor, which calculates how much beer you've consumed. Whenever you fill up your glass a tally is added to your table's total, which is then projected onto one of the many screens on the wall of the bar. Be careful though as the night can turn into a huge competition against the other tables and we know how bad-tempered grumps with hangovers can be.

: Mr. Grumpy says, "Prost! A great way to end a day's sightseeing, or—even better—interrupt it."

what do you get if you cross a trainspotter with a twitcher? anoraksia nervosa

Getting back to nature always makes a grumpy feel better about life. Buying him or her a pair of binoculars and booking a special **birdwatching** trip will ensure he or she is in harmony with the world once more.

Hungary, Sri Lanka, France … choose your destination and be prepared to see some fabulous birds as well as learn more about the heritage and culture of different countries.

I settled Mr. Grumpy in front of a marsh in South Africa where the brightly coloured yellow weaver birds, red bishops and fan-tailed widowbirds kept him mesmerised for days. The only downside was he took hundreds of photographs of them and it took us four weeks to print them all off on our little home printer.

: Mr. Grumpy says, "Peaceful and rewarding. No noise. No hassle. Worth five smiling faces but rules are rules."

Got an ultra-stressed grumpy, who hates beaches and bowls? Suggest a trip on a **boat**. Boating helps reduce anxiety, and there are a lot of fun activities that go along with it. It is a great way to stay active and blow off some steam at the same time. Whether it is a trip on the Norfolk Broads, a gentle meander on a canal boat, cruise to foreign parts, or a chartered yacht with crew, being on the water is ideal for grouchy folk. (Unless they suffer from acute sea sickness.)

what do you do with a sick boat? take it to the doc.

You don't need to stick to the obvious. Try out boats in other countries: take a dhow off Mozambique and watch the sunset from the deck while sipping wine with your loved one, cruise the Danube taking in wonderful cities rich in culture, or hire a small hobbycat at a seaside resort and bump over waves together.

Boats are often the best way to see a place. The Okavango Delta in Botswana's Kalahari Desert is one of the most ecologically important places on Earth. As the Okavango is flooded for much of the year, one of the best ways to see the region is by boat.

My advice, should you go there, would be to take a trip on a houseboat. This is by far the most luxurious option and guests can savour the passing scenery from the sundeck or even the Jacuzzi. Most houseboats offer deeper explorations into the delta by mokoro, a traditional style dug-out canoe, typical of the Okavango region.

This may seem too tame for some readers, in, which case I would suggest an overnight boating safari into the delta. A safari boat departing from Maun takes guests upriver to a simple overnight camp. Watch game and go bird spotting on a morning and afternoon safari, then partake in an evening sundowner on the boat. In camp the dome tents and shared shower tents are all erected prior to your arrival, and meals are prepared in camp too.

For adventure seekers looking for an action safari, check out trans-Okavango kayaking safaris. This is a real back-to-basics adventure where guests kayak down-river, setting up camp along the way. Kayak guides and safari guides travel with you and give a full safety briefing.

My grumpy guy does not generally like boats but was won over by a trip in a dhow thanks to calm seas, smiled during a small motorboat trip around islands off Montenegro, became most competitive in a kayak when we raced down the river Aveyron in south west France, and allowed himself to be persuaded to take a hobbycat out while on a beach holiday. The latter required energy and much jumping across a trampoline-like net to avoid being hit by the sail itself. However, it meant for a while he was not complaining about the heat on shore and was most entertained when I ingested a large amount of seawater when a wave hit us. In spite of these successes, I have yet to convince him to take a cruise or board a larger vessel. The film *Titanic* has a lot to answer for.

Your numbers have come up in the Rollover Lottery? Hurray! Hire one of the most expensive boats in the world, the mega-yacht "Imagine" and live the dream.

The name says it all, just imagine … . Imagine a world where you are surrounded by fine art, refined hand crafted interiors of the highest quality, and your every whim catered to by an attentive and highly trained crew. (I like that idea very much.) There are six guest staterooms (all mini-suites, of course) and one vast owner's suite with double Jacuzzi bath, adjoining private office, private balcony, and dressing rooms. On the Sun Deck, you can chill out at the swimming pool or Jacuzzi, both of, which have "wet-feet" bars, while the Sky gym offers the chance for a more serious workout, should you really feel like it. Of course, you could just recline on a sunbed with a glass of champagne, and watch the world sail past.

For a mere 565,000 Euros, you could bask in a week of opulence … Just imagine.

🦉: Mr. Grumpy says, "I still don't like boats. No grumpy faces for our boat trips but if you try to get me on a cruise ship, I'll cover the, whole page in frowning faces."

What about a really wild challenge? Charge off to Switzerland and hurtle head first down the Cresta Run in St Moritz on a luge (**bobsleigh**) at about 88 mph. The Cresta Run normally opens two or three days before Christmas and continues until the end of February.

It is a private club and unfortunately only male non-members are welcome. You will have to apply for temporary membership to ride in the early mornings on certain days, and this will last until the end of the season, entitling you to up to five rides on the run. Ladies, just ensure your man is well insured and relax at Da Vittorio with a glass of champagne and wait for him to come back, or not.

If you cannot get down the Cresta Run, sign up for a bobsleigh run at the Olympic Park at Lillehammer in Norway. Exodus holidays offer a thrill of a lifetime. Book a weekend with them and you will learn all about bobsleighs and speed down the course used by speed-loving athletes with an experienced instructor. This is one for the adrenaline-seeking junkies among you. Website details to be found at the end of this book. May the G-Force be with you.

😑😑😑😑😑: Mr. Grumpy says, "Nothing on this planet would possess me to get into those tight leggings and throw myself head-first down an icy run."

The game of **bowling** has a long history, with some scientists claiming it dates as far back as the Egyptians. Bowling holidays are very popular... yes, you read that correctly. You can go on bowling holidays almost anywhere and travel agents like Thomson offer holidays abroad where you can meet like-minded people, have free coaching, get involved in tournaments and even come home with a trophy.

Whether you are pro or a beginner, there is a holiday to suit you.

a little old man boards a bus with a bowling wood in each of his front pockets. he sits down next to a beautiful young lady, and she can't help but glance quizzically at the man and his bulging pockets. it's an uneasy few minutes before, finally, the little old man can take no more.
"bowling balls," he nods reassuringly.

For those of you, who would like to try a spiritual experience, spend a fortnight with novice **Buddhist monks** in Laos.

In the beautiful ancient city of Luang Prabang, northern central Laos, you can teach English to young Buddhist monks. The novices have chosen to become monks to escape poverty and have access to education. This is a volunteering holiday that will give you beauty, tranquility, and satisfaction. It takes place in an idyllic setting at the meeting of the Nam Khan and Mekong rivers, renowned for its Buddhist temples and monasteries. As well as working closely with novice monks, you will learn about Lao culture, history and food, visit the local sights and spend a weekend on the banks of the Mekong River, taking in fabulous waterfalls and breath-taking mountains.

Buddhists are not all serious people. Take a look at some of the laughing Buddha statues to see that they can be a jolly bunch. In the fourth century, Indian Buddhist scholar Bharata identified six degrees of amusement. These ranged from the "sita" (a faint smile) to the "atihasita" (, which is when you laugh so hard your jiggly bits wobble). My jiggly bits wobble a lot more than they used to so I might leave this option for my husband. He could do with a break from me and my dreadful jokes.

how many zen masters does it take to screw in a light bulb? a tree in a golden forest.

🙂: Mr. Grumpy says, "Buddhist retreat? Buddhist retreat? Not budding likely. Quiet, did you say? Nice organic food? No Smart phones? Oh, okay then."

I was traumatised in my early twenties when a boyfriend took me to a **bullfight** in Mijas. After a lengthy struggle, the matador killed the bull, chopped off its ear and tossed it into the audience where it landed slap bang in my lap. It dripped blood all over my white shorts and put me off bullfighting for life.

However, bullfighting is the most traditional of Spanish fiestas. The Spanish people consider them art forms, which are intimately linked with their country's history, art, and culture. Pressure groups attempt to lobby against bullfighting yet the King of Spain himself has allegedly stated that the day the EU bans bullfighting is the day Spain leaves the EU.

Bullfighting can be traced back to ancient days. They were popular spectacles in ancient Rome, but it was in the Iberian Peninsula that these contests were fully developed by the Moors from North Africa, who overran Andalucia in AD 711. Bullfighting became a ritualistic occasion observed in connection with feast days, on, which the conquering Moors, mounted on highly trained horses, confronted and killed the bulls.

All major Spanish cities have impressive bullrings but probably the most outstanding are those in Madrid, Seville, and Ronda.

I leave it you to decide if you wish to go and watch a bullfight. If you don't mind, I'll pass on that particular choice of holiday.

😀😀😀😀😀: Mr. Grumpy says, "After a close encounter with a large bad-tempered bull while minding my own business in a field, I think anyone who wants to goad these animals is asking for trouble. Let them get on with it. I don't want to see the outcome."

Bungee jumping holiday—no, I am not being serious. Well, only a little serious because there are some people out there, who really want to have a go at this activity. In August 2014, Margit Tall, a ninety-five-year-old woman who walks with a stick became one of the world's oldest bungee jumpers, joining the elite ranks of nonagenarian bungee jumpers including ninety-six-year-old Mohr Keet, who leapt from South Africa's Bloukrans Bridge in 2010, and Frances Gabe, who celebrated her ninety-first birthday in 2011 with a solo jump in Fresno, California.

Margit Tall did not even scream during the one hundred and fifty-metre plunge from a crane near her home in Helsinki, Finland.

Hats off to her. I certainly would not do it and neither would Mr. G. Free-falling from a tall structure connected only by a large elastic cord and watching the ground getting ever closer, is a no-no for us. If you want to add this adrenaline-inducing activity into your holiday itinerary, then good luck.

Seven Bungee Facts:

- Eccentric Oxford students carried out the first bungee jump with modern materials off the Clifton Suspension Bridge in Bristol on April Fools' Day 1979. Using nylon braided rubber shock cords and dressed in top hats and tails, four members of the Oxford University Dangerous Sports Club jumped off. They survived and were immediately arrested.
- Bungee jumping is so named after the strong elasticated cords that are normally used to strap down luggage.
- The highest commercial bungee jump in the world, according to the Guinness Book of Records, is 764ft (233m), off the Macau Tower in China. Jumpers experience four to five seconds of freefall at up to 125mph.
- James Bond film GoldenEye, starring Pierce Brosnan as 007, featured what was the largest bungee jump ever performed at the time in 2002. Stuntman Wayne Michaels jumped off the Verzasca Dam in Switzerland, a 720ft (220m) drop. That year it was voted the best stunt of all time in a Sky Movies poll.
- For $10,000 (£6,700) you can jump off a helicopter into the mouth of an active Andean volcano in Pucon, Chile. Breakfast buffet is included.
- Despite its inherent risk, there have only been a handful of deaths from bungee jumping.
- Jumper Carl Dionisio used condoms for his bungee cord when he made a 100ft jump in South Africa.

I am fairly certain you will not allow your precious grumpy to perform a bungee jump but if you do, make sure he or she has a hefty life insurance policy.

☺☺☺☺: Mr. Grumpy says, "Get out of here. I am not being suspended over a bridge on a piece of elastic."

Nature blessed butterflies with an array of colours to keep us humans entertained. Watching a brightly coloured butterfly entertains the eye and delights the soul of most humans. Children giggle and laugh as they chase butterflies along the field. We delight in their peaceful, delicate nature and marvel at their colours. So travel back to your childhood and consider **butterfly spotting** as a holiday.

Still largely agricultural, Macedonia (part of former Yugoslavia) boasts an impressive diversity of habitats and is one of Europe's best destinations for those interested in butterflies, as well as being outstanding for birds and flora. Forget looking for Cabbage Whites, Macedonia has much more to offer. To date more than two hundred species have been recorded there. You might come across a Grecian Copper, Krueper´s Small White, Balkan Clouded Yellow, Russian heath, Balkan Marbled White or Lattice Brown as you hike some fourteen kilometres from Millennium Cross to the serene Matka Canyon.

Expert guided tours can be arranged through various companies including Nature Trek, who offer a range of butterfly watching tours in other countries, including Italy, Sweden, Sri Lanka, Hungary, South Africa and France. Ten percent of all income generated by their annual programme of butterfly tours and one thousand pounds a year go to Butterfly Conservation to help preserve butterflies and moths and save habitats.

Travel during June and you will be sure to see an incredible array of these insects in the flower-filled fields of this stunning region. You might need to take a notebook to write down the fantastic names of the butterflies such as Tufted Marbled Skipper, Chapman's Blue, Southern Comma and Lesser Purple Emperor. You will not however, require that old butterfly net and container with holes in it that you might have used as a child.

☺: Mr. Grumpy says, 'After that last lunatic suggestion, this is a welcome relieve and I would most definitely go on this trip. Sounds delightful."

C

"there are two kinds of cruises: pleasure
and with children."
~ GEORGE BURNS

C is for camel riding, camping, canals, canoeing, canyoning, car holidays, caravan holidays, carnivals, castles, celeb hunting, Centre Parks, champagne sabering, chocolate-making courses, Christmas markets, circle dancing holidays, circus skills, climbing, coasteering, cookery courses, cowboy campout, creative courses, culture holidays, culinary tours, creative courses, cycling.

Camels are quite frankly bad-tempered and stubborn, so they make ideal companions for crabby old folk like my man and me. My first encounter with a camel resulted in it taking a bite out of me but that did not stop me from being fascinated by them. They may be grumpy but their faces always look slightly amused by everything. (The one that bit me certainly looked very amused.) If you have never ridden before on the "ship of the desert," try it out. Take seasickness pills first.

Camels have been invaluable to humans for thousands of years. These animals are very robust, can walk for miles a day and provide meat, wool, milk and even fuel as their dung can be burnt on a fire.

If your grouchy fellow fancies himself as Lawrence of Arabia, then I highly recommend a camel trek across the rolling sand dunes of the mighty Sahara Desert in Morocco or the Great Indian Thar Desert in Rajasthan. Alternatively, view the last remaining Ancient Wonder of the World on camel back as you ride between the Pyramids of Giza in Egypt.

Contrary to popular belief, camels do not spit too often at humans. They normally spit at each other to resolve herd hierarchy or food issues. When they spit at people it usually means they have either been mishandled at some point and have become territorial towards people, or they have never been properly trained and are afraid and use the spitting as a warning to "stay away." So, be nice to your camel and he will be your new best grumpy friend.

The Arabian Bedouin has one hundred and sixty words for "camel." No, "cigarette" isn't one of them.

As mentioned earlier, we grumbling folk usually crave peace and tranquillity. It can be found in abundance on Britain's waterways. A trip on a **canal** boat combines relaxation and exercise as you head off to open those heavy locks. It is usually the wife, who gets to work the locks, so best ensure you have been practising your bicep curls and tricep dips before you leave or you may find yourself hanging off the gate shouting for help while your other half tackles steering the boat, oblivious to your discomfort. If the weather is on your side, this is a perfect holiday for a grumpy.

If you do not want to take the chance of getting soaked and spending the time leaping on and off your boat to open and close locks, getting soaked through and wearing a luminous cagoule, then head the Canal du Midi in "la belle" France.

Savour the slow easy pace of travel, as you pass lush vineyards in the heart of the Languedoc wine region. Take pleasure in wine tasting, cycling, and sightseeing at medieval villages and ancient fortress cities all the way from bustling Toulouse to the golden sands of the Mediterranean Sea. The ancient city of Carcassonne is a must-see and a visit to at least one vineyard must be added to your agenda to fully appreciate this region and holiday.

Better still, hire a canal boat with crew—what more could you want? Remove your French dictionary from its mothballs and learn how to say, "Please could you put your foot down. I want to get to the vineyard for lunch."

There is a wide choice of canal boat holidays for you to consider. The UK offers some excellent waterways but if you want to go further afield, try Amsterdam. Low bridges, arching trees, and historic narrow houses line Amsterdam's many canals.

Or, how about visiting the forty-mile Black Sea canal from Ruse, on the Bulgarian section of the Danube River, to Constanta, a popular Romanian resort on the Black Sea? The canal is part of the wildlife-rich Danube Delta area, home to pelicans, herons, egrets, and up to three hundred other species of birds.

Sweden offers the Gota Canal that connects a series of lakes, allowing boats to travel almost all the way across Sweden from Lake Vänern, near Gothenburg, to the Baltic. Along the way are fifty-eight locks so it might be wise to choose a canal boat complete with crew to open them and manoeuvre the ship through.

In Germany, travel the Waterways of Brandenburg, between Berlin and the Baltic, cruising past castles and quaint towns. Stop off for a Bockwurst and beer or check out any of the super fish restaurants that are along the route.

France offers a 5,000-mile network of canals taking you from north to south, or anywhere in between. To the south, the Canal du Midi passes through a land of vineyards and walled cities, many in easy reach of the canal. Tie up outside a small town, then go ashore to sample local food and wine or bag a bargain at one of the many markets being held en route.

Grumpy tip: The medieval walled city of Carcassonne is well worth a visit but try to go early in the morning before the crowds arrive.

Think New York and you might think yellow taxis, Macy's, and the Empire State Building but New York also has canals—524 miles of waterways and towpaths between Albany and Buffalo, New York. You can rent a boat and sail it yourself, or hire a crew.

☺: Mr. Grumpy says, "There is a possibility I might get some satisfaction from this holiday, especially if I got to steer. I fancy getting away from the madness of the world in, which we live and pottering gently down a canal." He then went on and on about the traffic, roads, white vans and potholes.

You could of course, take your own **car** abroad and rejoice in driving on better roads than we have here. I had to put that in. I could not write a book aimed at us grumpies if I did not make some mention of potholes and traffic jams (again). Should you decide to brave travelling abroad, then head for the Monaco Grand Prix circuit. Monaco is the only proper road circuit in grand prix racing. Imagine manoeuvring your trusty Peugeot 206 or Citroen C1 (it is

France, after all) through tunnels, listening to the throaty burble of your exhaust pipe, as you press the throttle excitedly, pretending you are Louis Hamilton.

To be honest, there will be areas that you will be unable to speed around like F1 cars do, such as Casino Square, but it is worth following the rest of the circuit, taking in the boats and the jet-set lifestyle. Don't forget to stop off at the casino for a quick flutter in the hope you might win enough for an Aston Martin.

Be mindful that you will not be allowed to drive at one hundred and sixty miles per hour, not unless you want a speeding ticket. Finally, this suggestion is best not attempted during the summer months when it is very busy. In fact, you might be better walking the circuit, stopping at the Hotel de Paris and watching the fabulous display of cars stuck in traffic jams.

For those, who fancy some speed, take on the infamous Nürburgring track. Situated seventy kilometres south of Cologne and one hundred and twenty kilometres north-west of Frankfurt, anyone with a clean driving licence can purchase a ticket and drive this exhilarating racing circuit.

There is no general speed limit, although speed limits exist in certain areas in order to reduce noise and risks. Just be polite, don't overtake on the right, and watch out for my husband and me. We shall be bearing down on you, squealing at the thrill of it.

You might prefer a little adventure like hiring a Ferrari in Italy. Combine art, beauty, and driving by travelling to Florence. Head for the Piazzola Michelangelo, the main square overlooking Florence where you will find *Ferrari in Firenze*. Here you can book ten, twenty minutes, or an hour in a Ferrari driving the tree-lined streets of Florence. If you drive the Ferrari California, take your other half along. They can video you as you rev the engine and appreciate this beautiful Italian city in one of the most beautiful Italian cars.

The organisers and instructor speak English and will reply promptly to an email. Alternatively, you can book via your travel agent or head up the hill to the square and take your chance on the day. Be warned, you will be treated like a celebrity as you head off. Cameras will be snapping and people will be listening out for that throaty roar as you shoot off, so don't stall the car. The Ferrari is adored in Italy.

Should nostalgia be your thing, hire a classic car, load up a picnic and head off to a rural part of the UK to spend some quiet time with your other half. After all, when you are in a super classic car, you forget about the other traffic chugging slowly in front of you. Great Escape Cars offer a wide range of vehicles including a Jaguar E Type Convertible Steels, a Triumph Stag, an old Mini Cooper, and a Rolls Royce Silver Shadow among others.

For proper petrol heads, join a convoy of supercar owners, who drive from Muscat, Oman, to the Yas Marina Circuit in Abu Dhabi, just in time for the Grand Prix. Drivers head through desolate deserts and rugged mountain regions, with private excursions and exceptional meals incorporated into the schedule throughout. Participants pay £25,000 to join in, £30,000 if it includes supercar hire.

A similar run to Monaco ahead of the Monaco Grand Prix, offers a comparable itinerary. They would not let me enter my 2003 Volkwagen Polo—boo!

You can travel some iconic routes by car or motorbike, including Route 66 in the United States, known as the "Mother Road" that features in the well-known song (*Get Your Kicks on*) *Route 66*, penned by Bobby Troup but made famous by Nat King Cole in 1946.

A journey from Brisbane to Queensland in Australia is further than going from Lands End to John O'Groats but with the Great Barrier Reef as your constant companion, the miles will fly by.

The stunning Garden Route in South Africa can be done in a day, but you will want to stop frequently to take in the magnificent scenery and maybe view the whales at Hermanus.

Take in scenery galore if you head along California's Coast Road. This is a major north-south state highway that runs along most of the Pacific coastline and is one of National Geographic's Ultimate Road Trips.

One attraction you might not find when searching for car holidays, is the annual hill climb at Saint-Antonin-Noble-Val in the south-west of France. Each year this stunning medieval town holds a hill climb for enthusiasts and onlookers.

Even if you abhor cars, this is one town that will win you over.

I should know. I lived there for eleven years. It is one of the most picturesque towns in the region. It has even attracted the attention of film directors. The films *Charlotte Gray (2001)* starring Cate Blanchett and *The Hundred Foot Journey* (2013) starring Helen Mirren were shot there.

Saint-Antonin-Noble-Val is the oldest town in the Rouergue and Quercy region and takes its name from the early evangelist Saint Antonin, who introduced Christianity to the area.

It sits on the banks of the river Aveyron beneath magnificent cliffs. A medieval town with cobbled shady streets and historic houses, Saint Antonin retains an atmosphere of the Middle Ages. It has the oldest civic building in France and a splendidly unrestored medieval centre.

Travel uphill from the town towards the direction of Montauban and you will have some of the most spectacular views of the river and gorges. It is this route that is commandeered by the Course de la Cote when for two days in August, cars race to get the fastest time.

This is a great spectator sport. Sunshine, ambience, and then a gentle meander back down to the town for wine and foie gras. Have I tempted you?

: Mr. Grumpy says, "Go ...go ... go ...power!"

Carnivals, like the annual event in Venice, Italy have attracted visitors for years. The atmosphere is superb and even the most miserable amongst us will feel more cheerful after mixing among party-loving people dressed in bright costumes.

Trundle along to Tenerife in the Canary Islands for one of the largest of all the carnivals and fiestas in the Canary Islands. Originating in the eighteenth century, this is a huge event and is celebrated in every town and village on the island. The most spectacular carnival celebrations are to be found in Santa Cruz de Tenerife and Puerto de la Cruz. All-night parades and parties continue for up to a week and each year there is a theme–this year it is "the Future." The finale consists of the funeral and burial of the sardine, a giant *papier mâché* fish. Make sure you book accommodation well in advance or you will miss out on one of the most spectacular and colourful carnivals imaginable.

Probably the most famous carnival in the world dates back as far as the seventeenth century, when processions took place to celebrate the crowning of the Portuguese monarch John IV.

Today, the carnival in Rio de Janeiro, Brazil, attracts more than five million people to several days of parades known as "The Greatest Show on Earth." People come out onto the streets and dance and sing, and concludes in what is known as the Samba Parade. You will be amazed and enthralled by the extravagant and lavish finale of flamboyant late night parades through the Sambodromo.

I can almost hear the rhythmical beat as I type and soon shall have the urge to shake my booty which will make writing difficult. The samba originated from the blend of street music and African slave songs, and today its irresistible beats and rhythms have transformed it into the main dance of the Rio Carnival, and it is an inextricable part of the local identity. I guarantee you and your other half will be joining in if you go. Make sure you take an afternoon nap before the festivities. You could be in for a long night.

If Rio is samba and Venice is ballroom, then Trinidad's massive carnival in Port of Spain is soca and calypso. Huge steel pan bands are the driving musical force behind two days of celebrations in the island nation's capital.

Other carnivals you may fancy attending include the "Carnaval de Québec," Canada. Dance at the Ice Palace, try your hand at ice-sculpting, catch the night parade, go dog-sledding, or sluice down a snow slide. For three weekends in January and February, the city hosts one of the biggest winter festivals in the world.

And finally, do not forget Notting Hill Carnival, London. It boasts Europe's biggest street parties with street parades, sound systems and a huge range of food and drink options as the Afro-Caribbean communities celebrate to the sound of salsa, reggae, dub, and soca over the August bank holiday weekend each year.

🂠🂠🂠🂠: Mr. Grumpy says, "Can't say I fancy all that frivolity. Besides, I like to be in bed by nine o'clock."

Forgive me but I am going to scurry though the next suggestion—**camping**. My memories of life under the canvas are associated with a disastrous trip with a friend. Due to one of us consuming too much alcohol at lunch, we got lost on the way to the campsite and consequently arrived late. All the spaces were taken apart from one, which turned out to be on a slope. One of us—who had not been drinking and was not being sick in the toilet block—had to pitch the tent. That person did not do a very good job of it (well, I had never been camping before that day) thus at some point during the night we both gradually slid out of the tent and into a rain-soaked night. I have avoided camping ever since.

I have come up with a holiday that is a far cry from my terrible night of camping—a luxury tent camp in Moab, Utah in the United States. The website claims, "This is camping as it should be." Moab Camping offers a range of tents: Safari, Tipi, Deluxe (with stunning mountain vistas and views of Arches National Park) and Deluxe with Tipi. The Suite option comes with a bedroom wing inside the tent along with a king-size bed, a lounge area, and a sofa bed, and is in a secluded and more sheltered location boasting spectacular views of Arches National Park. There is even a wood burning stove in your tent with complimentary firewood. More importantly, there is a private en suite bathroom inside your tent and includes a hot shower, sink, flushing toilet.

Sounds a far cry from the toilet block I used all those years ago with cold and colder running water.

Glamping is the new camping and campsites like this have sprung up worldwide. If the last time you went camping was when you were ten and your memory is of sitting around a campfire singing *Ging Gang Goolie*, it might be time to try it again.

In an emergency, a drawstring from a parka hood can be used to strangle a snoring tent mate.

When I mentioned a holiday **canoeing** to Mr. G, his face fell in horror, probably due to having recently watched the film *Deliverance* where four men (two played by Burt Reynolds and Jon Voight) decide to canoe down a river in the remote northern Georgia wilderness but the trip goes wrong. You might recall the famous "duelling banjos" scene. Well, canoeing is not really like that.

In 2009, *Guardian* readers were invited to send tips of their favourite canoe trips. Top suggestions were:

- Canoeing on the Dunajec River in Slovakia "where the Polish peak of Trzy Korony (Three Crowns) looms like a chunk of white Toblerone."
- Östa Stugby camp, in Färnebofjärden National Park in Sweden
- The River Ardèche in France, chosen as a "top tip" for one of the best places to canoe.

I have to agree that France has many outstanding areas of beauty and rivers abundant with nature so I can see why this river was chosen. The paddle from Vallon-Pont-d'Arc through the incredible Ardèche gorges is indeed a trip where you will get back to nature and bask in serenity.

Such a trip is a short one—some thirty kilometres—so if you want to have a holiday in a canoe then you should consider a canoe wilderness trip. The wilderness has a certain appeal when you think of the bustling world we inhabit. It will indeed get you away from the madding crowd. There are some tremendous routes in the United States and Canada.

"What sets a canoeing expedition apart is that it purifies you more rapidly and inescapably than any other. Travel a thousand miles by train and you are a brute; pedal five hundred on a bicycle and you remain basically a bourgeois; paddle a hundred in a canoe and you are already a child of nature." — Pierre Trudeau, P.M.

Canoeing is calming and rewarding, much like kayaking (see under the letter K in this book) so give it some thought.

there once was a young man from crewe,
who wanted to build a canoe,
when he got to the river,
he found with a shiver
he hadn't used waterproof glue.

😑😑: Mr. Grumpy sings, "Row, row, row your boat, rapidly down the stream. Tip your missus overboard and listen to her scream."

From the tranquillity of canoeing to the adrenaline of **canyoning**. Rediscover your spirit of adventure and what it is like to be drenched through. Canyoning is a truly all-round adventure, following a natural water course through a precipitous canyon. Only for adventurous, madcap old fools, who suddenly feel like throwing caution to the wind (or, to the river).

Canyoning is generally only available in the mountains, where steep valleys and rushing mountain streams lead to the formation of canyons. The idea of canyoning is to follow the river downstream in any way possible. You follow the natural water course down through the gorge, descending waterfalls, sliding down natural water flumes, scrambling down gorges and jumping into deep, clear rock pools. In some sections you use harnesses and ropes to abseil down. It is challenging, exciting and is very physical so expect a few bumps along the way.

Try canyoning as a half day activity, as a long-weekend's introduction to canyoning or as a full week of canyoning working up towards the descent of technically challenging, vertical canyons at the end of the week.

Mad enough to give it a go? You need to have a decent level of fitness and a good head for heights but don't be put off by your age. I discovered several people over the age of fifty, who have actually enjoyed this activity.

😑😑😑😑😑: Mr. Grumpy says, "No way. No. No. No." I have to echo that sentiment. I loathe heights and I'm not fit.

Caravan and **camping car** holidays are extremely popular. I am sure you will have examined this possibility before today and have endured holidays in a caravan, maybe even driven to the coast in a Volkswagen campervan with the children when they were small or taken a caravan abroad.

My memory of caravanning includes struggling to get the bed down, then struggling to stay on it during the night, sitting squashed against a table playing cards with my parents while rain battered against the roof and eating lukewarm meals.

Caravans and camping cars are much improved these days. They have mod cons, showers and that all-important toilet. But have you ever been in a gypsy caravan, a "Wind in the Willows" caravan, or travelled the USA in a thirty-one foot long mobile home or RV—recreational vehicle—as they are known across the Atlantic, equipped with four double beds, a shower room, toilet, fridge-freezer, oven, hob, microwave, and satellite TV?

There are even bigger vehicles for hire and some have an ingenious compartment that, at the flick of a switch, will push out a, whole new living annex at the side of the vehicle.

The USA is perfect for this kind of adventure. If you cannot decide where to go and, which route to take, look at website RV Trips.

The idea of holidaying in a caravan or camping car may be one you should revisit now you don't have to worry about amusing young children on a wet and windy day. (Although amusing a Grumpy can be even more difficult.) Take a look at websites Under the Thatch, Unique Holiday Cottages, Rambling Rose, and others for a wide choice of caravans or accommodation that allow you to hide away from the madding crowds. Be bold and take to the roads abroad. Look further afield and consider the islands of New Zealand or some of the routes in Australia.

Today, the caravan is regarded as cool. From gypsy caravans and glampervans to eco-friendly pods, there is a caravan to suit everyone—even the grumpiest of people.

What do you do with your money when you are a super-rich member of a Royal Family in the United Arab Emirates? In the case of Sheikh Hamad bin Hamdan Al Nahyan, you have a caravan constructed in the shape of a globe, exactly one millionth smaller than the actual planet. It consists of eight bedrooms, nine bathrooms and four storage areas.

: Mr. Grumpy says, "Good holiday idea. I fancy driving an RV on new roads abroad, singing along to my ABBA CDs. Excellent way to see new places. You don't have to hang out with other people. No hotel bills either!"

Visiting **castles** can be most rewarding, especially if you are interested in history. Europe boasts hundreds of excellent castles.

If one is not enough for you, do a complete castle tour and have a castle-fest by following the Loire in France or the German Castle Road, a scenic route, over six hundred and twenty-five miles long. It starts in Mannheim and leads you all the way to Prague in the Czech Republic. The website for the journey is in English and has a very good map of the route, including exact distances between castles and cities. It also shows you, which castles have restaurants or hotels.

Find out what it would be like to be the queen or king of the castle and rent your very own royal digs.

Properties are available worldwide but for a contemporary twist on an ancient theme try the castle offered by LTR situated in the Scottish highlands, hidden away on a 60,000 acre estate that is a true Highland wilderness. You can hire this entire Scottish castle, for exclusive use. Its magnificent gardens, which combine modern luxury with the traditional feel of a Highland estate will astound you.

Stride about "your" estate, go walking in the nearby mountains or amuse yourselves playing snooker in the games room. There is a sauna that looks out over the loch, where you can also take a dip or fish for wild brown trout. After a few days here, you will not want to return home.

Did you know?

- According to the Guinness Book of World Records, Prague castle is the largest castle complex in the world.
- In 2007, Bran "Dracula's" Castle, in Bran, Romania, was put up for sale for seventy-eight million dollars. It did not sell and has since been removed from the market. If those Euro lottery numbers come up, it could be yours.
- Neuschwanstein castle in Schwangau, Germany, has been visited by over 60 million people and is the template for Disney's Sleeping Beauty castle. However, the French Chateau at Usse was the model for the castle in the actual fairy tale Sleeping Beauty, written by Charles Perrault.
- Leeds Castle, Maidstone, Kent, has a large garden maze and a dog collar museum containing over a hundred dog collars.
- Chambord Castle is the biggest chateau in the Loire Valley with four hundred and forty rooms, eighty-four staircases,

and three hundred and sixty-five fireplaces. Allow a little time for your visit here.

- Many people have drowned approaching Mont Saint-Michel, Normandy, France, thanks to the tides surrounding it. They can vary by almost fifty feet.
- In Limerick County, Ireland, they have more than 400 medieval castles. That has got to be some kind of a record.

Now you know.

🗿: Mr. Grumpy says, "A good idea. Oh you meant proper castles with moats and knights and crumbling walls. I thought you meant a holiday visiting bouncy castles. If I get to go on a bouncy castle, then ..."

I am dreadful at recognizing **celebrities**. I am dreadful at recognizing anyone, mostly because I do not wear my glasses and so every face is a blur until I get right up to it. As a consequence, I have missed opportunities to say hello to famous people even though they may have been dining at the table behind me (as was the entire England cricket squad), and am therefore not worried about being accused of stalking celebrities.

On the other hand, friends, who cannot wait for the next issue of *OK* magazine or *Hello*, squeal loudly when they spot a celeb, prod me and ask in hushed tones, "Is that ...?" If that sounds like you then tailor your next holiday around celebrity spotting.

There are hot spots for seeing some of the most well-known celebrities so book hotels where you stand the greatest chance of finding yourself next to one. *Sandy Lane* in Barbados is a magnet for celebrities—Simon Cowell, Jeremy Clarkson, Sir Cliff Richard, Hugh Grant and Beyoncé to name but a few. Even if you do not see any of your favourite names, the hotel will wow you and you might bump into the Beckhams while out and about at one of the restaurants. I do not know if anyone famous was there when we stayed, for the reasons mentioned above, but according to my travelling companions I missed Sir Cliff Richard and Michael Winner. Given my husband managed to get mistaken for Sir Clive Woodward, I am not convinced I missed anyone. If you go, take your *I Spy Celebs* book with you to make sure they are the real deal.

The Seychelles is an idyllic location for a romantic and peaceful break, and the very private North Island, with only eleven villas attracted Prince William and Kate Middleton, who spent their honeymoon here. Book here and you might stumble across Pierce Brosnan and Brad Pitt, among others, who take holidays at this resort.

Head to the One & Only Reethi Rah in the Maldives and you could rub shoulders with Gordon Ramsay, Tom Cruise, and Fergie (from one of the only pop groups I know—the Black Eyed Peas.)

Check into a celebrity-owned hotel, where A-list owners and their famous friends have been known to kick back. Book a room at the restored Bedford Inn in Upstate New York, owned by actor Richard Gere. Dine in the Farmhouse, and check out The Barn for a cup of coffee before embarking on outdoor adventures like sailing, horseback riding and hiking. Richard plays an active role here and is often seen at the hotel, which also attracts famous guests like Martha Stewart and Ralph Lauren.

Fans of U2 ought to stay at the cool, contemporary boutique hotel The Clarence, situated along the River Liffeyin the heart of Dublin and owned by Bono and bandmate The Edge. This hotel was transformed into a forty-nine-room boutique hotel in 1992. Grab a Guinness at the Octagon Bar and you stand a chance of spotting some famous names. Try to refrain from singing In the Name of Love loudly after two glasses of Guinness. Especially if you are unsure of the correct lyrics.

You may also howl with delight when you learn that Hugh Jackman (AKA Wolverine in the film X-Men) owns a hotel on the Gold Coast in Australia. Gwinganna (meaning "lookout") shares its name with the region itself, named by the local aboriginal people. The retreat offers visitors the opportunity to embrace health and wellness with fitness classes, a fully equipped gym with trainers, two infinity-edge pools, a yoga deck, holistic counselling, and nutritionists.

Rather than hope to come across the rich and famous at your resort or hotel, grab a Hollywood Celebrity Hot Spots Tour in Los Angeles. For two hours you will cruise Beverly Hills, Hollywood and West Hollywood, including on the Sunset Strip, in search of celebrities and learn some insider gossip about the most talked-about celebrities from well-informed staff on board the bus.

If you prefer, take the "Original Movie Stars' Homes Tour" with Starline, where guides take you on a narrated tour of the celebrity mansions through the exclusive residential neighbourhoods. This is a tour that has been featured on television and boasts a high success rate in seeing stars. You might pass homes belonging to Sandra Bullock, Bruno Mars, and Bruce Willis. If you peer closely over the walls into the back gardens of the mansions you might even catch a glimpse of Katie Perry or Halle Berry hanging out their washing.

Wherever you go, be it Hawaii, The Cote D'Azur in France or Mexico, I hope you have better luck than me at spotting a well-known person.

🗿: Mr. Grumpy says, "I have seen Sir Roger Moore and bounced on Beyoncé's bed. How many grumpy old men can say that with any truth?"

Centre Parcs is, as one person on a well-known travel site claims, "A haven for families with children." I assume most grumpy folk would therefore like to avoid it unless they want to go with their family.

Centre Parcs villages offer a wide range of activities for everyone and have five sites in the UK and several abroad

In fairness, I came across older people, who had a wonderful time there but proper crosspatches will be reluctant to admit they have had any fun at all there.

🗿🗿🗿🗿🗿🗿🗿🗿🗿🗿🗿🗿🗿🗿🗿🗿🗿🗿🗿🗿🗿🗿: Grumpy says, "Don't even dare to ask if I want to go! So what if it is nineteen over the limit?"

Celebrate your holiday in style by driving through the Champagne-Ardenne region of France and stopping off at Moët & Chandon's cellars, which are the largest within the **Champagne** region, spanning twenty-eight kilometres (approximately seventeen point four miles).

Épernay is the capital of Champagne, a town encircled by vineyards and home to many of the most famous names–Moët & Chandon, Pol Roger, and Perrier-Jouët. Most have their sumptuous headquarters along the stately Avenue de Champagne, which Churchill named «the world›s most drinkable address.»

Champagne is the costliest wine to produce. To produce champagne there must be two fermentation processes, with the second step trapping carbon dioxide and making the bubbles. In most of Europe, the name *champagne* is legally protected, meaning only the most expensive sparkling wine produced in the Champagne region of France can be marketed as champagne.

There are around 14,000 winegrowers in the Champagne wine region, so check up on what is available before planning your route. Many of the producers of the bubbly stuff offer bed and breakfast as well as a trip through the cellars finishing with a wine-tasting.

For those with a sense of humour, stop off at Bouzy. You must have your photograph taken, leaning against the sign, waving a bottle of champagne and an empty wine glass.

Champagne can be pricey. A bottle of Cristal will set you back anything from one hundred and fifty American dollars (ninety-nine pounds approximately) to three hundred dollars. A bottle of Krug Brut Vintage 1988 will cost you about five hundred American dollars but some will cost the equivalent of a car or a house.

An anonymous and young British businessman involved in foreign exchange trading pre-ordered a Nebuchadnezzar—equivalent to forty standard bottles of the expensive champagne—of Armand de Brignac Midas at the Playground nightclub in Liverpool's Hilton hotel. The bottle cost the equivalent of 200,000 American dollars and had to be carried to the businessman's table by a couple of waiters.

This is not the world's most expensive champagne. That accolade goes to over two hundred bottles of champagne from the Heidsieck vineyard. Produced in 1907, they were shipped to the Russian Imperial family in 1916, however, a shipwreck off the coast of Finland caused this champagne to be lost at sea until divers discovered over two hundred bottles in 1997. They were sold to wealthy guests at the Ritz-Carlton hotel in Moscow at a cost of 275,000 American dollars each, making this the world's most expensive champagne.

💀: Mr. Grumpy says, "It's obvious who has chosen this as an ideal holiday—it's the wife, isn't it? She loves the stuff. Personally, I'm not bothered but if it keeps her quiet..."

Still on the champagne theme and for a party trick that's guaranteed to impress, book yourself a place on the **champagne sabering** course at the St Regis hotel Bangkok. The hotel uses a saber from the Royal Thai Army in the head butler's nightly revival of this traditional art, which involves separating the collar from the neck of a champagne bottle with a traditional sword. Using a champagne saber is one of the most theatrical and amazing ways to serve wine so take your new-found skill back home and impress the neighbours at Christmas.

No one knows where the art of champagne sabering originated. It may have been Napoléon Bonaparte, who first put sword to bottle, back in the days following the French Revolution. Or perhaps it was the officers in his cavalry–celebrating some great victory by bashing open a bottle of bubbly atop a horse. There is another version of that story, where, following a defeat in battle, a bitter solider cleaved the head off a champagne bottle to drink away his misery.

A more romantic twist involves those same officers and Madame Clicquot, the young widow, who had inherited her husband's champagne house when she was twenty-seven.

Whatever the story, it is a neat trick to perform. Be careful not to break too many bottles with your attempts.

💀: Mr. Grumpy says: "This is more like it. Bring me a sword."

chocolate was introduced to the world by mexico, as was caesar's salad!

I have to confess at this point that Mr. Grumpy is a chocoholic. He cannot get through a day without some of the sweet stuff to chew on. We have a special cupboard and drawer filled with emergency rations in case we get snowed in and he is unable to get his daily fix. Should you be like him, then consider a **chocolate** holiday and visit the chocolate capital of the world—Belgium.

Brussels has more chocolate factories than anywhere else in the world. Check out the Museum of Cocoa and Chocolate to find out more about the history of chocolate, how Belgium adds that creamy taste to chocolate and try some truly scrummy creations.

Better still, learn to make your own chocolate. You need never fear a chocolate shortage. Wherever you live and whatever your level of expertise, there is a course to suit you, but why not travel to Europe and sign up for one of the courses available there? Depending on your interests you could take a short course on how to make truffles, moulded chocolates, filled chocolates, chocolate bars, chocolate dipped fruits and even chocolate fondue. Here is a small selection:

Choco Paris, France.
Belgian Chocolatiers, Brussels.
Chocolate Course, Museum of Chocolate, Barcelona, Spain.
Koeken Chocolade, Amsterdam, Netherlands.
Isertorten, Kaltbruun, Switzerland.
Chocolate Making in Umbria, Italy.

Belgians love chocolate. The Brussels National Airport is the biggest selling point of this sweet treat.

🙂: Mr. Grumpy says, "Chocolate? Yum. Belgian chocolate. Book it."

Tinny music—Slade's greatest Christmas hit—boomed from a speaker adjacent to a sleigh in much need of a repaint. Santa was absent. Probably embarrassed by the fact that the artificial reindeer pretending to pull the sleigh only had one antler. A man dressed in a raincoat, carrying a green bucket waved it at us, hoping for money.

"Is this it?" mumbled my husband. "Is this what Christmas is all about?" He waved his hands at the dismal scene.

It's little wonder that those of us, who are older no longer look forward to Christmas. We cannot comprehend why the real spirit of the season has been lost. We are dismayed by the trolley-loads of plastic gifts being purchased, knowing full-well that by the New Year, those toys will be discarded, broken or piled high in someone's wardrobe waiting to be taken to a charity shop or the local dump. We grumble about the same old trite tunes on the radio harping on about this being the most wonderful time of the year and give peace a chance.

Some of us have even grown to hate this time of the year. We miss those, who are no longer with us. It only serves to remind us of how alone we are. We have no reason to dress Christmas trees in glitzy baubles and decorate our lounges., who will see them? If we are among the fortunate ones, our children and grandchildren will pay us a flying visit, stopping only as long as they feel they must. The thrill of Christmas is no longer evident. We no longer get excited about this time of the year.

However, all is not lost. Think Glühwein, gingerbread houses, the smell of cinnamon and the sound of Christmas carols and nip over to Germany for a flavour of Christmas. No more chuntering about the materialism of Christmas or how the build up to it starts in August and how cheap and nasty it has all become. Here you will, for a while, recall the magic of Christmases past and suddenly you too will be transported back to your childhood.

Christmas markets take place all over the world but Germany is the most renowned for them. Cologne is proclaimed as the Christmas capital of the world and has some four million visitors during the festive period.

It hosts seven markets. The most famous of these is in front of the impressive Gothic cathedral—a UNESCO World Heritage site. The Nordmann fir tree, towering about twenty-five metres high, is the shining heart of the market, lit up with 50,000 LED lights, it is a bright landmark in Cologne during the advent season.

Among the one hundred and sixty stalls or "huts," you will be able to savour the smells and delights of German specialties: gingerbread, Stollen, roast chestnuts and of course, the infamous mulled wine—Glühwein. Take in—and no doubt take home—the prettiest Christmas decorations imaginable. Shop for fabulous wooden gifts and crafts. Marvel at the skills of the tradesmen carving fantastic creatures into wooden trunks, or blowing glass baubles. Watch and listen to several of the one hundred performers playing or singing Christmas music. Stop off for a local tasty treat and mix with a crowd, whose festive cheer is passed onto you by some invisible process of osmosis.

Our favourite market was Altplatz. It is the area of the "House

Gnomes", who were believed to assist the tradesmen of this area. A nostalgic children's roundabout whirls merrily in one corner of this bustling delightful market. Stop and watch a puppet show, or admire all the huts and soak up the truly festive atmosphere or grab a pair of ice skates and weave about the ice rink beautifully surrounded by Alpine buildings and gnomes being transported on a small lift. If you are worried about staying steady on your skates after a few mugs of Glühwein, then try the curling there in a convivial atmosphere.

Cologne is not merely about markets. Some of the window displays are incredible. The Steiff bear display at the Galerie Kaufhof department store kept us mesmerized for ages. Featuring a large display of a circus with every toy animal playing a part, it was a magical world of childish fantasy.

At this point, if you have not reverted to an excited ten-year-old, then head to Don Gelati. This stylish café, opposite the cathedral, specializes in Spaghetti Ice creams, topped with a latticework of caramel. They are scrummy. I don't normally eat ice cream but caved in and had an After Eight special—a wondrous creation. Mr. Grumpy dug into an enormous cherry affair that made him smile… yes, smile for some considerable time afterwards. Even if ice cream is not your thing, you must visit here. It is perfect too for a cappuccino or sandwich but trust me those ice creams are delicious.

Even Mr. Grumpy, who grumbles "Bah Humbug!" every year, was enchanted with the Rudolfplatz that transports you to the world of the brothers Grimm, with fairy tale figures and festive illuminations.

For a genuine Christmas atmosphere and to rekindle that enthusiasm for Christmas you may once have had, head to Cologne. For a few days you too can believe in Santa Claus and feel the warmth of human kindness.

Get your Grumpy into the festive spirit and book a trip for you both.

Top travel tips for Cologne:

- Visit the German Christmas markets at the very beginning of the season before it gets flooded with visitors. (Opens about 24th November.) We went for the second and third day. Plenty of atmosphere and room to get about.
- One of the best hotels to stay in is the Excelsior Hotel

Ernst. It is slap bang opposite the cathedral, offers a warm welcome and a delicious buffet breakfast.

- Wear warm clothes. It can be very cold, especially at night.
- Look for Don Gelati ice cream parlour opposite the Dom. Try one of their incredibly tasty ice creams. I had an After Eight ice cream that contained five After Eight mints as well as several balls of ice cream. The parlour also serves light snacks, is very clean and modern and can provide you with a splendid cappuccino.

: Mr. Grumpy says, "Even a hardened grumpy guts like me will like the Christmas markets in Germany. It's a must-do. Ho, ho, ho! Where's my Stollen?"

Circle dancing comes from the tradition of communities dancing together and claims to be of benefit to older people. In fact, if you have ever seen *Zorba the Greek* starring Anthony Quinn, you will have an idea of what it entails but don't let your other half near any china plates when he is practising.

The list of benefits is lengthy but suffice it to say, it is great for improving physical, spiritual and mental health, and perfect for meeting new people. Ideal for first-timers and single people because you dance with a group of people, whereas some other forms of dancing require a dance partner. You do not throw any plates but you do dance in a circle. If you can convince your other half that this is going to be a lot of fun, then book a circle dancing course at home or abroad. There are glowing testimonials for many of the circle holidays you can find online.

I could not convince my husband to take up circle dancing. The last time he joined in and danced in a group was when he was dragged into a conga line at a New Year's party, many years ago. Someone balanced a large fake pineapple on his head, then I threw myself at him and asked him to marry me. I have not seen him dance since.

Years ago I decided to learn to juggle. I used my mother's bowl of fruit to assist me and it took a while before she worked out why her apples were always bruised. Today, along with other budding performers, I can acquire a, whole host of **circus skills** including fire eating, acrobatics, trapeze, and learning to walk the tight wire. It's no good shaking your head at this suggestion. Circuses are not just for children and some of these skills are excellent for older people.

For example, not only does juggling improve your coordination, vision, and reflexes but it also increases grey matter in certain area of your brains. People, who have learn to juggle are less aggressive, more sociable and communicative and find concentration easier. On top of that they also develop much better balance and coordination.

Clearly, learning other circus skills will also have similar benefits but if you do want to attempt any of these, you can always opt for clown school.

There are circus schools across the world that allow wannabe clowns and acrobats to pick up the basics. And, if they really want to, they can stay on for longer-term courses. Many of the courses and camps are aimed at children, but the Trapeze Arts Circus School in Oakland, California, and Sydney Trapeze School cater for big kids and old grumpy pants, although after a holiday learning to fly through the air, you will feel much lighter-hearted.

I have moved away from fruit now and can juggle rubber balls. I think I might try flaming torches next. That should light up my other half's face.

What do you think about my next suggestion—a **climbing holiday**? I have to admit that although I immediately thought, "Not a chance!" my inner child got rather excited about a trip to climb Mount Kilimanjaro. It got more animated when I discovered that holiday firms, besieged by adventurous grandparents, who are increasingly choosing all-action holidays, are now offering life-changing holidays for us older folk.

Holiday companies like Shearings and Get-Lost have come up with many fabulous adventures, so if you would like a holiday of a lifetime, there are oodles of possibilities.

Rock climbing is a fantastic way to get fit. Don't let your age put you off the idea of rock climbing because there are many different levels of the sport and you can choose suitable heights and surfaces to match your fitness and abilities. (So, no booking that holiday to Mount Kilimanjaro until you are ready to face the climb.) Climbing is not all about strength, there is a good deal of skill and grace involved, meaning it can be the perfect sport for picking up when you are a bit older.

Climbing holidays are ideal for those, who want to challenge themselves physically and achieve a special goal in older age. We challenged ourselves a few years ago, when we booked into Cathedral Peak Mountain Lodge in the Drakensberg Mountains, South Africa.

Cathedral Peak is surrounded by stunning mountains and you are spoilt for choice of walk. There are eighteen different walks and free guided hikes, ranging from gentle riverside ambles suitable for the fatigued grumpy to guided hikes to Bushman paintings and beautiful waterfalls, or for hard-core hikers, the day hike to the top of Cathedral Peak (3,007 metres), one of the best day walks in the Drakensberg Mountains.

We managed a few of the easier routes and I must admit, I felt a lot fitter by day five. This is an inspirational destination with some of the most spectacular ranges of mountains you could come across. After day five, we gave up and took a helicopter flight over the tallest mountains. It was a heck of lot easier than using crampons.

My inner child is still clammering to climb Kilimanjaro but my ancient knees are creaking a warning. I wonder, which will win the battle. Race you to the top!

the group leader gave a group of hikers, who were climbing mount everest some very important advice, "if by chance, you see the yeti, run. whatever you do, don't touch the yeti."
that night, one member was alone in his tent, when he saw the great yeti standing at the entrance. the man was so scared, he shot out of the tent at speed, but on the way out, he touched the yeti. the yeti set off after him.

the man ran as fast as he could. he ran past all the climbers, down the mountain, but the yeti continued to follow him. the man raced to a nearby village, rented a bike and cycled all the way to the nearest city. he sat down to catch his breath and lo and behold, the yeti was thundering up the street after him.

the man cycled to the station, leapt onto a train and headed out of the city as fast as he could. he booked into a hotel but when he looked out of the window, who did he see running into the hotel? yes, the yeti.

he nipped out of the back of the hotel, caught a taxi to the airport and caught a plane out of the city back home to america.

a few days later, he is back at work when he sees the yeti thundering down the corridor to his office. the man starts running again but trips and falls. the yeti comes up to the man and stops on front of him. the man struggles to his feet and angrily says, "you've chased me for days. i give up. what do you want?!"

the yeti reaches out to him with his giant hands and says, "tag, you're it."

😊😊😊😊: Mr. Grumpy says, "Ladders are my limit. I can't climb any higher than the top rung. Not for me."

Mr. G said this was a daft suggestion—**coasteering**. I agree it is not the most sensible of ideas I have had but many people take pleasure in this activity including one of my hairdressers. Strange but true, quite a few of my ex-hairdressers have left hairdressing and taken up exciting activities. One took up tango in Argentina, another climbed Mont Blanc, and this one went coasteering every weekend and finally left to do it as a full-time job.

Sorry, did I not explain what it is? First you squeeze into a wetsuit, don a safety helmet and old trainers then traverse a coastline where sea meets land by any means possible (climbing, scrambling, jumping, swimming etc.)

According to website coaststeering.com *"Coasteering is a magnificent way to explore personal limits, overcome fears, increase personal confidence and of course enjoy a few hours of pure adrenalin-soaked fun whilst bonding with family and friends."*

If you have never tried this activity and fancy a holiday bonding with your beloved while navigating around a coastline, then you are in luck. Coasteering NI is on a quest to find someone "older" to go on an adventure with them. You need the following criteria and be:

- Outgoing
- Adventurous
- Up for a laugh
- Mega keen to try coasteering
- Have their doctor's approval
- Aged 68 or older
- Able to come coasteering on Sunday 1st September (of their own free will)
- Agreeable to all video and photographs being used for PR

Oh bother, I have checked and it seems we have all missed the deadline. Still, if you email them. I am sure they are still on the hunt for that special person.

😀😀😀😀😀: Mr. Grumpy says, "LOL. Really? People do this for fun?"

What is your favourite dish to eat? Is it Greek? Italian? French? How about learning to cook it in the country from, which it originated? **Cookery** courses are a wonderful way to combine sight-seeing, relaxation, and education. Learn new techniques and skills and create traditional recipes.

Travel website Responsible Travel offers an array of courses and destinations including Mexico, India, Umbria, Vietnam and Scotland among others.

Be bold and explore the Lemon Grass Trial in Thailand, where you can have a two-week private tour feasting on local delicacies, learning from local people and picking and catching produce before you cook it. From Bangkok to the Central Plains and Isan to Krabi, you will travel across Thailand on a real foodie trail.

Or, take your cooking skills to another level in exotic Marrakech, where you can learn the art of slow cooking and the secrets of spices while immersing yourself in North African culture. You can stay and cook in an intimate riad and dine in some of the city's finest restaurants. Learn to prepare slow-cooked Moroccan tagine, couscous dishes and cook with rare spices.

A culinary experience and/or a cookery course could be the ideal holiday for those, who are bon viveurs. Make sure you take an elasticated pair of trousers. I do not expect you will lose any weight on one of these holidays.

"Waiter, this Lobster has only one claw."
"I'm sorry, sir. It must have been in a
fight."
"Well then, bring me the winner."

😒: Mr. Grumpy says: "How do I work this iPad thingy? I want to book Mrs. Grumpy onto a course. I am desperate for some decent food."

There are so many **creative courses** on offer, it would take another entire book to list them all. My favourites include:

- Discovering the art of knitting the Icelandic way. Icelandic sheep are an ancient North European breed, whose double-layered coat is uniquely suited to cold and wet conditions. In Iceland they are raised primarily for their meat, but the wool is a valuable by-product. The inner layer, or *thel*, is insulating, superlight, and very airy, while the outer layer, or *tog*, is long, strong, and water repellent. Carded together, these two layers make *lopi*, which is a versatile wool used to knit the traditional Icelandic sweater called *lopapeysa*. You can learn how to produce and use lopi, the wool that is gaining cult-like popularity among knitters worldwide. You will also be able to meet farmers, learn about wool drying and spinning and design your own jumper, as well as attend knitting classes. (You could then present the said jumper to your other half as a special Christmas present. Surely, he will be glad you did not waste money on a shop-bought gift!)

- A carpet weaving holiday in Turkey where you are able to stay in a peaceful Nomadic village on the Aegean Coast and learn the traditional techniques of carpet weaving from its local women At the end of the week you should have created your own carpet, which you can take home, that is, if you have not spent most of the week eating Turkish food, exploring the city of Bodrum and relaxing on the beach.
- Crime writing in Tuscany where you will learn about how to pen a bestselling crime novel. I really should book myself onto that one.

Be as creative as you want. There will be a course somewhere in the world to interest you and plenty nearer home if you are on a stricter budget.

My grumpy laughingly suggested I should enroll on a Turkish belly dancing holiday in Istanbul, given I have a large, wobbly belly. After due consideration, I have enrolled us both.

🧔: Mr. Grumpy says, "I might be persuaded to go along to a course in Spain where I could learn the flamenco guitar, or a good photography course abroad where I could learn to come to grips with the digital camera I got for Christmas several years ago. I still don't know how to make the flash work." Mrs. Grumpy says, "We shall see how smiley it is after his belly dancing course."

Surrounded by red canyons and big skies, the backdrop to Mustang Monument: Wild Horse Eco Resort in a sleepy Nevada backwater is pure Wild West fantasy: from the hand-painted storybook tepees down to the colourful indigenous cowboys and Indians that populate the ranch. Mustang Monument is as far as you can get from the traditional idea of a **cowboy camp-out**. Its glamorous tepees are kitted out with four-poster beds and have a twenty-four-hour butler service. Despite the luxuries, the essence of the retreat is communing with nature and good old-fashioned adventure.

It is run by Madeleine Pickens, the British wife of Texas billionaire oilman T. Boone Pickens, who, concerned that the US government was considering a massive cull of some 35,000 mustangs, purchased the land spread across three valleys and two mountain ranges in what was once prime horse country to provide a sanctuary for them.

Madeleine wants people to sample the simplicity and beauty of the American West, the joys of falling asleep under the stars and waking up with wild horses. You can be a part of that and live the life of a cowboy/cowgirl with a stay here.

For all you Wild West and horse lovers, I can think of no better holiday.

It is the sport that so often captures the imagination of us Brits at the Winter Olympics—**curling**. It looks easy. You simply slide a stone—made of granite—down the ice, towards the house (the circular target), while your partner frantically sweeps the ice in order to increase the speed of the stone and/or affect its path. When you try it out it transpires this is not an easy sport at all. You find your stone over-shoots or under-shoots the target every time. Visit St Anton am Alberg, Austria and you will be able to practise curling until you get it right. Those, who are sick of housework and brushing floors need not bother.

Once they hit the big five-oh, many of my friends seemed to gravitate to **cycling** as an activity. In fact, cycling is an activity encouraged by the Ageing Alliance. They recommend it to help us prepare for ageing and stay fit. Certainly, those, who have taken it up seem very enthusiastic about it and all look fit and healthy.

One friend in particular, is addicted to cycling, having only taken up the sport five years ago. He has gone from riding in an amateurs' club to travelling the world on his bike. His last trip was to Nepal and his next is to Mount Kailash at the centre of the Earth, where he will cycle the roof of the world. I guess you cannot beat that.

Start small like him, and, who knows where you might fancy riding next: Cycling across the wild and pristine southwestern region of Sardinia, Mexico, Californian Winefields, through the rolling hills of world renowned wine estates in Napa Valley, alongside towering Redwood trees and across the Golden Gate Bridge. Or, how about cycling the back roads of China, rural south-west China, taking in some of the most famous images of China, including the giant pandas of Sichuan and the karst scenery of Yangshuo through breath-taking scenery, terraced rice fields and to ancient villages, alongside rivers and streams, lined with bamboo? Cycling is the perfect way to explore Rajastan.

Check into MesaStila a luxury twenty-two-villa property in Central Java, Indonesia that offers a cycling package (two days minimum, four days maximum) and you will return home fit enough to take on Bradley Wiggins. Here you can push your pedalling prowess to the limit through Yogyakarta's spectacular terrain, where volcano-ringed plantation fields provide a fiery backdrop to your journey. Out of the saddle, lose yourself in the resort's hammam steam room and take your pick from one of the daily recovery or relaxation massages; or cool off after your bike ride with some laps in the octagonal-shaped infinity pool fed by fresh spring water. Alternatively, celebrate your cycling success with a favoured vintage from the bar's wine cellar.

It will soon be that time of year again, when French streets are filled with cheering supporters waving tricolour flags as the Tour de France teams thunder through their towns and villages. You too could ride a stage of the Tour de France.

Take on L'Étape du Tour. It is the one stage of the tour that is open to amateur riders every year (the real tour covers it a week later). Roads are closed, as they are for the rest of the tour, and riders have a police escort. My aforementioned friend rode it a couple of years ago and loved every moment although his legs felt like lead for days afterwards.

Or brag about visiting Macchu Pichu by bike. Oh alright, not all the way by bike—that would be a gruelling ordeal rather than a holiday. You can take a bus up the hardest climbs but you can omit that detail when you tell your awe-struck friends about your trip. World Expeditions offer a thirteen-day holiday during, which you will be able scream happily as you zoom down thrilling slopes and gasp as you cycle past outstanding sights.

To appreciate these holidays, all you require is stamina, a love of cycling and some rather sturdy cycling shorts.

a tandem rider is stopped by a police car. "what've I done, officer?" asks the rider. "perhaps you didn't notice sir, but your wife fell off your bike half a mile back." "oh, thank goodness for that," says the rider. "I thought I'd gone deaf!"

: Mr. Grumpy says, "Loved cycling in France. Would give this a go again but I think my old steed is a little rusty and the tyres are perished. I might need some practise first."

I gave up cycling after falling off my bike in France—actually, more over my bike as I hurtled over the handlebars when my chain snapped, and landed somewhere in the middle of the D958 to Montricoux. Hitherto, I'd loved the freedom that cycling brought and we both cycled miles over hills, taking in endless vistas over beautiful gorges and revelling in the fact that the roads were almost traffic-free. I took the accident as a sign that I should stick to four wheels or two legs, ergo the next suggestion holds much appeal— **Cypriot Underwater Walk**.

Cyprus, a popular destination for many people over fifty, offers some surprising activities for grouchy folk, who want tranquillity. Walking underwater, admiring the sea life, rock formations, and feeding the fish, seemed like a proper get-away-from-it-all adventure. You wear a special diving helmet attached to air by a long tube. No snorkel, no diving mask and best of all you can keep your glasses on so you can enjoy perfect vision. Walk along the sandy floor of the sea in your own private bubble. You cannot get much more peaceful than that.

: Mr. Grumpy says, "Walking underwater wearing an upside down goldfish bowl on my head—I'll pass."

D

twenty years from now you will be more disappointed by the things you didn't do than by the ones you did do. so throw off the bowlines, sail away from the safe harbour. catch the trade winds in your sails. explore. dream. discover.
~ mark twain

D is for dance holidays, diamonds, dinosaur dig, dog holidays, dogsledding, drumming.

Does your other half dance like a stiff penguin? Loosen him up and book yourselves onto a **dance holiday**. Try a tango course in Buenos Aires, a salsa holiday in Cuba, learn the flamenco in Spain, or rock 'n' roll in Rotherham ... you get the idea. Best not to book a Gangnam course in Seoul, Korea, though. We would not want that video to go viral, would we?

my wife and I both love to dance. she goes on tuesdays, I go on thursdays.

😀😀😀😀😀: Mr. Grumpy says, "I don't do dancing. I don't mind watching though. Does a trip to the Moulin Rouge in Paris come under this category?"

They may be a girl's best friend but when I did an internet search for "**Diamond tours**" I ended up with a load of bus company information and the possibility to go and see the great entertainer, Neil Diamond, in concert. I was tempted by the latter.

Amsterdam is the place to go to see sparkling, expensive rocks. You can book a tour with a company or plan your own. If you make the arrangements, ensure you visit Coster Diamonds, the diamond factory that re-cut the Koh-i-Noor at the request of Queen Victoria.

Coster Diamonds was one of the most eminent diamond factories in the city and still operates to this day. Book a guided tour or a workshop tour. Guided tours of Coster Diamonds demonstrate how the diamonds are cut and polished, after, which visitors can browse the diamond showrooms to see the results of these processes. The free tours last about forty-five minutes. There is both a cafe and souvenir shop on the premises and, of course, the shop where you can buy a large gem for yourself.

The Diamant Museum is a venture of Coster Diamonds, which, in addition to its free factory tours, operates this small but attractive museum. The museum follows the story of the diamond, from carbon crystals to the cut and polished jewels that are prized the world over. There is much to see and learn about here including replicas of some fabulous stones and an audio-visual exhibit on famous jewel thefts. You can also learn how to spot a fake.

Gassan Diamonds opened shop just after World War II, in October 1945. Samuel Gassan began as a small importer and exporter of gems, but after trading for ten years, he noticed how much a short introduction to diamond craftsmanship spurred sales. He introduced tours to the factory and now offers tours to 350,000 people each year at its historic, canal-side premises: a restored steam-driven diamond factory. The half-hour tours cover the basics of the famous "4 C"s—carat, colour, clarity, and cut.

🐵: Mr. Grumpy says, "Quite interesting but don't linger in the shops. Make sure you keep one hand on the door handle when you enter so you can beat a hasty retreat."

Explore a diamond mine in South Africa. Premier Diamond Mine is still one of South Africa's largest diamond mines, and it is here that the Cullinan diamond was found in 1905. This world famous diamond remains the largest gem diamond ever found to date. The diamond was sent to the Asscher Brothers in Amsterdam, where it was cut into nine smaller diamonds, which either form part of the Crown Jewels, or are still owned by the British Royal Family.

The Premier Diamond Mine started underground mining in

1945 and is now owned by De Beers. It was renamed the Cullinan Diamond Mine in 2003. Here you can see the massive crater where the Cullinan Diamond (named after Sir Thomas Cullinan) was found, and get an in depth look into the daily routines of a working mine. There is a museum on the premises and the Diamond Shop— of course.

African Sky offers a tour that takes in this mine and the surrounding area along with some other interesting sights.

Travel on a historical tram from City Hall, Kimberley, capital of the Northern Cape Province to Kimberley Mine Museum. This open-air museum has been authentically restored back to the time of the diamond rush in 1880.

Wander past dwellings once inhabited by diggers, the tobacco shop where Perilly produced his famous hand-made cigarettes, Barnato's Boxing Academy, Digger's Rest an old pub and the old farmhouse belonging to the DeBeers family.

The DeBeers Diamond Hall displays—amongst other things—the famous Eureka diamond, the first officially-recorded diamond in South Africa.

Marvel at the Big Hole. It is two hundred and fifteen metres deep and one point six kilometres in diameter, making it the largest man-dug hole in the world.

Sift through diamond-bearing gravel, looking for your own treasure. We can all live in hope!

Finally, go on the Sparkling Tour through the Diamond Works, Cape Town, a journey through the history of diamonds and tanzanite. Meet the designers, cutters, and goldsmiths that work here, and view some impressive pieces.

Digging up a **dinosaur** is not high on my bucket list, but the prospect of being part of a proper scientific dig to discover dinosaur bones holds a certain appeal. I suppose I have *Jurassic Park* to thank for that, or I fancy myself to be Christmas Jones in one of the James Bond films. (Give yourself a pat on the back if you know, which film.)

GeoWorld Travel, which specialise in Geo- and Polar tourism offered the opportunity to be part of dinosaur digs in Portugal in 2013 and Wyoming, USA in 2014. Places filled up quickly, and now that those digs are completed, you will need to keep checking the website for dates of the next big dinosaur dig. Some significant dinosaur bones were unearthed last time and finds have been exhibited in major museums.

Should you be unable to get onto one of these digs, follow in the footsteps of the prehistoric creatures that once roamed this ancient land. Australia's Dinosaur Trail encompasses the towns of Richmond, Hughenden, and Winton, which all have their own unique dinosaur stories to tell.

In Richmond, visit Kronosaurus Korner Fossil Centre, home to Australia's best-preserved dinosaur skeleton. After visiting Kronosaurus Korner you may like to try your hand at finding your very own fossil, that is, if he has got lost in the centre!

☺☺☺☺: Mr. Grumpy says, "Sounds like too much effort for me. I do enough digging in the garden and if I want to find any fossils, I'll look at the back of the freezer. Guaranteed to find some forgotten ready-meal fossilized in there."

For a special holiday to see the Northern Lights or to travel to the Yukon, book a holiday with man's best friend and go **dogsledding** with huskies.

Husky safaris take place in Finland and Canada but for a true adventure that will stay with you forever, head off on an organized Arctic expedition with a dogsled team. You can travel across Sweden's wilderness and challenging terrain transported in true explorer style by a team of trained huskies. This is not a casual holiday trip and you will need to be fit and healthy to take up the challenge, but imagine the sense of accomplishment at the end of your trip.

Despite common usage in annoying commercials or movies, mushers do not say "Mush" to their dogs. Where did this come from? One theory is that French trappers were overheard saying "marche" to their dogs. The term "musher" stuck and is used to describe someone, who runs sled dogs.

One of many things a leader must know is their right, "gee" from their left, "haw." These commands have been around since teams of oxen were used to plough fields.

how can you tell if you have a stupid sled dog?
it chases parked snowmobiles.

🙁: Mr. Grumpy says, "To prepare for this, take an over-excited Labrador to the park, throw a ball for it and keep hold of its lead. If you can stay upright for more than ten seconds, you'll love this holiday suggestion."

Drumming is incredibly good for you. Drumming can achieve physical and mental relaxation, relief from stress, some relief from depression, temporary relief from pain or muscle stiffness, a greater clarity of thought, improved social networking, and more efficient team working.

It is also proven to help cancer patients, people with Parkinson›s disease, people with Alzheimer's, people with learning difficulties, people with physical disabilities, and older people.

Even the most uptight curmudgeon will take pleasure in beating out a rhythm on African drums. So why not consider going to Africa to learn to play them? There are drumming residential courses in Gambia where you will have intensive instruction in beautiful surroundings.

Mr. G and I had one night of learning to play the drums. It was extremely therapeutic. Unfortunately, both of us got carried away with the beat and ended up in a drumming jam session that lasted far too long for those unfortunate people forced to listen to us.

how can you tell when a drummer's at the door?
he doesn't know when to come in.

🙁: Mr. Grumpy says, "Surprisingly therapeutic. Practise your drumming skills by tapping your fingers rhythmically against the kitchen tops while waiting for your wife to get ready to go out."

E

LIVING ON EARTH IS EXPENSIVE, BUT IT DOES
INCLUDE A FREE TRIP ROUND THE SUN.

E is for elephants, elf hunting, expensive holidays, and extra-terrestrial highway.

Ever since watching Disney's *Dumbo*, I have been a sucker for **elephants**. I have watched them roaming in the wild, sat in silence as a huge bull grazed near our jeep, observed a baby elephant learning to dig up roots with its mother and aunts, and am as infatuated with them now as I was as a child.

There are all sorts of holidays involving elephants, from tracking down and observing them, going on an elephant safari and riding one of the huge beasts, watching elephant polo to elephant conservation volunteering.

Elephants have been a part of Indian culture since time immemorial. The elephant-headed god, Ganesha, is revered and devotedly worshipped throughout India. They, therefore, play an important part in religious events, marriage ceremonies, processions, and in times past, they were a significant part of the battlefield.

Nepal and Rajasthan are the only two places where polo is played on elephant-back.

These giants of the animal world are representative of the strength and power of kings and emperors. It was, therefore, natural that polo, the king of sports and the sport of kings, was adapted for play on elephant-back.

Jaipur is the only place in the world where you can witness this exclusive sport being played throughout the year. Unlike horse polo, which is fast-paced, elephant polo is more relaxing and leisurely. It is enthralling to watch the enormous pachyderms pursuing the ball at their own majestic pace.

To witness elephants in all their glory, attend the annual Elephant

Festival, held every year in the Pink City, Jaipur. This event is organised on the full moon day of Phalgun Purnima, which falls in the month of February/March. It is celebrated on the day before the festival of colours called Holi.

For the Elephant Festival, mahouts (the keepers) wash the elephants then groom and adorn them with colourful and embroidered velvets rugs, parasols, huge elephant jewellery and anklets decked with bells. They paint intricate traditional Indian motifs onto their bodies, and add ear danglers and coloured brocade scarves. Tusks are bejewelled with gold and silver bracelets and rings. Shining head-plates are placed on their heads, giving them a regal air.

This festival begins with a magnificent procession of these regal creatures accompanied by their mahouts and much noise from musical instruments. Following this, the elephants participate in elephant polo, elephant races and a tug-of-war between the elephant and nineteen men and women. (My money will be on the elephant wining.)

The festival attracts thousands and is an important event in the calendar. Book a holiday to coincide with this festival to appreciate how beloved and revered these intelligent giants are.

Sadly, elephants are still being hunted and killed in huge numbers for their ivory tusks. There are conservation projects that help preserve the creatures. Many of these are reliant on volunteers to help with the elephants and the camps.

Responsible Travel has a wide range of volunteering holidays in Namibia, Cambodia and Thailand. Volunteers, who take up the latter challenge are allowed to work with one elephant and her mahout, walk with their elephant through the area surrounding the camp, learn from the mahout how to verbally command the elephant to follow directions, help to shower the elephant, feed her and keep her living area tidy. It is a golden opportunity to discover more about these gentle giants and take back much more than just holiday memories.

The Elephant Sanctuary in South Africa also provides a safe haven for elephants that have been rescued.

The sanctuary believes in educating and interacting, consequently you can purchase packages that give you further exposure to the elephants. The basic package is called "Walk Trunk-in-Hand," during, which a guide introduces you to the elephants, you learn about their backgrounds, behaviours, characters, and more, while being able to touch, feel, feed, interact, and walk trunk-in-hand with the elephants. If you want to, you can add on an elephant riding package.

Should that not be enough for you, try their Brushdown package where you take part in the morning grooming of the elephants. Afterwards you join the training and stimulation program the handlers do with the elephants every day. For a full day with elephants add a Sundowner Package where you help groom the elephants and get them ready for bedding down for the night with the Brushdown program.

The focus here is on happy elephants. I think they succeed.

what do you get when you cross an
elephant with a parrot?
an animal that tells you everything it
remembers.

: Mr. Grumpy says, "Don't tell Mrs. Grumpy but I received a love letter from an elephant a few years ago—honestly, I did. Wonderful, intelligent creatures who somehow touch even the grumpiest soul."

I appear to have gone all J.R.R. Tolkien on you with this suggestion—**elf hunting**. I am not unique in my love of folklore, fantasy and other worlds. Icelandic folklore is a rich field, ranging through stories of magic, elves, trolls, and ghosts and spirits of all kinds, so it is not surprising to discover that Iceland claims it has a magical world of elves, dwarves and other spiritual beings, collectively called the "Hidden Folk". Scandinavian folklore is full of elves, trolls, and other mythological characters. Most people in Norway, Denmark, and Sweden have not taken them seriously since the nineteenth century, but elves are no joke to many of the 320,000 Icelandic people. Centuries-old folklore says that, whole families of the beings live in the rocks that are part of a town's centre, and on a trip to Iceland you can enter their magical world. You can join a tour that takes visitors to their homes, stopping at places like Hellisgerdi

Park and the base of the cliff, Hamarinn, where it is said the Royal Family of the Hidden Folk lives. Along the way, the guide retells stories about the magical hidden worlds and describes the town's development in harmony with the Hidden Folk.

😑😑😑😑: Mr. Grumpy says, "Brings a whole new meaning to the phrase, "away with fairies.""

Many holidays are expensive, but if you happen to have one million pounds shoved under your mattress and don't know what to spend it on, treat yourselves to the most **expensive** holiday in the world. One holiday company, VeryFirstTo.com has come up with a bespoke package holiday for anyone, who has that sort of cash to splash.

You can expect to embark on the epic two-year odyssey around the world, visiting more than one hundred and fifty countries. The trip includes overland travel and flights (in business class cabins or superior, of course), with guided tours at the different sites. There is no "slumming it" on this trip. Chill out in between journeys at a range of luxurious hotels, including Sandy Lane in Barbados, the Hotel George V in Paris, The Plaza in New York, the Cipriani in Venice, The Ritz-Carlton in Moscow, and the Taj Mahal Palace in Mumbai.

However, if two years' travelling is too much for you, spend less and book a trip into space with the same company. It will only set you back £69,000. I can see you rushing for your chequebooks for this one.

😑: Mr. Grumpy says ... Mr. Grumpy is speechless.

This is an unusual idea—travel the **Extra-terrestrial** Highway, in Nevada, USA. This is actually Highway 375, designated the Extra-terrestrial Highway in 1996. Drive the route and you will not see little green men but will rejoice in the scenic beauty of the desert's varied terrain.

Visit Rachel, the town closest to Area 51, the popular name for the top secret government research, development and testing facility located within the 3-million acre Nellis Bombing and Gunnery Range—also a hotbed for conspiracy theories on alien life.

Stop at the Little A'Le'Inn in Rachel with UFO parking spaces, alien mural, and a sign reading, "Earthlings Welcome." Owner Connie West claims she has catered for all sorts of people. She once had to kick out two men, who showed up wearing nothing but silver and green spray paint.

"It's life, Jim. But not as we know it."

☻☻☻☻☻: Mr. Grumpy says, "Whatever!"

F

F is for fishing, flamenco dancing, football, France, free diving.

Women are extremely good at **fishing**. Especially fly fishing. It is something to do with patience and pheromones. Fishing also has huge health benefits, so ladies, think about this choice for a moment before skimming over it and seeing what else you can choose. Surprisingly, fishing is the most popular participation sport in the UK. See, you might be missing out on something extraordinary.

I am not suggesting sitting beside a lake, huddled under a small umbrella on a cold rainy night, or balanced precariously on a small boat on a windy reservoir, because I have tried those and I would not consider them an escape in any shape, way, or form. I propose something more exciting—a guided Thailand fishing adventure that will give you the opportunity to pit your skills against the mighty Mekong catfish, salmon fishing in Russia or saltwater fly-fishing in the Bahamas. They may seem slightly far-flung destinations but if you want to do more than sightsee or loaf about on a beach, then sign up for some fishing. You and your spouse can spend time together while enjoying the same activity. That is until one of you catches a huge fish and the other is left with nothing but an empty rod and a tale about the one that got away.

Add some danger to the fishing holiday by hopping aboard a canoe and discovering how to fish for piranha in the forgotten wilderness of the Peruvian Amazon.

Watch out though because even when dead they can do you

damage. You need to eat them using your fingers so you can feel for their tiny forked bones that can lodge in your throat and choke you.

☺: Mr. Grumpy says, "A far cry from catching minnows in the local river. The best part of this trip would be watching Mrs. Grumpy attempting to descale and gut my catch—might have a go at marlin fishing. That should keep her very busy."

I mentioned dancing in an earlier chapter but it is worth mentioning **flamenco dancing** holidays again. Flamenco dancers try to express their deepest emotions by using body movements and facial expressions. Flamenco courses are run in cities all over Spain and are suitable for all levels. This is a sexy, passionate, uplifting dance. It will help release tension, improve fitness and you will both look amazing at the annual pub Christmas party when you practice the flamenco in front of DJ Dave's disco.

It appeals to me. How often is a woman allowed to make lots of noise with her shoes, wave a long dress seductively, clap her hands and occasionally kick without getting into trouble?

One of my friends went to Argentina on a flamenco dancing holiday and never returned. She ran off with the bare-chested dance instructor, who taught her how to play her castanets. I rest my case. Book now.

There are more flamenco academies in Japan than in the whole of Spain.

☺☺☺☺: Mr. Grumpy says, "Frilly shirts and grumpies do not go hand in hand unless they have consumed copious amounts of sangria beforehand— Olé!"

Did I hear a collective groan from the grumpy old ladies reading this book? **Football holidays** may not result in you having to sit back and listen to your other half complain about his team's performance or hang about in pubs cheering on your side while watching a large television screen. I know many of you ladies are football supporters too so take your passion for the sport further afield (excuse the pun) and consider a football-themed holiday.

Brazil is the ultimate football holiday destination. You do not even have to purchase match tickets to catch footballing action as the game is played on street corners, local playing fields and even on beaches. However, if you want to see some professional action, head to Rio's Maracana where tickets are usually available as the 90,000 capacity stadium rarely fills its seats.

For a more intimate, local experience, try the Brazilian Peladao from August to December, hosted in the rainforest city of Manaus. It may be an amateur tournament but it attracts vast crowds.

For those armchair football critics among you, make use of your keepy-uppy skills and teach football abroad. Volunteer coaching while on a gap year or career break can be incredibly rewarding, particularly if you work with disadvantaged youth in developing countries. There are quite a few organisations that can organise trips to South Africa, Ecuador, India, or Ghana where you can work with children in local school, training grounds, or even slums. You don't have to have a year to spare either, with trips as short as two weeks.

Back in Old Blighty, Ryan Giggs and Gary Neville's Hotel Football, right next to Old Trafford in Manchester opened in March 2015. This is a hotel for footie fans and the second venture for the duo, who also own Café Football. The one hundred and thirty-eight room hotel also features a five-a-side pitch on the roof and houses a supporters' club.

Standard rooms not only have Hypnos beds and rain showers, but come equipped with a 40" Samsung smart TV and, of course, full Sky Sports package. The bar has specially brewed Cafe Football beer, an extensive wine and champagne list and a creatively themed cocktail menu.

Book here and you might stumble across a few famous names in football or some WAGS.

If it is autographs you seek or if you fancy watching footballers training, stay at the Hilton Hotel at St George's Park, Tatenhill, UK, home for each of the twenty-four England teams. It is fully open to the general public and, set in the heart of the National Forest, is the perfect destination hotel for short breaks and leisure stays in the UK.

I was fortunate (or unfortunate) enough to require some physiotherapy treatment and was sent to the centre at St George's Park. I shared the waiting room with some top names from footballing but was too shy to ask them to sign my knickers for me.

😑😑: Mr. Grumpy says, "More atmosphere than watching the match at the pub with the lads. Remember to sit at the correct end though. Finding yourself wearing Liverpool kit while seated among Real Madrid supporters can be awkward."

In France, a kiss or kisses (on the cheek) is the common way of greeting between family and friends, and even between men. The number of kisses varies—if you are in Brittany then it is one kiss, four kisses if you are from Paris and up to five in Corsica.

I could write another entire book about **France** and why you should visit it. Having been fortunate enough to travel to many destinations, I find myself constantly returning to this country because it has everything you could desire as a holiday destination, especially if you are a grumpy guts.

It is probably best if I do not write too much here on the subject or you will be here for a very long time. For relaxation, sea, wine, sun, food, stunning scenery, wine, activities, wine, history, culture, pretty perched villages, wine, good roads, lifestyle and wine, there is little to beat it. The language is sometimes a problem but you can always resort to the good old-fashioned method of shouting loudly in English at the French if they do not comprehend your requests. No, seriously, try to learn some basic French. The French are very polite people and if they think you are making an effort, they will be agreeable.

There are a few things to beware of, including: dog mess on pavements, lengthy lunchtimes—which means most shops are shut from midday until three in the afternoon—and badly-driven old Citroen cars (usually more prevalent after lunch when the drivers have imbibed wine with their lunch).

Why do I love France? It fulfils all my holiday desires. There, I can explore in potholes, go canoeing, cycling, sailing, learn about gastronomy cooking, stay in a chateau, tour vineyards, see cave art, paint where famous painters have been before me, hang out on a barge, go camping, ski, hike, sunbathe, go hot air ballooning, walk in some charming streets, eat fabulous food, sample some fine wines, soak up more history than possible, visit museums, admire architecture, and delight in a laid back lifestyle along with some phenomenal scenery and ace weather. I think I have made my point.

2015 is the 200th anniversary of Waterloo and the 600th anniversary of the battle of Agincourt. There is to be an attempt to break the world record for an arrow storm over the weekend of 25th and 26th July with one thousand archers firing simultaneously, as well as a re-enactment at the Agincourt site.

If you have never visited France then go and see why I love it so much. Every region has something to offer and is rich in history, culture, and beauty.

🐢: Mr. Grumpy says, "Delicious cheese, freshly baked bread and fine wine. I rest my case."

How long can you hold your breath? A long time? Consider trying out a holiday where you can learn to **free dive**.

People have been free diving for centuries: for food, sponges, pearls and other objects of value, or for items lost overboard ships. It has even been argued in the "Aquatic Ape" hypothesis that humans spent several million years of evolution in a semi-aquatic existence explaining some unique physical characteristics.

Revel in a freedom that does not come with scuba diving and head to a resort where you can immerse yourself in clear waters unencumbered by diving equipment.

Check out Nihiwatu resort in Indonesia. It offers diving, free diving and fishing and luxury.

🐢🐢🐢🐢: Mr. Grumpy says, "Good idea. When your wife next hints you should buy her pearl earrings or a pearl necklace, book a freedive trip for her and say whatever she finds, she can keep. Contrary to what she thinks, I am very good at holding my breath. I have had lots of practise holding it while waiting to get a word in edgeways with her."

G

the guitar of the noisy teenager at the next campsite makes excellent kindling.

G is for gaps for grumpies, gambling, gaming holidays, glamping, gliding, golfing, Genghis Khan training, grizzly bear watching.

One website offers **gap year** holidays for grumpy people but first you have to check you qualify for grumpy status. The website states:

As well as a commitment to make a real contribution you will have that spark, that desire to be heard that marks out a grumpy. You are too old for night clubbing (Peter Stringfellow – no need to apply) but a long way from that stair lift. You don't want the comfort of SAGA and you would never say "that's a nice cardigan in the window."

If you fit the bill then sign up for a gap year adventure and join an ever-increasing number of over-fifties, who are doing just that.

An article in the *Daily Mail* in 2012[2] indicated that over fifties are now taking gap years. Indeed, I have several friends, who have done exactly that. In one case, a trip to visit Australia resulted in the couple moving there permanently.

Gap years used to be for adventurous young travellers and gap year students, many seeking to escape the watchful eye of their parents. Now, inspired by their offspring's exciting stories of countries far and wide, older visitors are heading in their droves to those same destinations.

Older generations are turning their backs on previous favourite destinations such as the Canary Islands, mainland Spain, and Portugal, in favour of Australia, Canada, New Zealand, Caribbean, Seychelles, and the Maldives.

Almost one in ten of those questioned in a 2012 Thomas Cook

---

2   www.dailymail.co.uk/femail/article-2117436/Over-50s-gap-year-trail-follow-footsteps-globetrotting-children.html#ixzz3H4xOuUx2

survey admitted to booking a holiday to a particular destination in the hope of appearing younger or more adventurous than they really are. I bet they came back from their trip looking and feeling younger too.

The ultimate gap year is currently being undertaken by Lee Wachtstetter, who has spent seven years aboard the Crystal Serenity cruise ship. The eighty-six-year-old widow sold her five-bedroom Fort Lauderdale-area home on ten acres after her husband passed away and became a permanent resident on the cruise ship.

Mama Lee, as she is known on board the ship, stopped counting countries visited once she hit one hundred but says she has been to every country where there is a port. Mama Lee has undertaken almost two hundred cruises including fifteen world cruises. That is what I call taking a gap!

☺: Mr. Grumpy says, "I could do with a gap from my daily routine, house repairs, bills, obligations, and gardening. I'd prefer a gap decade though."

Blow the kids' inheritance once and for all, or indeed triple, even quadruple it by hitting the slot machines and casinos at Las Vegas. I have yet to hear someone say they did not have fun on their trip to Vegas and almost everyone I spoke to, who had visited this incredible spot wanted to return to do it all again.

I gave up **gambling** after a one-armed bandit punched me in the face and smashed my front teeth (that might require some explanation to those of you too young to remember old fruit machines) but from the tales I hear, I ought to give these newer slot machines a go. For one thing, they are addictive and for another, they no longer have large handles to pull down.

Go for glamour with a hint of James Bond about it and test out the casino in Monaco, where you will be able to hobnob with the rich and famous as well as bankrupt the family, although the actual residents of Monaco are not allowed to gamble there. If you have a winning streak, take your money over to the Hotel de Paris and indulge in a sumptuous meal to celebrate, then nip down to the car showrooms and purchase something exciting to travel home in.

☻☻☻: Mr. Grumpy says, "I won thirty pounds at a casino in 1983. I don't intend playing again and breaking my winning streak."

I do not know where you stand on **gaming**, but should you be one of the millions, who goes online to play against others worldwide, or spends hours attempting to reach the next level in your latest computer game, check out the new holiday offered by Game, the retailer. It is a four-month, round-the-world adventure, described as a "pilgrimage" for gaming enthusiasts. It includes thirteen locations in eight countries, each of, which has inspired a big blockbuster game.

Travellers can expect to head to Edinburgh and London, Kyoto, Seoul, Los Angeles and New York. They will also visit Ko Tapu Island, a setting frequented by Lara Croft, the busty protagonist of Tomb Raider Underworld. Given I am a little obsessed by her and, indeed, emulate her whenever possible, I ought to consider this holiday. It is Lara Croft—Fridge Raider we are talking about, isn't it?

Glamping is the new camping, not a weird modern dance as I thought it might be. Gone are the days of struggling to erect a two-man tent on a sloped hill in the wind, only to discover once you are in your sleeping bag, you are gradually sliding out of the structure and then have it collapse on you in the middle of the night. Nowadays, you can chill out in yurts, tipis, cabins, safari tents, shepherds huts, gypsy caravans, eco domes, or tree houses. Creature comforts including electricity are standard. Accommodation is often luxurious. Glamping is, after all, a combination of *glamorous* and *camping*. The comfort levels and price of these also range wildly so there really is something for everyone and for every budget.

So, if you like the idea of camping but hate the thought of getting dirt under your fingernails, glamping might be right up your street or should I say bracken path? Alternatively, you could always rent a hotel room near a wood or park and stare out of the window.

In my grumpy old opinion, glamping is just a silly way to hang out in the woods, one that happens to be supported by pop sensation Justin Bieber. In an interview with *Love Pop Magazine*, the boy wonder discussed his love of glamping.

"You sleep on a bed. It's a mattress bed! In a huge tent with TV and everything. You have electricity and stuff but you're still in amongst the wildlife. It's pretty cool," Bieber explained.

I guess that says it all. If you want to go down to the woods today, and do not want to be in for a big surprise, then possibly glamping will suit you. Watch out though. You might find Justin Bieber lurking in the bushes.

😠😠😠😠😠: Mr. Grumpy says, "No. No. No. No. Have I made myself clear on this matter?"

You might by now be wondering if I have lost the plot with my next suggestion—**Genghis Khan** warrior training. For this, you need to head for Mongolia where you are shown what it was like to be a warrior under Genghis Khan. It will certainly make for some rather unusual holiday photographs. You dress in full costume, stay in nomadic tents and spend the days training in thirteenth-century battle skills. You will learn bow and arrow making, how to shoot from horseback, lighting campfires, and field cooking. Guess that makes a survival course with Ray Mears sound tame by comparison. If you want to bring out the macho in your man then send him off to train in Mongolia and don't snigger at the photos of him dressed in a long skirt. He might be tempted to test out those newfound battle skills.

😠😠😠😠😠: Mr. Grumpy says, "Mongul madness."

Germany is one of those destinations that people do not immediately consider when booking a holiday, yet Germany is full of history, architecture, superb scenery, activities, culture, excellent food, and some of the nicest cities you could imagine. Having visited various parts of it over the years, I have constantly been impressed by the efficiency of staff and transport systems, standard of cleanliness, and the politeness of those we have encountered. There, that is my bit done for the German Tourist Board.

😠: Mr. Grumpy says, "Great choice of destinations in this country with far more to see and enjoy than I first thought. Learn essential German before you go—"Ein bier. Noch ein bier. Danke.""

I do not want to get into promoting courses rather than holidays but **gliding** seemed too much fun to not include it. Gliding is the one of the most peaceful recreational sports you can take up. Attend a five-day course in the Cotswolds and you will be able to soar majestically above the fields and get a bird's eye view of all below.

Once you have your licence, travel to Spain, Lanzarote or to France to Saint Hilaire's free-flight festival, held at the end of September, where you can practise flying at other awesome sites in the French Alps such as Annecy and Chamonix.

Soar like a veritable eagle in southern Nevada with Soaring Center Glider Flights, a well-established company, who fly all year round.

Unwind as you sit back in utter tranquillity and look down on a world that seems so distant all your troubles will disappear, at least for a short while.

: Mr. Grumpy says: "It took hours before I was pinged up on what can only be described as a large rubber band. I couldn't find any thermals and came straight back down. Those five minutes were very nice and I imagine if I had stayed longer, I would have enjoyed soaring like a giant eagle."

my husband's on the golf diet. he lives on greens.

Golf is a sport that can be practised or learnt at any age but is particularly popular with the over fifties. Golf holidays in the Mediterranean mean that this sport can be played at any time of the year. There are spectacular professional golf courses in Italy, Greece, Malta, and Spain. The climate and stunning scenery make golf abroad a much more enticing prospect than golfing in the UK. There are tailored packages for over fifties golf holidays that combine sun, sea, and golf for that ultimate golf holiday.

If you play golf then you have an extensive range of holidays available. From Spain to Portugal, Ireland to the home of golf itself—Scotland—a trip will be available to suit you, no matter what your handicap. Portugal's Algarve has many championship quality courses where tourists can play for reasonable fees. A country, which is just starting to advertise itself as a golfing holiday destination is

Cyprus, where many new courses are springing up and holidays are available at reasonable prices.

We attempted to play a course but Mr. Grumpy kept losing his balls, including his special neon-coloured balls, in the water. He gave up in frustration. I was forced to give up because I failed to hit the ball at all; merely clods of earth and turf. Before we decided we were not cut out to be golfers, we were invited to play on an impressive course on Grand Cayman. Having missed the tee six times, I was demoted to caddie while my other half looked important waving at me impatiently to hand him the correct club. It was a good course with some excellent sand banks and large lakes—very large lakes. Sadly, Mr. Grumpy drove every one of his golf balls into the first lake and left the course in a foul mood.

Never mind about all the aforementioned courses, if you or your other half have a penchant for this sport then treat yourselves and sign up for the Tiger Tour, a nine-night trip with stopovers at three outstanding New Zealand lodges: The Farm at Cape Kidnappers, Matakauri Lodge and The Lodge at Kauri Cliffs.

Located in the heart of Hawke's Bay Wine Country, the Farm at Cape Kidnappers features a world-renowned 18-hole course designed by architect Tom Doak. With easy access to one of the adventure capitals of the world, Queenstown, Matakauri Lodge is dramatically situated on the shores of Lake Wakatipu, where you tee off at Jack's Point and later board a helicopter to take in the fjords and glaciers of Milford Sound. (That sounds exciting.) The twenty-one-hole golf course at Kauri Cliffs has six daredevil holes situated alongside cliffs that plunge down into the sea. Transfer between properties is via private jet and the tour also includes horse riding, sailing, quad biking, and vineyard tours among other activities.

It is fair to say that although neither of us is any good at golf we think we might like to have another go at it if it means we can go on this trip.

how many golfers does it take to change a
light bulb?
fore!

Website Holidays Please offers the ultimate **gourmet break holidays**. If you are feeling peckish, love fine wine, travelling and Michelin-starred meals, then how about a six-month holiday visiting twelve countries around the world during, which time you eat in all one hundred and seven three-starred Michelin restaurants? You will stay in top accommodation and travel business class (guess you might be needing those extra-large seats after a few weeks chomping through all the food). Did you ask how much? It is a mere £182,000 and that includes all your meals and wine. (Probably not all of my wine requirements.)

More seriously, we discovered a perfect gourmet retreat at Cleopatra Mountain Farmhouse, South Africa, where guests are treated to seven-course meals lovingly prepared by Chef Richard Poynton, wife Mouse and his team. Cleopatra Mountain Farmhouse is most definitely *the* romantic gourmet getaway. It has only eleven rooms but each is superbly and individually furnished. The lodge is hidden away in the KwaZulu-Natal, Drakensberg and with its stunning mountain views, river walks, situation, wildlife, and hosts, is a must visit.

Most guests only stay a night or two, but being rather greedy grumps we booked for five days and I can confess that every meal was exquisite.

Before the meal, the team gives a talk about each course, where it was sourced (all vegetables, spices and herbs come from their own garden), and how it has been prepared. You are invited to visit their wine cellar with an appealing choice of South African wines, to select an appropriate bottle to accompany your meal and then you are seated with a wonderful view of the lake, can watch the weaver birds settling for the evening, and live like an epicure.

Chances are your cholesterol levels will have risen if you stay for five nights, but the stay is well worth it.

When I decided to include holidays for foodies, I thought I would be writing largely about those in France but more and more countries are offering these holidays. Gourmet holidays in the Baltics, Russian, or Nordic regions are more in demand, especially after the restaurant Noma in Denmark was named the best restaurant in the world.

This is a wonderful way to add flavour to your trip (that was Mr. Grumpy's pun, not mine) but ensure you do not overdo it. A moment on the lips...

🙂: Mr. Grumpy says, "It's been so long since I ate a proper cooked meal, I'm not sure I could eat one." (I pointed out to him ready-made meals from certain supermarkets *are* proper meals.)

Should you have mastered Genghis Khan warrior training techniques, you might feel like putting them to the test and go **grizzly bear watching**. Then, should a bear becomes too curious by your presence, at least you will be prepared.

British Columbia, Canada is prime bear watching territory. The province is home to the rare white Kermode (Spirit) bear, more than half of Canada's grizzly bears, and a quarter of Canada's black bears.

Feel like an extra in a David Attenborough wildlife programme and perch in an elevated viewing platform to witness grizzly bears pouncing on and devouring spawning salmon or drift silently in a riverboat to catch a glimpse of an elusive white Kermode bear lumbering along a mossy riverbank.

Bear viewing in British Columbia ranges from spotting a bear next to the highway to luxury wilderness adventure trips. You may be able to watch bears without a guide, but guided bear-watching trips are by far the best way to ensure a safe, successful experience of viewing bears in their natural habitat.

One of Earth's great wildlife areas, the Great Bear Rainforest—a land of island archipelagos and long fjords that reach back into the glacier-capped Coastal Mountain range—is home to many unique populations like the white Kermode bear.

If you travel to the heart of the Great Bear Rainforest to see and photograph grizzly bears, try the floating Great Bear Lodge. It allows with a maximum of ten guests and is a super place for observing the wildlife and being part of the wilderness of British Columbia. Biologists lead the twice-daily bear-viewing sessions.

Travel with Great Bear Tours in Port Hardy, on northern Vancouver Island, and you will begin your trip with a spectacular seaplane flight to the Great Bear Lodge. This company was voted by National Geographic Adventure as one of the Best Adventure Travel Companies on Earth.

Glendale Cove in Knight Inlet is home to one of the largest concentrations of grizzly bears in British Columbia, Canada. It is not uncommon for up to forty bears to be within a few miles of the wilderness lodge during the peak autumn (fall) season when the salmon are running up the Glendale River. Their website gives details of when and where to go and see these wonderful creatures.

what do you call a wet bear?
a drizzly bear.

😁😁😁: Mr. Grumpy says, "Have you seen the teeth on those animals? And you thought I was bad-tempered."

H

I need a six~month holiday twice a year.

H is for haunted houses, healing hotels, helicopter trips, heli-hiking, heli-skiing, hiking, horse riding, hot air ballooning, house sitting, humorous writing, hunting, husky riding.

There are spooky goings-on in many hotels, houses and castles. If you are fascinated by ghostly sightings, apparitions, the sound of footsteps or poltergeist activity, then book a stay in a **haunted house**. I imagine it would like being a member of the *Scooby Doo* team, racing about (without Scooby Doo) attempting to discover if there is a real ghost in the house although it is probably nothing like that. Indeed, looking at the numerous places available, it seems this is a holiday for those, who love the paranormal and being scared. A British website called Haunted Rooms offers a wide choice of haunted happenings throughout the UK and Ireland.

You may prefer to hunt ghosts in a haunted pub. That would be my choice. Mind you, after several glasses of sherry, I am capable of seeing all sorts of strange happenings.

This could make for some interesting holiday photographs to show off to the neighbours.

how do well~groomed ghosts keep their hair in place? with scare spray.

: Mr. Grumpy says, "Woo. Woo. Boo! Wouldn't it be cheaper to let me wear a sheet and scare you? Has a certain appeal, especially if it takes place in a pub."

Scaring yourself senseless might not be my best suggestion for a holiday so for utter relaxation, to come away feeling rejuvenated and even inspired to look after yourself, track down one of the large number of **healing hotels**.

This is all about holistic and natural approaches to looking after your body so you can expect yoga and Ayurvedic treatments. Focus on well-being, ageing healthily, healthy nutrition, detox, and fitness. It may not appeal to all, but be assured once you arrive at one of the resorts you will have no difficulty in adapting.

You will be pampered and transformed during your stay. Thermal baths and spa, massages, and fitness programmes in beautiful settings will ensure you feel far less grumpy, well, that is until you check out, get your bill and discover one of you spent far too much on extra treatments during the stay. (Sorry, Mr. Grumpy but those hot stone massages were simply divine.)

If you Google "Incredible **helicopter trips**" you will be spoilt for choice with my first suggestion under this heading. If there is one thing that will make a grumpy exhilarated and animated, it is a breath-taking flight in a helicopter.

We have been fortunate enough to see some amazing scenery from helicopters and flying over the Drakensburg Mountains in South Africa is one memory that will stay with me forever. Friends have waxed lyrical about similar flights in New Zealand, India, over Niagara Falls, over the Grand Canyon, along the coastline from Nice to Monte Carlo, and in Egypt. Choose a location and view it from a helicopter. It will be unforgettable.

You might not want to have an entire holiday in a helicopter but you can buzz off on all-day exhilarating helicopter tours like the ones over Lake Las Vegas, Lake Mead, Hoover Dam, and Fortification Hill, an extinct volcano. Pause for a glass of the bubbly stuff or other beverages and a light snack before flying back over Downtown Vegas and the Strip. Or, book a helicopter safari to take in the diverse and vast wilderness of Kenya. Cheli and Peacock is one of many companies that allow you to plan your own bespoke safari. Not cheap, but it will put a smile on any grump's face.

: Mr. Grumpy says, "Blow the cost! It's well worth the money. How many smiley ones am I allowed to use, because I'll put them all up?"

Combine this activity with the one below and go **heli-hiking** in the Columbia Mountain Range. This range, older than the Rockies by a couple of hundred million years, runs parallel to the Rockies. The Columbia Range is a stunning and little-known collection of peaks and ranges and is very hard to get to. By travelling to the remote destination in a helicopter, you can expect to encounter no one else. The perfect antidote to our busy, crowded existence.

Once deposited by your helicopter, you travel with a guide at a pace to suit yourselves, ending up at a point where you will be collected again by helicopter. You should see sights that would otherwise be impossible to view. Trails vary from easy to difficult, so as long as you are in good health for walking, this will be one to savour.

Not exciting enough? How about **heli-skiing** then? Heli-skiing is not just the domain of the super-fit, although it is advisable to be able to ski. Sign up with CMH Heli-Skiing and you can expect to team up with other fit retirees, who may be beginners or seasoned professionals. You will stay in Bugaboo Mountain Lodge, nestled into the Purcell Mountains of the Canadian Rockies. By day, you will be whisked up remote mountains to 1,000 square kilometres of untouched terrain; by night, you will indulge in a rooftop sauna, in-house massage, packed cellar and three-course gourmet cuisine, before awaking with weary limbs to do it all again.

CMH has long been the playground of the rich, the famous, and the fanatical, but they are drawn not so much by love of skiing, but love of what the place offers: pure escapism. What grumpy person would not fancy that at least?

I am embarrassed to admit I always want to sing about knapsacks on backs when I see a group of hikers. I can be rather childish at times and do not mean to scoff. **Hiking** is a fabulous way to see a country and is beneficial to your health. How beneficial? Feast your eyes on this list and consider taking a hiking holiday:

- Improved cardio-respiratory fitness (heart, lungs, blood vessels)
- Improved muscular fitness
- Lower risk of coronary heart disease and stroke
- Lower risk of high blood pressure and type 2 diabetes
- Lower risk of high cholesterol and triglycerides

- Lower risk of colon and breast cancer, and possibly lung and endometrial cancer
- Increased bone density or a slower loss of density
- Reduced depression and better quality sleep
- Lower risk of early death (If you are active for seven hours a week, your risk of dying early is forty percent lower than someone active for less than thirty minutes a week.)
- Weight control; hiking burns up approximately three hundred and seventy calories an hour.

Now you have decided to give it a go, the National Geographic website offers twenty dream trails for you to consider, including the one hundred and four mile Tour de Mont Blanc:

"Circling Mont Blanc—the rooftop of Western Europe—is one of the most special hiking experiences in the world. You travel through three different countries (France, Italy, Switzerland) and over several mountain passes with some of Europe's most dramatic glaciers on display. You can soak it in and take your time over seven to ten days or fast pack in three days. No matter how you choose to do it, it is an adventure of a lifetime!" —Topher Gaylord

Should that not be long enough for you, they offer the one thousand, eight hundred and ninety-four mile Te Araroa, Maori for "The Long Pathway," in New Zealand. Split into one hundred and sixty trails, this hike should take one hundred and twenty days to complete. Hope you have some thick soles on those hiking boots!

two hikers encountered a big black bear. afraid, the hikers began to run. the bear gave chase. as they were sprinting away, one of the hikers said to the other hiker, "do you think we can outrun this bear?" the other hiker said while panting, "I don't know. I just have to outrun you."

: Mr. Grumpy says, 'Good way to see places and stay active. Take plenty of plasters for your feet."

As Roy Rogers claimed, "A four-legged friend will never let you down." He was referring to horses in case, like me, you thought he was singing about dogs. Much like boating or helicopter flying, **horse riding** also allows you to explore regions and areas you might otherwise not have seen. Again, do your research and you will find many places world-wide offering horse trails and rides, including Kyrgyzstan, Mexico, and Argentina.

Feel like an authentic cowboy and stay at a dude ranch like Bitterroot, USA. This ranch is situated near Yellowstone Park and provides a variety of riding opportunities including tuition with certified instructors, a cross-country course, team sorting, herding cows, cattle drives, roundups, pack trips and trail rides. The Fox family have been running this operation for more than thirty years and, as their website states: "provide a relaxed and friendly holiday atmosphere for their guests."

Although I have a penchant for Stetsons, I am allergic to horses so I cannot really comment on this holiday but friends who ride say that travelling through an unspoilt area on the back of a horse is very therapeutic. I shall take their word for it and leave you to decide if it is a holiday for you.

Facts about horses:

- Horses use their ears, eyes, and nostrils to express their mood. They also communicate their feelings through facial expressions. I am sure I could make one demonstrate feeling frustrated with the idiot on its back—me!
- The horse is one of the twelve Chinese signs of the zodiac. Anyone born in the year of the horse is seen to embody the characteristics of the animal, namely intelligence, independence and a free spirit. That said, I was born in the year of the rat. Make of that what you will.
- Horses have nearly three hundred and sixty degree vision. However, they have blind spots directly in front and behind them. Ergo, it is extremely dangerous to stand behind a horse as they are liable to kick out if they get scared by anything. Kicking out is their way of defending themselves.

☺☺☺: Mr. Grumpy says, "Horses bite, don't they? And buck? Think I'll give this a miss."

This next holiday idea makes me squirm in delight—**hot-air ballooning**. Once you are up in the air, you will transform into the calmest, happiest holiday-maker.

The hot-air balloon was invented by the Montgolfier brothers so it would be appropriate to take a flight over the magnificent Loire Valley in France. You will be hard-pressed not to find a company willing to take you up, up and away. Check out the various websites to book your flight, which always ends with a celebratory glass of champagne. This is something of a tradition and originated from those early days of flying. As hot-air balloons became a fad, the French aristocracy soon discovered that local farmers appreciate rich folk setting balloons down on their land. The aristocracy claimed the peasants were afraid because they thought the balloons looked like dragons, but while the smoke that powered early balloons may have appeared dragon-like, it is far more likely that the farmers did not want hot-air balloons crushing their crops. In any case, champagne smoothed things over, and the tradition of drinking champagne after a flight was born.

Should you prefer to keep your feet on terra firma and look at balloons, join the tens of thousands of people, who watch balloons, from traditional globes to complex special shapes, inflate in a mass ascension at the Albuquerque International Balloon Fiesta. A similar event take place in Bristol.

In 1783, the first hot-air balloon was set to fly over the heads of Louis XVI, Marie Antoinette, and the French court in Versailles. Its passengers were, sheep, ducks, and roosters. This odd assortment of animals was chosen to test the effects of flight. Sheep, thought to be similar to people, would show the effects of altitude on a land dweller, while ducks and roosters, which could already fly (albeit at different heights), would act as controls in the experiment. The balloon flew on a tether for eight minutes, rising 1500 feet into the air and travelling two miles before being brought safely to the ground. The animals were unharmed although I would bet those ducks ended up as tasty confit de canard.

😀: Mr. Grumpy says, "Super. It's very relaxing and gives you excellent photographic opportunities. Watch out for rough landings on uneven ground. Mrs. Grumpy fell out of the basket---as I said, great photo opportunities."

Living like a local in free digs sounds ideal so if you have not got sufficient money saved in your piggy bank for a holiday, consider **house-sitting**. There are plenty of house-sitting websites. You generally have to pay to register, need to upload your photograph and profile and add references. Once you have done that you search for potential sittings. Choose anywhere you fancy and sit back to see if you are contacted.

If the owner likes the sound of you and you like them, arrange a Skype interview before signing any contract. Chances are you will not get paid but you will stay somewhere for free.

Be careful as it is huge responsibility. You are going to look after someone's home and even their pets. Some owners expect a lot so ensure it is all laid down in the contract beforehand. Be prepared to treat the place as if it were yours, take care of it and hand it back looking pristine.

Hurrah! I have discovered a holiday to make you really laugh and where you can learn to write **humour**.

The course is led by stand-up comedian, writer and funny man Tony Hawkes, who has made many appearances on television and radio including shows like *Have I Got News For You* and *I'm Sorry I Haven't a Clue.*

Tony is holding a humorous writing course on the Aegan Island of Skyros, at the Atsitsa Bay in September.

Other courses exist worldwide but this one combines humour and relaxation in a wonderful retreat by the sea, in the shade of pine trees.

how many comedians does it take to change
a light bulb?
one million . . . just joking. two. one
comedian to open for the other, who
changes the bulb.

I

> "It is impossible to travel faster than Light, and certainly not desirable, as one's hat keeps blowing off."
> ~ Woody Allen

I is for ice blokarting, ice climbing, ice cream making, ice-diving, ice hotels, igloo building, internet, islands, Istanbul.

How about zipping across a frozen lake at high speeds in a small kart with a sail? In the Lithuanian winter, when lakes freeze, locals replace the wheels on their blokarts (small land yachts usually with three wheels) with ice blades.

Baltic Adventure provides lessons for beginners and claims the **ice blokarts** are so easy to use, you should be self-piloting within minutes – and gliding silently across the ice with the wind in your hair and a, whoosh of adrenaline coursing through your veins. They also suggest you do not consume any alcohol before taking control of a blokart. That seems wise. Mr. G and I were dangerous enough in Dodgems at the fairground after a couple of shandies. I can only imagine what mayhem we would cause in a blokart.

I shall only briefly mention **ice climbing**. Although you can learn and practise on an indoor ice wall, this is for those, who are keen on mountaineering and want to develop an in-depth practical knowledge of all the skills required to tackle winter mountaineering terrain. Should you be one of those and would like to take on some of Scotland's most famous winter routes, then look at Ice Factor's website or consider a trip to Norway.

Norway has some of the best ice climbing in Europe, with over one hundred and fifty frozen waterfalls around Rjukan alone. Whether you have climbed on rock before, or attempted nothing more adventurous than a staircase, Kelso Travel will show you the ropes. Their ice climbing trips take place on frozen waterfalls and are suitable for all levels of expertise.

Responsible Travel offers intensive five or eight-day trips introducing the techniques of ice climbing and exploring some of the best ice in the French Alps. There are waterfalls, ridges, and gullies for all levels from the complete novice to the seasoned climber. Both trips are progressive courses aimed at teaching you the basics of ice safety and security and ice climbing techniques.

I was struggling to see the appeal of this holiday until I read this description of it on their website, *"... the satisfaction as your ice screw winds easily into the ice, the achievement of reaching the top ... combined with being in an otherwise totally inaccessible place with stunning Alpine scenery surrounding you."*

I now comprehend why this might be a perfect holiday for a grumpy guts.

La Grave is one of the most challenging resorts in the Alps. Every winter it attracts mountaineers from across the globe, who converge on the small resort in search of thrills. The ice-climbing here is regarded by most as the best in France, with some seriously tough climbs for experts. There are, however, some smaller ice falls near the village for those taking their first tentative steps up the ice. Book here and you will able to boast you have climbed in this prestigious and notoriously difficult area. No one needs to know how far you really went.

🌚🌚🌚🌚🌚: Mr. Grumpy says, "I have trouble walking on slippery pavements. This is a no-no for me."

Mr. Grumpy loves nothing better on a sunny day than a large—no, make that a very large—tasty **ice cream**. In truth, he likes nothing better than scoffing a large ice cream even on days without sun. You can imagine how happy he actually was to discover a trip that combines making and eating ice cream in beautiful Italy.

If you, too, drool at the thought of ice cream, head to Sorrento to attend ice cream classes with television personality Mario Gargiulo. Mario will let you in to the secrets of his trade, a wonderful Italian skill passed down through three generations. What is there not to like about this trip?

Gelato is Italy's version of ice cream, with three major differences:

- Gelato has significantly less butterfat than ice cream's typical eighteen and twenty-six percent. However, less fat does not mean less taste. With the lower butterfat content, gelato is less solidly frozen than ice cream and consequently it melts in the mouth faster. The result is that the customer will taste gelato's full flavour immediately.
- Gelato has a much higher density than ice cream. Ice cream is produced by mixing cream, milk and sugar, and then adding air to the product. Manufacturers add air to ice cream because it nearly doubles the quantity of their product but it cuts the quality in half. No air is added to gelato. The result is a higher quality dessert with a richer, creamier taste.
- Gelato is served at a warmer temperature than ice cream. While both gelato and ice cream are served well below the freezing temperature of thirty-two degrees Fahrenheit, gelato is served ten to fifteen degrees warmer than ice cream. Because it is less solidly frozen, gelato's taste is further enhanced as it melts in the mouth.

What is there not to like about this holiday choice? Now, I need to stop him singing, "Just one gelato, give 'eet' to me."

: Mr. Grumpy says, "I don't need any education to eat it."

Feel your heart pounding as you plunge into the freezing water below the ice. Look upwards towards the bright sunshine masked by a thick layer of ice. As sensations go, **ice-diving** is strange one. You can sense the ice-cold water around you but you remain comfortably warm in your drysuit.

As odd as this may seem, ice-diving is exhilarating and will make you feel fully alive. One of the great things about ice diving is that anyone can have a go. You do not need to have dived before. In fact, around a third of all people, who ice dive say it is their first diving experience. This is because although it seems like a dangerous pursuit, it is actually very safe.

At Avioraz Morzine, France, you can try a circuit-style dive connected by an air supply. Several holes in the ice are connected by a rope, creating an established route for divers to follow, all accompanied by an instructor. You will get to feel the underwater currents and rivers, as well as see the spectacular light shows created by the light passing through the ice.

Combine an ice-dive with a skiing trip in France and sample one at high alpine frozen lake at Tignes, Lake de Montriond near Chamrousse or at the frozen Lac du Lou, Val Thorens.

Head to the cold of Norway and plunge the icy depths with divers and explore wrecks and reefs well below the sheet of ice.

It is a remarkable opportunity to attempt something different and if you are a person, who prefers the cold to the hot, why not discover what it is like? You can even dive at night for added atmosphere.

Whilst I can see the attraction of a dive in the dark, skinny-dipping in these temperatures is definitely off the agenda.

💀💀💀💀💀: Mr. Grumpy says, "Not even on my radar of things I want to do. I'll leave this one to those, who want to and penguins."

Ice hotels fascinate me. The idea that you can stay in a sumptuous palace built entirely of snow and ice that magically melts and disappears each spring is incredible. The original Icehotel in the small village of Jukkasjarvi in Swedish Lapland opened its reindeer-skin-clad doors twenty-five years ago and has been astounding visitors with its stylish design ever since. The design is different each year. The 2014-15 season celebrated the 25th year of construction and alongside twenty-three Ice rooms there were eighteen Northern Light rooms, sixteen Art Suites and two Luxury Suites.

The Icehotel complex boasts a surreal Icebar, a champagne bar and a first class restaurant. I wonder if they serve *Chilli* Con Carne there.

Imagine snuggling up to your loved one in an ice room? In truth, you will be in one sleeping bag clad in thermals, fleece, and woolly hat, and he or she will be in another, under a warm reindeer skin cover. A member of staff will wake you in the morning and bring you a warm glass of lingonberry juice. (Sounds remarkably like something from a *Star Trek* episode or am I confusing it with

Klingons?) You can start your day with a sauna or hot shower. I am assured three days maximum is enough to spend in the hotel, and outside activities, including skidoo riding will keep you entertained during the day. This is right at the top of my carpe diem list. Husky rides, reindeer watching, gazing at the Aurora, a stay in a magical hotel ... Have I convinced you to book yet?

😑😑😑😑: Mr. Grumpy says, "Although it looks stunning, the thought of waking up blue-lipped and frozen to the bed is one I would like to avoid. Delighted to send the Missus on her own though."

Continuing the cool theme, consider a holiday in an **igloo** and even learn how to build one. You can get back to nature in the cold wilderness in Finland, Lapland, Sweden and almost anywhere where winter is long, cold, and snowy.

The igloos are constructed by building a large dome of snow, which is dug out by hand with a spade to create a hollow space inside. Sleeping platforms are constructed. These are higher than the tunnel entrance to make the most of the warmer air rising for comfortable sleeping conditions. Not that there is a lot of warm air to rise.

Igloos are cosy, accommodating up to four or five people. No need to take your duvet because these igloos are usually equipped with special insulated mattresses and warm sleeping bags suitable for the cold night time temperatures. They are lit with candles inside, thus creating a romantic and unique atmosphere. Romantic it may be, but I doubt there will be any frisky activity going on.

This is only for those people, who are fit, active and, who fancy the adventure. The rest of us will be quite happy to stay in a warm hotel or for something extra special we might consider a stay at the Kakslauttanen Arctic Resort in Finland. It not only offers stays in one of the log cabins (complete with saunas) at the resort but you can spend a night or two in a glass igloo where you can have the thrill of gazing through your roof for a possible sighting of the Aurora Borealis. The igloos have ensuites and some even have showers. Watching the Northern Lights from the comfort of your cosy bed has to be more entertaining than tuning in to the evening news on your television or watching the late night football.

Grandivalira Igloo Hotel, Andorra, sits at 2,350 metres, is entirely built of snow, and is rebuilt each winter. There are five igloos in total for up to six people sharing. The actual hotel boasts a bar, a restaurant and a hot tub to soak in after a day on the slopes. The temperature in the hotel is about zero degrees centigrade so you will have to wrap up warmly at night.

The hotel offers snow activities during the day as well as skiing so pack a bag and find out what it is like to live like an Eskimo.

how does the eskimo mend his house? with iglue!

: Mr. Grumpy says, "You complain when I turn down the heating yet you want to go and stay in an igloo!"

In my opinion, you need the **internet** to successfully research, plan and book a holiday. I am biased because as a writer I use the internet every day. I have to send emails, press releases, answer interview questions, plan tours, and send copies of my work to publishers. Also I am active on all social media platforms. My other half is convinced I am addicted. Of course not. Erm, maybe he is right.

Wherever we go, I make sure there is WiFi connection, if not at where we are staying, then nearby. If the connection goes down or is slow, I panic. I might be missing an email inviting me to host my own comedy show or an important interview with Oprah.

With the advent of small portable tablets, being connected has never been easier. You no longer need to drag down to an internet café or the lobby of a hotel to request a code then log in on their system. I had to check in on a return flight from Russia and had a difficult night, trying to understand the Cyrillic keyboard available in the internet room.

Whilst I would advise travelling with such a device so you can check in online, read numerous books using the Kindle App. or stay in touch with family and friends, I would counsel against over-using it. You are on holiday. Forget what is happening back home. It was a lesson I was not keen to learn.

Last year, my eyes got very bad through over-working. A trip to the doctor confirmed I had severe eyestrain and needed to rest them. Mr. G booked a trip to a cottage in France for us so I could rest up. I checked to see if it had internet—it did.

My husband was not keen for me to use the computer so I developed all sorts of ways to stay in touch with my cyber friends in spite of my ban from the internet.

First, I sneaked my iPad into the bathroom and pretended I was having a bath when I was really on Hootsuite scheduling tweets. There were people I could not let down– a fellow author had a book tour and launch, which needed promoting, as did new authors, who had joined the same publishing house as me. Also, a good friend and blogger was about to get married. I could not miss the photographs of that event that were sure to appear on Facebook.

The Grumpy One sussed me. He did not confiscate the iPad though. Wiley Old Hubby confiscated the modem and that was that— no signal.

The first week of the ban was dreadful. I missed my blog and my cyber chats. I hatched a plan for week two.

At the airport, I sent Hubby through security ahead of me while I pretended to ferret about in my handbag looking for the toiletries in the plastic bag. He removed his jacket and belt and went through the metal detector. To his surprise it sounded. The guard sent him back to take off his shoes and try again. It was at that point that I grabbed my iPad, hidden in the depths of my bag, shoved it into a tray, covered it with my bag and strolled through the detector. My husband had "pinged" again and was being frisked by a guard. He looked vexed. The guard sent him through once more and he set off the alarm yet again. That gave me time to collect all the belongings and shove the iPad back into the bottom of my handbag.

Hubby joined me, a perplexed look on his face. "There was a twenty pence piece hidden right in the corner of my trouser pocket. I don't know how it got in there. I must have picked it up and forgotten I had it. It made the machine bleep and I had to be searched," he said.

I tsked in sympathy and scooted off to buy him a coffee to take his mind off it. Ha! It had worked. The coin I had carefully pushed deep into his pocket had managed to distract him from my ploy. I patted the iPad in glee.

At the cottage in France, I waited patiently until Hubby was in the shower then extracted my iPad from its hidey-hole. Just as I logged onto Facebook, the signal disappeared. Cursing, I hid the iPad again. I would try later.

Showered and ready for action we were about to go out when the cottage owner appeared.

"Just to let you know that we've lost the telephone lines and internet. An enormous lorry containing logs has come down the road, caught the cable and sent it flying across the field. A neighbour has contacted French Telecom but they can't come out until the end of next week. We are sorry. We hope you didn't need the internet," he said.

Mr. G brushed away the apologies. "No, no problem. We don't need the internet this week. We are incommunicado for a few days, aren't we?" He shot a look at me. I nodded woefully. It was not meant to be.

So, after two weeks of no typing, no reading, nor chatting to my cyber friends I became fitter (thanks to Mr. G making me walk every day) and my eyes got a lot better.

Moral of the story: Holidays are for rest and renewal, not for messing about online.

Does your iPad rule your life? Maybe it is time to try out the "digital detox" course in the idyllic setting of St Vincent and the Grenadines. Turn off your Smart phone and go cold turkey on the beach, surrounded by the tranquil sound of the Caribbean waves. The holiday, available from Black Tomato, includes a de-teching guide, a session with a life coach and a private catamaran transfer to Palm Island in St Vincent, just to ease that transition into a non-digital world.

These internet-free breaks now also called "sublimity breaks," are very much in vogue. There must be more grumps, who despise technology than I first suspected. More folk are taking off to recharge their soul rather than their iPad.

Ermito Hotelito del Alma, a converted fourteenth-century monastery in 7,500 forested acres in Umbria has no televisions, no phones and no Wi-Fi. On top of that, you will not have to fight for the duvet cover at night because beds are for only one person.

The "cells" are designed for individuals to switch off completely. Add vegetarian meals prepared with fresh organic vegetables from the gardens, a spa in a heated pool dug from the rock, a steam room, Gregorian chanting and you are sure to discover inner peace.

☺: Mr Grumpy says, "I could live here. No news, no hassle, no nagging wife!"

Finally, if you like the idea of complete tranquillity while sunbathing, spend time on the "Silence Beach" at D-Hotel Maris in Turkey. The hotel imported 250,000 tons of sand from Egypt to create beaches to rival those in the Maldives. The most picturesque, Silence Beach, was introduced for couples, who prefer the sound of silence. It has proved a success with its stylish white cabanas and total silence. Only books, sun, gentle waves and your beloved grumpy one in the cabana next to you.

There certainly would be no modern-day distractions on a private **island**. Denis Island in the Seychelles. The hotel won the World Luxury Hotel Award 2014 and has everything you could desire from a getaway retreat.

The twenty-five well-appointed villas offer "unpretentious comfort with the talcum-soft beaches just steps away."

Villa options vary, so chose one to suit you. Most come with daybeds, iPod decking stations and writing desks for those, who wish to capture it all on paper.

Relax on sun loungers on the beach and admire the turquoise ocean or snorkel around the coral reefs. There are no mobile phones or televisions to irritate or distract you. This lush island lends itself to tranquillity and romance. There are not many places where guests can take open-air baths or al-fresco showers in private garden courtyards—very romantic indeed. Ideal for those, who feel like spending quality time together.

This is one island that takes relaxation seriously and if secluded hospitality is for you, look no further.

Menjawankan Island, Indonesia is a cheaper option than Denis

Island. Kura Kura resort here has thirty-six cottages and pool villas. That may sound a lot of rooms but the island sits on twenty-two hectares of land, sand and jungle. You can surely find some peace and quiet here.

There is not a lot to do here except swim in the emerald-coloured lagoon and laze on the beach catching up on the latest best-sellers. Super for stressed-out folk.

I have chosen **Istanbul** (formerly Constantinople) purely because in 2014, it knocked Paris off the number one spot of the world's top destinations.

Despite announcing record tourist figures for 2013, the French capital lost out to Turkey, dropping to seventh in that year's Travellers' Choice Destinations awards, voted for by millions of holiday-makers. Surprisingly, Istanbul was a newcomer to the top ten and swooped in to grab the number one position.

Istanbul is the largest city in Turkey, located on the Bosporus Strait, and covering the entire area of the Golden Horn—a natural harbour. Because of its size, Istanbul extends into both Europe and Asia.

The city boasts towering minarets, superb palaces, mosques, museums, churches, and more. History, architecture and art are all to be discovered here too.

If you fancy getting a real flavour of Istanbul, there are several magnificent steamy Ottoman bathhouses to choose from, including the spectacular sixteenth-century Ayasofya Hürrem Sultan Hamam, in Sultanahmet Square. Imagine acres of marble, the sound of running water echoing around stupendous domes, and a massage to beat all massages. You will feel like a sultan or a sultana. No, not a variety of pale dried white grape.

Refreshed and ready for action you might fancy a little fun. Try Istrapped, a live room escape game. The description reads, "The door slowly closes behind you. You are suddenly enclosed within a room containing numerous locked doors. All you need to do is find the clues, combine and use them to help you solve the final puzzle - the key to escape. Using real objects to solve puzzles and open doors, you will truly feel like you're the lead character of a movie, book, or a game." Sounds like a blast and of course, if your other half has been playing up and complaining, you can always send them in on their own.

Anyone, who has visited Istanbul will probably agree that it is an astonishing city where east meets west. It has a European feel, a Mediterranean way of life, friendly people and one of the top cuisines in the world.

Istanbul, Turkey, is the only city in the world located on two continents.

J

"I've just been on a once-in-a-lifetime
holiday. I'll tell you what, never again."
~ tim vine

J is for jeep tours, jungle trekking, jousting.

Jeep tours in Madeira, Cyprus, Africa, the Azores, Greece, Egypt, through wadis in Dubai, or any place where getting off the beaten track is fun, are hugely popular.

Drive the jeep yourselves, with or without a guide, or sit back and be driven (and rattled about) by an expert. You will certainly be able to see more than you would by sticking to conventional routes.

Some of you might fancy a trip in a superjeep. These huge four-wheel drive vehicles are specially modified with high ground clearance, gigantic tyres and the latest safety and navigation equipment enabling them to travel just about anywhere. It is better than staying at home and ogling the exciting vehicles on *Top Gear.*

If you and your spouse are adrenalin junkies, who love motors, take a superjeep safari in Iceland across remarkable landscapes for a truly thrilling ride.

: Mr. Grumpy says, "Enjoyed my jeep safari hugely. Somehow a jeep is more fun than a car, especially when you go shooting off-road chasing after a lion in it. Hang onto your camera, hat, and anything else that might break loose though."

"Mr. Grumpy, I presume?" Explorers and lovers of nature might like to take a **trekking holiday** through a jungle. A couple I know, in their late sixties, trekked in the Amazon rainforest and raved about it for months afterwards. However, you really need to be fit, healthy and do your research before you embark on any trekking trip. Take medical advice, prepare beforehand and make sure you travel with a group.

Humidity, insects and bashing through forests is not for me, even though the beauty of the rainforest is renowned. I would be more likely to scream, "I'm a grumpy! Get me out of here!" Nevertheless, this holiday is not one where you will have to survive in the jungle, make up your own camp using whatever materials you find, and survive by eating insects. (Note: some insects are quite tasty. I ate locusts and mealworms and thought both were delicious. In hindsight, going zorbing immediately after consuming them was a bit stupid.)

Elder Trek offer treks during, which you can explore and enjoy Costa Rica's natural wonders. A typical jungle trek holiday consists of an active program of hikes, river safaris, and horseback rides for active nature lovers seeking exotic wildlife, active volcanos and some of the best bird watching. You may also visit an indigenous village known for its pottery making. For those with a head for heights, walk on the famous Arenal Hanging Bridges and to relax those aching feet at the end of a day out, take a well-deserved soak in the thermal pools at Eco-Termales Hot Springs.

a monkey and a hyena, best of mates, were walking through the jungle when the hyena was attacked by a vicious lion. the monkey escaped up a nearby tree and watched his friend being mauled and ripped to bits. once the fight was over, the hyena was barely alive. he groaned, looked up through bruised eyes, turned to the monkey and said, "why didn't you come and help me?"

and the monkey replied, "the way you were laughing i thought you were winning so i didn't bother."

~ tommy cooper

😁😁😁😁: Mr. Grumpy says, "I am not a coward but nasty biting insects and humidity are to be avoided at all costs. I'm opting to forgo this trip."

For *Game of Thrones* fans, look no further than Bavaria for my next suggestion—jousting holidays. You are not going to be able to spend an entire week **jousting** but every July, a little corner of Bavaria in southern Germany turns back the clock and transforms into a medieval society at the world's biggest jousting tournament in Kaltenberg.

This is truly medieval with performers mingling with the thousands of visitors–many of, whom are also dressed in medieval attire–playing music, dancing, and telling stories. Eat meat cooked over open fires and bread pulled steaming out of enormous clay ovens, washed down with mead and ale served in stoneware mugs.

A town crier announces the start of the jousting and everyone converges to watch the staged performance that transports you to the days of yore. Cheer as knights knock each other from horses in the knowledge that no one will be actually hurt.

😁: Mr. Grumpy says, "I like Germany but I'd prefer to go and look at German cars and drink beer."

K

"knock knock!
who's there?
tibet!
tibet, who?
early tibet and early to rise!"
~ aha jokes.

K is for kangaroos, kayaking, kites, kiteboarding, kitesurfing, kiting, Komodo dragons.

I admit I am cheating now. I have no unusual holiday suggestions of places where you can go and hang out with **kangaroos** although there are marsupial safaris should you wish to go and view these extraordinary creatures. Nor am I suggesting you go to watch them boxing. I am not even going to suggest you go in search of the fictional Waratah National Park in New South Wales where Skippy the bush kangaroo purportedly lived. I am merely going to suggest you look up Kangaroo Island—described as "one of the last unspoiled and unique wilderness wonders of the world."

Kangaroo Island is home to over eight hundred and fifty species of plants and native animals—wallabies, goannas, echidnas and koalas. Walk with sea lions on the sands of Seal Bay. Watch penguins, fur seals and dolphins frolicking in the pristine waters surrounding the island. You may even spot the shy platypus, one of nature's more unusual mammals.

Kangaroo Island is Australia's third largest island, seventy miles south west of Adelaide. It is one hundred miles long, thirty-four miles wide and inhabited by about four thousand five hundred people.

Take a guided tour in a four-wheel-drive vehicle to appreciate this absolute haven of beauty. A third of the island is a national park, with stunning natural features such as the wind-sculpted Remarkable Rocks and Admirals Arch in Flinders Chase.

This incredible place combines dramatic coastal scenery, secluded pristine beaches and an abundance of native wildlife. It's the place to see the best of Australia if you don't have time to see the, whole country.

🪃: Mr. Grumpy say, "What's that Skippy? You think we should come over immediately. There are some tinnies[3] stuck down a mine shaft that need rescuing and drinking? We're on our way."

sanδy, a texan farmer goes to australia for a vacation. there he meets glen, an aussie farmer and gets talking. the aussie shows off his big wheat field and the texan says, "oh yeah. we have wheat fields that are at least twice as large." then they walk around the ranch a little, and the glen shows off his herd of cattle. then sanδy immediately says, "we have longhorns that are at least twice as large as your cows." the conversation has, meanwhile, almost δied when the texan sees a herd of kangaroos hopping through the field and so he asks, "and what are those?" "sanδy", the aussie replies with an incredulous look, "δon't you have any grasshoppers in texas?"

Kayaking is therapeutic and calming. Slip through waters, listening only to the splash of your paddle, while absorbing the landscape about you. That is, unless you go in a double kayak with your other half. You could well end up squabbling or worse. At least, that is what happened to us.

We set off down a river in southwest France with a group of six

---

3   Tinnies = Australian for beer or lager cans.

others. We were divided into four kayaks, two in each. All four of us launched from the bank and headed to the beautiful bridge over the river at Saint Antonin-Noble-Val. That is, three kayaks headed towards the bridge. Ours went around and around in circles, creeping ever sideways towards the reeds and grasses.

"You're not paddling enough," my husband grumbled as we drifted sideways.

I paddled harder.

"You're paddling too hard now. Stop it."

I paddled with less vigour. The other three kayaks were now under the bridge. Hubby growled in frustration.

"You have no idea what you're doing. This is stupid. Why can't you paddle properly?"

"I know exactly what I'm doing. I've done this before."

"Well, why are we going around in circles?"

"You're not paddling…"

"Yes, I am!" he yelled. "It's you. You're hopeless."

It might have gone on like that all morning as we drifted down the river in a kayak going around and around. Fortunately, one of the husband and wife teams came back to sort us out and split us up. I swapped places with the other woman. She knew exactly what she was doing. She and her husband were passionate about kayaking and regularly headed to rivers to tackle rapids.

It worked. Well, sort of. I shot off down the river with my new kayaking partner both of us paddling steadily. I glanced behind as we raced under the bridge to see the kayak bearing my husband still going around in a circular movement and heard the woman say, "Maybe it would be better if you hung up your oar and left the paddling to me."

Kayaking is a super way to appreciate nature and as long as you and your other half can work together, take a kayak trip. You can, of course, get a single kayak then you will resist the urge to capsize him or her into the water.

If kayaking is fun then sea kayaking is thrilling. A sea kayaking holiday removes you entirely from modern life and immerses you in the wilderness, yet is entirely accessible to beginners—and it is that combination that makes it like no other. Imagine yourself paddling deep in the Amazon of Ecuador, surrounded by primeval rainforest, jungle populated only by indigenous communities and exotic wildlife, or sea kayaking amidst the incredible wildlife of The Galapagos Islands. Darwin was influenced by the Galapagos in his concept of evolution and studied extensively its plant and animal life; such as finches, iguanas and giant tortoises.

Head to the turquoise waters of Turkey to discover steep rugged cliffs, deserted sandy bays, deep clear water, and natural hot springs, as well as many types of wildlife. The region is dotted with fascinating ancient ruins, often in the remotest of locations.

Explore Johnstone Strait off Vancouver by sea kayak, camping in the amazing Canadian wilderness and possibly seeing killer whales up close. Hmm maybe not too close.

Watch waterfalls pouring into the sea and be overwhelmed by towering glacial mountains on Milford Sound, a massive fjord formed over millions of years of glacial activity. It is the biggest tourist attraction in New Zealand, attracting over half a million visitors each year.

Or, if all of that is a tad too adventurous, explore the sheltered sea lochs and inlets of western Scotland, one of the best destinations in the world for sea kayaking as it boasts hundreds of miles of secluded beaches, beautiful blue waters and an incredible marine and bird life.

two eskimos sitting in a kayak were getting cold so they decided to light a fire in their boat. It promptly sank, proving once again that you can't have your kayak and heat it too.

: Mr. Grumpy says, "I don't want to do it again if I have to share the same kayak as my wife. Great scenery on the way down the river and it is rewarding. I was not so keen on the sore muscles the following day."

Kiteboarding, kiting, kitesurfing, snowkiting ... in fact, anything to do with boards and kites might not be an obvious choice of holiday for you. However, read on before you decide it is not for you.

"Let's go fly a kite ..." Bet you haven't flown a kite for a few years. The last time I flew one—a red plastic effort—I had to run up and down a hillside several times until I finally persuaded it to get airborne. It swished about once or twice then dived into the only tree in sight where it lodged itself onto a top branch. I had to shimmy up the branches to retrieve it. I might have trouble these days getting my leg up onto a low branch let alone hauling myself up an entire tree.

This suggestion is not as childish as you might first think. Kite flying is popular worldwide, in countries such as Greece, Chile, Brazil and especially so in many Asian countries, including India, Pakistan, and Vietnam. During springtime you may visit important kite flying festivals where you can observe "kite fighting" in, which participants try to snag each other's kites or cut other kites down.

Uttarayan is a kite flying holiday that takes place on the 14th of January each year in some Indian states. For weeks prior to this festival, shops sell brightly coloured kites and kids practice kite fighting., whole communities and neighbourhoods go out on their rooftops to fly kites. It makes a great spectacle and brings out the inner child in you. You might even find the most hardened grump wanting to purchase a kite to fly back home.

In Vietnam, you will discover sound-making kites. These are smaller kites that have small flutes attached instead of tails, allowing the kites to hum as they fly. There are other forms of sound-making kites. In Bali, large bows are attached to the front of the kites to make a deep throbbing vibration, and in Malaysia rows of gourds with sound-slots are used to create a whistle as the kite flies. (Source Wikipedia.)

China, alongside India, has flown kites for centuries. Weifang, Shandoing, China is regarded as the kite capital of the world. It is home to the largest kite museum in the world, with a display area of 8100 square metres. Weifang also hosts an annual international kite festival on the large salt flats south of the city. For those, who would like to earn more about kites head here or to any of the other kite museums worldwide in Japan, UK, Malaysia, Indonesia, Taiwan, and the USA.

Extra impressive kites can be seen at the Yokaichi Giant Kite Festival, which is held every May in Higashi-Omi, Shiga, Japan, or head to Bali. The Balinese are crazy about kites. Kite flying and kite making is serious business and subtlety is not really an option. Forget childhood memories of a tiny polygon kite with trailing ribbons; in Bali it means colossal handmade flying machines that take a small army to get off the ground.

It all reaches fever pitch at the Bali Kite Festival held between July and August during the windy season. This event attracts over 1,200 competition kites and up to 10,000 spectators. These Balinese kites, constructed by each competing village, are a sight to behold. Most eye-catching of all are those in the "non-traditional" category, which range from the frivolous to the frankly bizarre. Past examples have included a green goblin on a tricycle and a Mercedes truck with turning front axles.

Kiteboarding or kitesurfing is a combination of most water sports and kiting. It has become a global craze and is exhilarating. Sign up with a professional outfit and you will be able to learn all about kite boarding and be well briefed in safety before you take to the seas.

This is for those, who are active, but age is not a barrier. Lou Self from Phoenix decided to take up kiteboarding when he turned fifty-eight. More than a decade later, kiteboarding is still his passion. His longest ride was more than four hours.

Known as Arizona Lou you can read more about his passion of kiteboarding, his other hobbies, and about his kiteboarding records on his website.

As tempted as I am to sign Mr. G up on a kiteboarding holiday so I can watch him perform aerial displays attached to a large kite, I know this is not for him. He preferred observing the kitesurfers in Mallorca, who gave a spectacular display of their skills and entertained us on a blustery day, rather than join them.

The history of kiteboarding dates back to the thirteenth century Chinese when it was utilized as a means of transport. Kites were used as a method of utilizing wind to gather thrust and energy to propel their canoes over bodies of water.

😠: Mr. Grumpy says, "Pretty, but not for me. Too many years spent running up and down hillsides trying to launch my son's kite have put me off."

The **Komodo dragon** was considered a mythological creature by the western world right up until 1912. Since then the lizards have earned a reputation as a fearsome predator living on the secluded island of Komodo in Indonesia. The Komodo National Park located in the centre of the Indonesian Archipelago was set up to conserve the species. Due to loss of habitat the future of the Komodo dragon is uncertain. More ferocious than the worst mother-in-law, these creatures are worth viewing.

Nearby Rinca is less familiar than Komodo Island, for, which the park and dragons get their name but claims to be even better for viewing dragons. The geography of Rinca is slightly different to that of Komodo, having a savannah type topography, which the dragons prefer to jungle and trees. There are four different walks you can take, accompanied by a ranger. They vary in levels of difficulty so decide, which suits you best and make sure you take water.

The largest Komodo dragon discovered was over three metres long and weighed one hundred and sixty-six kilograms. They can run up to thirteen miles per hour. Komodos sometimes eat their own young. To avoid being eaten by the adults, baby Komodos hide up in trees. Komodos may be monogamous and form "pair bonds", a rare behaviour for lizards.

😐😐: Mr. Grumpy says, "I'll resist the urge to write about mother-in-laws here."

L

WHATEVER CAROUSEL YOU STAND BY, YOUR
LUGGAGE WILL COME IN ON ANOTHER ONE.

L is for laughter yoga, log cabins, luxury trains.

Laughter is exceptionally good for you. Laughter lowers blood pressure, reduces stress hormones, increases muscle flexion, boosts the immune system by raising levels of infection-fighting t-cells, produces disease-destroying antibodies, triggers the release of endorphins—the body's natural painkillers and (phew) produces a sense of well-being. And, guess what? Faking laughter can fool the body into producing those mood-enhancing hormones so you can transform from a grumble guts to a happy soul by forcing or faking laughter. So, I hope you laughed at my last joke. If not, please go back, read it again and make an effort.

Being a sceptical pair of grumps, neither of us believed **Laughter Yoga** would do anything more than make us raise our eyebrows and complain further. We were wrong. One session of Laughter Yoga had us giggling like children and feeling a, whole lot better about life afterwards.

Laughter Yoga sessions vary from teacher to teacher but by and large they encourage you to laugh. You may start off falsely but it will not be long before genuine laughter takes over and you begin to truly enjoy yourselves. Nothing is funnier than a grumpy trying desperately not to laugh, then exploding in spontaneous guffaws.

The Laughter Yoga movement was founded by Doctor Madan Kataria and began in a park in Mumbai with only five participants. Today, there are over 10,000 laughter clubs in seventy-three different countries and Laughter Yoga is celebrating twenty years in 2015.

You might be surprised at the number of celebrities, who endorse Laughter Yoga including the great comic actor, John Cleese, who attended a laughter yoga class in Mumbai.

It has been accepted by the medical and scientific profession worldwide so consider a holiday that will give you a terrific sense of well-being, improve your health, and put a genuine smile on your face.

☺☺☺: Mr. Grumpy says, "I am not going to Laughter Yoga again. I would rather watch my collection of *Fawlty Towers* DVDs. They make me laugh every time I watch them."

A holiday that involves nature and seclusion appeals to many curmudgeons. It certainly appeals to mine. For a holiday away from the masses, look into renting **log cabins**. Mostly found in idyllic locations and away from it all, these retreats can often offer you luxuries such as a lakeside hot tub.

Log Cabin Holidays in the Cotswolds offer eight cabins near the lake each with cosy real log fires, bespoke fully equipped kitchens, good powerful showers, stand-alone roll-top baths, king-size beds, and some special touches like large fluffy towels and locally made Cotswold biscuits on arrival. Included in every booking is the use of your own row boat, logs for the fire and all of your luxury five-star towels and Egyptian cotton bed linen.

This is no back-to-basics holiday but a perfect getaway from the hustle and bustle.

You can find larger, more comfortable cabins worldwide including some superb cabins in Zermatt, Colorado, Whistler, Lake Placid, and La Forêt Enchantée in Western Australia. However if it is *luxe extraordinaire* that you want, one of the most luxurious log cabins in the world has to be Chalet Edelweiss in Courchevel, France. Resembling a small private wooden hotel, it is the ultimate in log cabin retreats with eight bedrooms all with private bathrooms, open log fires, seven storeys with latest furnishings, and a dedicated team of staff that includes two ski instructors, two private chefs, two butlers, a waiter and waitress, a massage therapist.

Prints by Miro, Damien Hirst and Roy Lichenstein dress the walls and the ski room has a collection of winter Olympic posters from 1924 to 1992.

The chalet boasts its own private nightclub, accommodating one hundred people, state-of-the art cinema, and a spa floor that no other chalet rivals. Just in case you feel like inviting your entire family, neighbours and strangers from your local town to join you, also book Chalet Les Gentianes located next door to Chalet Edelweiss. The chalets connect to give you additional space should your chalet be insufficient in size. Les Gentianes also has a cinema room and a spa floor with massage and gym. Log cabins do not come much more upmarket than this.

: Mr. Grumpy says, "They're like giant "man-sheds". That's a thumb's-up from me, then."

Go back in time, to an age when travel by train was luxurious and romantic and book a **luxury train** holiday.

No section about luxury travel by train would be complete without mentioning the authentic Venice Simplon-Orient-Express with its 1920s vintage Art Deco cars, stunning in their navy and gold livery and white roofs.

Made famous in the Agatha Christie story, the train still runs on the legendary route from Paris to Istanbul. Many other itineraries are also available. They include Istanbul to Venice, Krakow, Dresden, Prague, and Paris.

The train continues to portray elegance, beauty, sophistication, and romance. How many of us wish we could step back in time? If we book a trip on the Orient Express, we can.

Travel from Pretoria to Cape Town, South Africa on board the infamous Blue Train. The Blue Train combines the luxury of the world's leading hotels with the charm of train travel. Think of it as an all-inclusive luxury rail cruise with an opportunity to view South Africa's spectacular landscapes and visit interesting tourist attractions along the way.

You will not go short of luxury on board this train. Irish linen, crystal glassware and Sheffield steel cutlery enhance your feeling of well-being. Marble-tiled, gold-plumbed bathrooms, stately, cigar-stocked lounges, gourmet dining and personal butlers may distract you from the observation deck. As the sky darkens over the landscape, the day's smart-casual dress code gives way to a parade of elegant evening wear or traditional attire. Time to brush off that dinner suit, dicky bow and cummerbund you have had in mothballs the last few years.

Fancy listening to a pianist play Tchaikovsky as you sip vodka in an opulent lounge and gaze through panoramic windows at the vastness of Siberia? Then Russia's Trans-Siberian Railway and the lavish Golden Eagle Trans-Siberian Express, a five-star hotel on wheels and Russia's only fully en suite train, is for you.

The Trans-Siberian Railway is one part of the massive Russian railway network. It connects the European rail network at one end with the Chinese rail network at the other. You will take in outstanding scenery, lakes, the Urals, steppes and some fascinating cities en route.

All cabins have power showers, underfloor heating, air conditioning, DVD/CD player with LCD screens and audio systems and in the classy restaurant caviar and fine wines are standard.

Delight in the ancient "Land of the Maharajahs" surrounded by the regal grandeur of a bygone era.

Launched in 2009 with lavish Indian decor, gourmet cuisine, and impeccable service, the Royal Rajasthan on Wheels runs from Delhi on a seven-day journey exploring the majesty of Rajasthan, Madhya Pradesh and Uttar Pradesh.

The deluxe and super deluxe cabins are all superbly furnished with ensuite bathrooms, luxurious beds, sumptuous sofas, built-in wardrobes, and huge glass windows. There is a spa, a well-stocked bar, two opulent lounges, and two olde-worlde restaurant cars.

What more could you desire? Watch out for Poirot sitting across from you in your carriage. It could mean your trip is going to be murder.

☻: Mr. Grumpy says, "The ultimate trip for those of us who played tirelessly with Hornby railway sets when younger."

M

you can't buy happiness but you can buy a plane ticket. that's kind of the same thing.

M is for maps, meditation, model holiday, monkeys, motorbike trips, motor shows, movies, Meccano, music festivals.

You might be wondering why I put **maps** in this section. It was purely to stress the importance of one of you being able to read a map. I am not being condescending. As I have got older and my eyesight has failed, I can no longer read the names of the streets on those tourist maps or on the ridiculously small printed maps you get at reception. The days of navigating us about an island or through a foreign country are over and as for getting about cities, well, unless I have my super strength goggles with me, I am stumped. Of course, those of you with Smart phones might be able to utilize the useful apps that can guide you about but if you are a true grumble guts, chances are your phone, like ours, resembles a giant brick.

Purchase a sensible-sized map with clearly printed roads and streets. It will be a wise investment.

In recent years, I have managed to misdirect us on a couple of occasions thanks to misreading a map. (And a slight problem regarding my use of the words "left" and "right". I seem to get them muddled up.) However, be warned. Going off-piste in a city can have surprising results as we discovered on one trip to Berlin.

My other half was not only taken by the history, architecture and sights of Berlin but was somewhat attracted to the large Mercedes showroom he saw on the trip from the airport to the hotel.

He insisted we walk to the showroom, which was some way from the hotel and take in the sights as we walked. He also decided to take control of the map so I did not have to keep putting on my glasses to read it and then remove them every five minutes. Husband managed to get us lost and a couple of miles off the correct route so the trip to the showroom became a four-mile hike. (I know because I wore my pedometer.)

Having taken such a lengthy detour to get to the showroom, I took command of the map for the return journey as both of us were getting sore feet and becoming fractious.

Mr. G maintained we would see more of the city by walking rather than catch a ride in a taxi. We marched down all the main streets and I pointed out all the major attractions and peered continuously at the map working out the shortest return route. Mr. G trundled along beside me, in his own world dreaming about driving down an autobahn at speed in a fast Mercedes-Benz.

"Turn here," I commanded and we entered a street blocked by some tape.

"Oh, it says route blocked. No entry," I told him reading the sign.

"No, it can't be. What's the alternative route?"

I checked the map. It would mean retracing our steps at least a mile back up the road then going out of our way another mile to get back on the road, which lay more or less ahead of us.

"I'm not going that far. My feet hurt."

"We could get a taxi," I offered.

"No taxi rank here. I suggest we ignore the sign," he said ducking under the tape.

"The Germans are quite strict," I pleaded. "They don't cross the road if the little man on the crossing is on red. They obey the rules and signs," I continued.

"Well I'm not a German and I shall just pretend I didn't understand the notice," he replied and stormed off.

Further along there was another larger notice and some wooden barriers.

"I think we might have to turn around," I announced. "This looks blocked off for some reason."

"I'm not going back now," mumbled the grumpy one, climbing over the barrier. "Flipping roadworks," he complained.

We continued along the quiet street. I stared at the map trying to work out an alternative route. When I looked up I noticed Hubby had become distracted by a large glass-fronted building. Mr. Grumpy pressed his nose up to see what was going on. He was staring at a group of well-dressed men and women seated behind a large circle of tables.

"What are you doing? Come away. Don't distract people in a meeting."

"Do you know," he said. "I think that might be Bill Gates?"

"Don't be ridiculous," I replied checking the map again. "Why would he be in Berlin?"

"No, it is him. And I think I know that chap there too."

I sighed. He must have had too many beers. I turned to check the name of the street ahead and at that precise moment about thirty armed policemen appeared from out of the back of a parked van and politely but firmly asked us to move on.

"Vot are you doink here?" they said.

"Sorry, we're just trying to get back to the hotel. My husband thought he saw someone he recognised," I joked. "Bill Gates." I laughed nervously.

"Yes, vell, he is here mit der Israeli Prime Minister, Herr Netanyahu. You," said one policeman pointing his finger at us, "you cannot come dis vay, so, please, avay you go. Komm."

We were escorted back through the cordon we had penetrated and past the bright green tanks, which were parked on the main road. Somehow we had not seen those.

Half an hour later, as we sat on a bench to rest our feet, we watched the cavalcade of black Mercedes cars carrying the delegates, thunder down the main road, blue lights flashing and accompanied by motor cycles, sirens and what appeared to be the entire German police force.

"See I told you it was Bill Gates," said Hubby as he rubbed his feet. "I wonder if we could find a taxi now."

A few years ago, I found myself sitting on a mat, legs crossed, eyes closed, chanting, "Om". I felt ridiculous. I wanted to snigger. I fought my urge to giggle and get into the act of meditation. I am glad I persevered. There was no denying the positive energy that surged through my body after I left the class and the sense of well-being that sent me scurrying back to my room feeling youthful and surprisingly relaxed.

Meditation is often something clearly dissociated from "fun". However, meditation relieves stress and those, who meditate regularly can expect a happier and longer life, meaning they will have more fun, more often, than if they were to avoid meditating.

I took a short meditation course in the UK and would say to you all, do not be sceptics about this. Meditation might make you think "hippies", the Beatles, or Buddhist monks, but give it a chance and you might find it transforms you.

Not convinced you? How about if I tell you that celebrities including Richard Gere, Orlando Bloom, Herbie Hancock, Gwyneth Paltrow, and Tina Turner all meditate. They recognise the importance of inner peace and mental awareness, something us grumpies often no longer have.

Meditation holidays are becoming increasingly popular worldwide, as more and more people choose to combine their holidays with meditation, to relax and wind down from the frantic tempo of their everyday lives.

Some of those people head abroad to places like popular Corfu where nature is rich and the olive groves radiate absolute peace and quiet—a perfect place for meditation and to feel at one with the world. You will find several retreats on this pretty island surrounded by crystal clear waters. I defy you to not come away inspired, relaxed, revived, and dare I say it—content?

Combining a place with an abundance of nature, sea, fresh air, quiet and beauty will help hugely with meditation. If you are stuck for ideas Travel Quest and the Retreat Company offer directories of places to go to meditate.

Or, you could consider Serenity Retreat, on the island of Lefkada, Greece, set up by Zen Buddhist meditation teacher Kim Bennett. Retreat-style holidays take place from May and combine personal development courses with excursions, therapies, meditation sessions and guided walks. Relax on the beach, potter around the village, spend time alone, or meet like-minded people. The courses are optional, and are designed to nudge you into new ways of thinking about your life.

For those, whose budgets are very tight, Freely Given Retreats, Devon, UK offers meditation retreats to newcomers and dedicated meditators alike on a donation basis, so you pay only what you can afford. Retreats teach "insight meditation," a form of mindfulness, and are held mainly in silence. The charity is supported by Jenny Wilks and Kirsten Kratz, Buddhist teachers from Gaia House in Devon, and retreats are held at High Heathercombe, inside Dartmoor National Park.

😒😒: Mr. Grumpy says, "I don't "get" meditation. Isn't it just thinking? Or daydreaming? I'll leave it to those with enough imagination to concentrate on thinking about nothing."

Here is a most unusual idea for someone, who like **models**, especially radio-controlled model airplanes—visit the Radio Controlled Flying Hotel on the island of Corfu. This purpose-built complex for Radio Controlled Model Aircraft enthusiasts has all you need for them or those, who have never flown model craft before, and instructors to assist you. It offers an array of models for people to fly including electric or IC models, trainers, sports aerobatics, powered and unpowered gliders, slope soarers, scale, full control four channel: aileron, elevator, speed and rudder or three channel control, elevator, rudder and speed control. You can choose airplanes or helicopters.

While one of you is flying high, the other might offer to co-pilot for the day or hang out at the infinity pool. Others facilities that might help clinch the deal include a bar and a "Man Crèche." Over and out!

😒😒: Mr. Grumpy says, "I quite like the idea but would much rather be behind the controls of a real plane. Looks like fun for a while."

You spent your life looking after your children. Now dare to be different and go on holiday to look after **monkeys**. Actually, you will be looking after and nursing orphaned and rescued capuchin and howler monkeys as well as lemurs and parrots, taking pumas, ocelots, and jaguars for daily walks in mangrove forests, preparing birds for their release in the wild, and guiding visitors if you take part in a community wildlife project in the tropical heart of Bolivia. Inti Wara Yassi rehabilitates victims of the country's black-market trade in exotic pets. The refuge is run entirely by volunteers, who feed and care for big cats, birds, and other creatures that arrive abused and malnourished, as well as build and clean cages. Volunteers share rooms in the refuge's two hostels.

Rather than work all holiday, primate lovers might prefer the chance of a lifetime to track down and watch the rarest ape in the world—the western hoolock gibbon (No, I did not make that up) of Bangladesh. They are rarely seen and usually only with the help of a trained local tracker and a qualified zoologist. In addition to the western hoolock gibbons, the forests of Bangladesh are home to very rare monkeys like Phayre's leaf monkey, pig-tailed macaques, capped langurs, rhesus macaques, common langurs, and the very special nocturnal slow loris. Bet you did not realise there were so many species of ape.

Primate tours are an excellent way to see the creatures in their natural habitat and get a real sense of adventure as you track them down.

For some serious monkey business, take a tour in Costa Rica, home to lush rainforests and to the capuchin monkey, Costa Rica's most popular monkey. These small brown monkeys with a distinctive white face can be very mischievous, often observed stealing food from picnic sites. Howler monkeys, renowned for their distinctive noisy call are also common here. They are the main attraction on the popular Monkey Trail Costa Rica. Look out for spider monkeys. They are long and slender with colour that ranges from black to gold. You might even see squirrel monkeys. These orange-furred creatures with big dark eyes are highly endangered and are protected by the government.

Because of its intelligence, the white-faced capuchin monkey has been used to assist paraplegics.

My soul encounter with a monkey was in South Africa at Simbambili Game Lodge in Sabi Sands, next to Kruger Park. We had been warned that the cute black-faced vervet monkeys might attempt to steal food from our rooms and to ensure doors were locked and windows shut when we went out on safari. Rangers would walk us to the dining room each morning, in case we came across any elephants or stray lions. One morning, having arrived at breakfast, I discovered I had forgotten my camera. There were no rangers available to escort me but my hut was not far away so I raced off to fetch my camera.

There were no lions but there were two vervet monkeys on the roof of my hut hanging over the side, watching a third attempt to pull open my front door. He tugged and tugged. I yelled at them.

If I had been able to communicate with them like Doctor Doolittle I might have understood their conversation. I am fairly certain it went along these lines:

"Vince, have you got that door open yet?"

"Nah. It's trickier than the last job we did. I think they locked the door. Don't worry. I'll work at it and I'll have it open in a jiffy. The silly tourists are at breakfast, so I've got plenty of time to break and enter."

"Oh hurry up, Vince. I'm dying to get my teeth into those apples I saw through the window."

"I'm going as fast as I can, Vern. Nearly there … just one more twist and I'll be in."

"Oh blast! Here comes one of the residents now. Quick. Pretend you were just passing by."

"What? Oh bother. Why didn't you warn me? I thought you were supposed to be on lookout, you muppet."

", who are you calling a muppet? You might be the one, who can pick locks, Vince, but, who's the brains behind this operation? Yes, me, Vernon Velvet."

"Shut up, you two. This tourist is a bit daft. She thinks she can shoo us away. Look, she's waving her arms at us, or she's pretending to be a windmill."

"What's a windmill?"

"Never mind. She obviously doesn't realise she's dealing with the Velvet Gang. We'll have to enlighten her."

"Did she bring the ranger with her? I can't see him."

"Nope, no ranger. I think we've just found the real muppet. Come on lads, let's show her we're not the pretty faces she thinks we are. Give her the Velvet Gang hard stare. Yeah, that's got her worried. Go on Vince, snarl at her.

"Ha! Look at her. She's worried now. That's it Vernon, make those angry gibbering noises. We'll start advancing on her and if she doesn't run away, we'll jump on her head and steal her hat."

"Steady up, lads! Look out. Ranger One approaching and he's got the stun gun. Whistle nonchalantly. Come on men. Just walk away and pretend we are going back to the trees. Leave them to it. We'll return when she's gone off on the jeep safari and finish off the job. No one can stop the Velvet Monkey gang."

Exit monkeys muttering and looking remarkably like a group of hooligans, who had been reprimanded by a policeman.

The moral of my story is never annoy a monkey. It might take offence and decide to sort you out. If you go on a primate tour, respect the wildlife.

q. what do you call a 2,000 pound gorilla?
a. sir

:: Mr. Grumpy says, "Wiley little critters that stole the rubber from my windscreen wipers when I was parked up at a forest car park. Approach with caution."

One year, unsure of what to do for my other half's birthday, I decided to try out a **motoring show** holiday. I booked a trip to Geneva and arranged for us both to attend the Geneva Motor Show. Turned out it was a cracking idea and I recommend it to you if either of you are interested in cars. Even I became excited at the unveiling of brand new models of top brand cars. Each stand was decked out like a mini concert with performers and music, dry ice, and action. Those, who ordinarily yawn when their other half starts talking horsepower, miles per gallon and engine size will enjoy the shows. Best of all, you can then go and explore a new city after the show.

Motor shows take place in Tokyo, Detroit, Los Angeles, Paris, Frankfurt, Geneva, and London. Frankfurt is the largest of the shows. Make sure you check dates because quite a few of these shows take place every other year.

Other, even more thrilling car events, include Top Marques. Top Marques takes place every April in the prestigious Principality of Monaco. It is the only live supercar show in the world. VIP visitors have the unique chance to test drive the world's most bespoke cars on the Formula 1 track. The event has grown to such proportions that it now represents everything that encompasses luxury living so while one of you is drooling over supercars, the other might be able to sneak off inside the Grimaldi Forum's Watch Pavilion where they can be enchanted by exclusive timepieces, precious jewels and brand new luxury products (this year they will include Remmus, a self-rotating lounger, which follows the sun). Or, nip outside to put a down payment on a new luxury yacht.

Billed as the "most exclusive car show in the world" by the New York Times, Top Marques Monaco has become a must-attend event for supercar and lovers of all things luxury. VIP tickets can be purchased from the Top Marques website. How you get your new supercar and bling back home after the show is up to you.

Classic car enthusiasts will relish the sights and sounds of the Monte Carlo Classic Historic Grand Prix with of some amazing cars from the golden age of motor racing. Another hugely popular event, in a fantastic setting, this should make for an ace holiday. Line the streets to see drivers tackle the twists and turns of this famous street circuit, which still uses the same roads as the very first race on 14th April 1929. Hang out with the yachts and listen to the scream of engines, echoing around Monaco Bay. Or, grab a glass of wine at Café de Paris where you can rub shoulders with the rich and famous in Casino Square and admire the endless display of supercars. It will make for a special holiday for both of you.

🐵: Mr. Grumpy says, "Good idea. Hours of fun looking at the sleek new models and the cars they are sitting upon."

Movie-inspired packages are becoming increasingly popular and there is one to suit most budgets. Nowhere says movies quite like the U.S.A. and a visit to Universal Orlando Resort is a must for film fans.

Save the city from certain doom with Spider-Man□. Be transformed into a Minion on the hilarious 3-D ride based on *Despicable Me* and experience The Wizarding World of Harry Potter□. Then go behind-the-scenes on the legendary Studio Tour at Universal Studios to explore Hollywood's largest working movie studio.

With so much to see and do what is the greatest attraction there? There are lots but for me it has to be being able to See Wisteria Lane from ABC's hit series *Desperate Housewives*. I admit, that is very sad.

Warner Brothers Studio in Burbank, California offers an exclusive tour through one of Hollywood's most famous motion picture and television studios. At the moment of writing, Warner Brothers are celebrating the 75th anniversary of DC comics so book a Deluxe Tour, which will immerse you behind-the-scenes of Hollywood, while seeing Batman's original costumes, props and artwork in the Warner Bros. Museum. You will also venture to the Picture Car Vault, which is dressed as the bat-cave. My old grump's ears pricked up at that suggestion.

The average weight of Batman's armour is about forty pounds.

Lovers of Bollywood should shimmy over to the Film City in Hyderabad located in Anajpur village, India where numerous films in Hindi, Tamil, Telugu, Malayalam, Kannada, Gujarati, Bengali, Oriya, Bhojpuri, and English are produced every year. Several television commercials and serials and a huge number of popular movies and television serials are made there.

Spread over one thousand acres, the Ramoji Film City is a city unlike any other city. Approximately 1.5 million tourists come to the Film City annually. With its parks, gardens, sets, spectacular live shows, and amusements it is a wonderland for all, who are enchanted by the Indian film industry.

The British film industry also has an illustrious past and tours around Elstree, Ealing and Pinewood studios can be booked but if you are in London take a Brit Movie tour. Choose from *Sherlock Holmes, Harry Potter, Doctor, who, Game of Thrones, Downton Abbey, The Only Way is Essex, Paddington,* and *James Bond* walking, bus or car tours. All can be arranged by Brit Movie Tours.

Those with a penchant for new movies might like to join the glitterati at the Cannes Film Festival taking place every May. This is the place to see up and coming films, directors, and big names and is *the* place to be seen. Even if you only take in a couple of the films there will be plenty to keep your eyes wide open.

There are film festivals worldwide including the Edinburgh International Film Festival, Robert Redford's indie showcase, and the Sundance film festival in Utah, USA. Germany offers the Berlinale, Berlin, where *Fifty Shades of Grey*, the film adaptation of the bestselling book, celebrated its international premiere as *Berlinale Special* Gala at the 65th Berlin International Film Festival. Venice hosts a magnificent film gala event, as does Toronto.

Plan a trip to any destination where there is a film festival and pack your tuxedo. You never know when George Clooney or Kristen Bell is going to pop up.

If you are quick off the mark and have £198,000.00 to blow, you can take the film buff's ultimate trip. This once-in-a-lifetime opportunity offers couples the chance to visit many of the most iconic film locations in the world over a period of three months including the Thai island from *The Beach*, the vast deserts shown in *Lawrence of Arabia*, the delicatessen from *When Harry Met Sally*, and the streets of Paris explored in *Amélie*. VeryFirstTo is offering this extraordinary trip. I suspect you have to provide your own popcorn.

😩😩😩: Mr. Grumpy says, "The last film I watched was *Fatal Attraction*, way back in 1987. I dozed off during the sex scene on the kitchen sink. Guess this sort of holiday isn't for me."

Forget Glastonbury. That is not what I mean by a **music festival** holiday. I cannot imagine any grumpy person wanting to hang out with the masses in a muddy field among spaced-out, smelly youngsters, watching unheard of acts playing raucous music. Wait a minute. The rumour-mill says AC/DC, Ironmaiden, Kate Bush Fleetwood Mac and—swoon—David Bowie might be playing this coming year. How soon are tickets available?

I was thinking more of the jazz festival in Antibes, France, the Valletta International Baroque Music Festival on Malta, The World Festival of Sacred Music in Fes, Morocco, the Canary Islands Music Festival, or the Bohuslav Martinu Festival featuring the Czech Philharmonic Orchestra in Prague among others. Kirker Travel offers a variety of music festival tours that combine sightseeing and relaxation.

According to research, music triggers activity in the nucleus accumbens—also known as the accumbens nucleus or as the nucleus accumbens septi—a part of your brain that releases the feel-good chemical dopamine and is involved in forming expectations. It is no surprise then that listening to music makes you feel happier and more relaxed.

Music has been proven not only to release stress but improve health, relieve anxiety, elevate mood, ease pain, improve cognitive performance, improve sleep quality, and help individuals eat less. As long as you do not drag your other half to a Foo Fighter's concert—the noisy group known for playing extremely loudly, drew complaints from people living fifteen miles away during one concert—a music festival holiday could be just the tonic for a stressed grumpy pants.

☻☻: Mr. Grumpy says, "I'm down with the kids. I know who Caro Emerald is. I watched a Tom Jones tribute act a few weeks ago. I saw Meatloaf and Eric Clapton play at the NEC—not at the same time—and sang along. Might give this a go if the right act or group is playing."

N

"I may not have gone where I intended to go, but I think I have ended up where I intended to be."
~ Douglas Adams

N is for nature, naturists, netball, learning to be a Ninja, Northern Lights.

Let us begin this section in a sensible manner and discuss the pros of a **nature** holiday. Wildlife and grumpy folk seem to co-exist harmoniously. Many of us, unable to cope with the stresses and strains of our modern world, often like to seek refuge in the wild.

A growing body of research links spending more time in nature with a reduction of stress and depression, faster healing time, and less need for pain medication. Being in contact with nature is beneficial to mental health, encourages optimism, and improves mood. Heaven knows we grumps need all the help we can get and a visit to the local park is not enough to stop us from feeling grouchy much of the time.

Whilst there are a vast number of possibilities that come under the category "nature holidays," I would like to send you in the direction of Naturetrek Wildlife Holidays, who offer some fascinating trips including a unique opportunity to explore Chitwan National Park in Nepal with an optional extension to visit Koshi Tappu Wildlife Reserve, a thirteen-day wildlife safari in search of the mammals, particularly the primates, of Kibale Forest, Queen Elizabeth, and other national parks, as well as the Mountain Gorillas of Bwindi Impenetrable Forest in Uganda or a deluxe holiday exploring Sri Lanka's wildlife and cultural highlights in the utmost comfort and style, plus an optional extension to Sinharaja Forest.

Whatever you want to observe, whether that be dragonflies, whales, or wolves, this company has a trip that will suit you with destinations worldwide. Download a brochure from their website or join their free roadshow that tours January and November throughout the UK to meet the team, discuss your holiday plans, and watch a series of illustrated presentations by their top wildlife tour leaders on their most popular wildlife destinations.

In the UK, Wild North Discovery offers more than just walking and discovering new wildlife. You can learn wilderness cooking, willow weaving or pole lathe and basketry. Activities take place in the North Pennines in Northern England and the Northwest Highlands of Scotland, two areas of outstanding beauty filled with wildlife and excellent walking.

Wherever you decide to go, I am convinced a holiday surrounded by nature is perfect for grumps of all ages. Sit back, listen to the birdsong and enjoy!

🖼: Mr. Grumpy says, "Yes, yes, yes. Anywhere that is away from roads, people, television, those darn mobile phones and the flipping internet. Book me a month away."

Do not get nature and **naturist** mixed up or you could find yourself in an embarrassing situation. Letting it all "hang out" is one way to feel free and unencumbered. There are resorts, beaches, cruises and indeed luxury resorts where you can strip off and strut about in your birthday suit.

On the basis that mine needs a good iron, I shall not be joining the many, who feel comfortable in their own skin.

Travel AOL listed some of the best naturist holidays in the world and I have to admit a few are tempting enough to attract me to bare all:

Specialists in cruises, eWaterways, offer nudist cruises to see Croatia's diverse landscape. Their website states, "Croatia has a huge range of "clothing optional" beaches and with its warm summer temperatures is the perfect destination to shed a few layers of clothing. All of your fellow cruise passengers will also be comfortable without clothes on, and the sailing itinerary will take you from one secluded beach to another."

Haulover Beach in Miami is internationally famous for its New Year's Eve parties and other amenities throughout the year. The designated nude area stretches for over 800 yards, and is overseen by its own police and lifeguards. Hundreds of nude party people descend on the beach each New Year, to take part in the drum circles, dancing, and seafood dinner. Running into the ocean for a midnight skinny dip is a traditional way to welcome the New Year at Haulover. It is a three-day two-night beach festival—billed as the most extreme thing to do for New Year's Eve in the world.

The climate in Palm Springs is pleasant in the winter, making this an ideal destination for naturists. The Terra Cotta Inn—A Couples Nude Sunbathing Resort and Spa Resort here is very popular with first-time naturists. They have barbecue and spa facilities as well as an outdoor pool and Jacuzzi, all of, which come into play in their notorious clothing-optional New Year's Eve celebration.

Sun your buns in California at this highly rated resort and get a genuine all-over tan.

Rather than get naked on a beach, go to a resort. The privately owned commercial naturist park in Wai-Natur Naturist Park in the Wairau Valley, Marlborough, New Zealand is an acclaimed award-winning park.

This haven for naturists is set in a region of outstanding beauty. There is a fitness centre, heated swimming pool, and spa pool on site, as well as a cabin with ensuite bathroom, on-site caravans for hire, and five acres of park-like gardens within, which guests may camp.

The site hosts a variety of events including "nudie foodie" cruises and in February 2015 the annual Nude Golf International is held at the Wairau Valley Golf Club.

😁😁😁😁😁: Mr. Grumpy says, "Move along. Next suggestion please."

"Cowabunga!" what about this for a cool suggestion? **Learn to be a Ninja** in Japan and at the same time visit the "Land of the Rising Sun."

Having only seen Ninjas in films and a series of *Teenage Mutant Ninja Turtles*, I was surprised to learn that historically a Ninja was a covert agent or mercenary in feudal Japan. Time, legends and folklore have transformed Ninjas to more modern-day versions of those, who can become invisible or walk on water.

Black Tomato holidays offer you the opportunity to learn to become a Ninja with a special holiday. Have a go at Japanese archery and master the sword during Kenbu—a Japanese dancing art, which uses the sword and other weapons as a central part of the dance. (Considerably more exciting than doing the Twist.) Then explore Kyoto with a private guide and witness a classic tea ceremony before being whisked off to Tokyo on the fantastic "Bullet Train." Once there you will receive one-to-one martial arts lessons from one of Japan's most legendary sensei in his private dojo.

Ken means sword and Bu means dance in the Japanese language.

The price tag of four thousand, nine hundred and ninety-five pounds per person per person might put you off this particular trip. If so, but you still wish to be schooled in skills essential to ninjutsu warfare, such as the arts of espionage, sabotage, and infiltration, then learn what it takes to become a modern-day fighter spy at camps in Iga, east of Osaka or nearby Nabari.

Iga has a proud ninja history stretching back to the 15th century. It was here, on plains protected by mountains, that many ninjas—a more working class warrior than the samurai—rose to become the Iga-ryu, a force of clans to be reckoned with in feudal Japan. Nowadays, the warriors' skills are being used to boost the area's flagging economy.

Purchase a ninja-training hour for approximately ten pounds at these camps and you can expect to learn how to throw ninja stars, scale walls, and haul yourselves across rivers by rope.

There are many tourist spots in Japan where visitors can sample ninja techniques or can learn secret mechanisms in ninja houses including Koka Ninja Village or the museum at Iga-ryu, however, for a Ninja experience unlike any other, climb aboard a "Samurai and Ninja Safari" jaunt around the Japanese capital.

The tour may appear to be standard as it heads through the streets of Tokyo past points of interest but be prepared for a dramatic change halfway around when street performers dressed as both samurais and ninjas will burst out of the shadows and leap into battle, assailing each other with a range of acrobatic kicks and athletic blows.

😑😑😑😑😑: Mr. Grumpy says, "Who came up with this idea? It's bonkers. Not that I would say that to any Ninja's face."

I had to put the **Northern Lights** in this section purely because they are astouding and seeing them is on most people's bucket lists.

Many of the Arctic trips I have mentioned also include watching the Northern Lights but search for Northern Lights online and you will find all the information you need on this subject, or speak to a travel agent.

It might interest you to know that you can book Aurora flights. These flights depart from many of the airports throughout the UK including Birmingham, Bristol, Manchester, and Glasgow on various dates.

Once you have taken off into the dark skies you head to the Shetland Islands where the aircraft takes up a holding pattern (flies around in very large circles) and you hopefully witness the spectacle of the Northern Lights. Guest astronomers are on hand to talk about the stars visible in the clear night sky and tell you more about the Aurora Borealis.

There is no guarantee that you will see the lights. Much depends on weather conditions but at least if you take an Aurora flight, you will not be chilly.

This is still very high on my carpe diem list. I am trying to decide between heading to the Yukon, Canada, or Lapland to view them. It is important not to make seeing the Northern Lights the focus of any holiday, so best to choose a trip I have mentioned before and keep those fingers crossed that the sky will light up like a giant lava lamp for you.

😑: Mr. Grumpy says, "I wasn't too keen until you said we could watch the Aurora Borealis from an airplane window. I'm happier about that. I don't fancy hanging about in the cold waiting for the Lights to do their thing. Much better to be inside a nice warm airplane with a glass of beer."

O

O is for ocean rafting, olive picking, opera, orienteering.

Similar to white water rafting without the rapids, **ocean rafting**, is suitable for almost anyone and age.

Award-winning company Ocean Rafting in Queensland, Australia, offers three ocean rafting excursions and safaris. Visit the Whitsunday Islands, uninhabited islands with beautiful natural scenery brimming with marine, bird and animal life. There are two exciting tour options, the Northern Exposure and Southern Lights.

Each excursion of tour is taken in an eleven-metre, semi-rigid inflatable vessel. All four of Ocean Rafting's were originally designed and built as rescue crafts and are driven by 500hp engines. Each vessel carries a maximum of twenty-eight passengers, and seventy percent of the vessel is shaded, providing comfort from the tropical sun.

In general, ocean rafting cruises such as the "Bali Hai's 3 Island Ocean Rafting Cruise", that travel around Bali and its three Islands of Nusa Lembongan, Ceningan Island, and Nusa Penida usually take up to one day. It is not long but you get sufficient time to enjoy the thrill of the ride, go snorkelling and view the magnificent coral reefs.

Hawaii Activities offer fast-paced ocean rafting adventure from Maui to Lanai with a landing at Manele Harbor and snorkelling at Hulopoe Bay Marine Reserve. You may even see spinner and bottle-nose dolphins that are often encountered off the island of Lanai along with lots of tropical reef fish.

Ocean rafting then is a fast, exciting way to travel to snorkelling destinations or beaches that are away from the crowds. Incorporate it into your holiday to inject a little excitement.

😡😡😡: Mr. Grumpy says, "I'll wait for you on the beach. Have fun."

Are you looking for a new challenge? A chance to spend a week or longer doing something different? Often people with many **olive trees** to harvest, or old groves to restore would welcome help in return for varying deals: normally think in terms of a day's work in exchange for free board.

There are olive groves all over southern Europe. I expect, like me, you tend to think that this is one for backpackers or the young but no, it can be an ideal holiday away from it all. Choose a small farm for their harvest and this trip will give you the true flavour of living in a rural community.

It is educational, invigorating, and will ensure you stay fit and active. There is often time for trips to nearby cities or relaxation time as some farms have swimming pools so it is not all work. And don't forget the delicious local food, often accompanied by some of the finest olive oil in the region.

The largest type of olive is called a "donkey olive."
The smallest is known as a "bullet."
The average life of an olive tree is between 300 and 600 years.
The oldest certified olive tree is more than 2000 years old.
Olives are rich in Vitamin E and "good fat."
Your five daily portions of fruit can include sixteen olives, which make one portion.

😡: Mr. Grumpy says, "Another one of those holidays that fools you into thinking you have a purpose in life again. On that basis alone, I'd book it."

A night at the **opera** is always a glamorous affair but imagine a night out at the Semper Opera in the centre of the historic area of Dresden and close to the banks of the Elbe or a night watching one of the world's greatest opera stars at The Metropolitan Opera in New York City? Picture yourself in your finery sitting in La Scala, renowned for its beauty, history and high musical standards.

Combine a cultural trip with the pleasure of a night in one of the world's most historic and magnificent opera houses to make your holiday even more memorable.

I highly recommend the opera houses in Prague, especially the ornate and stately National Theatre. It is grand in every sense.

If you would like to visit one of Europe's leading opera houses but prefer to travel independently, Kirker Holidays are able to book tickets for any opera in any one of over fifty classical cities.

Kirker specialise in cultural tours for the discerning traveller and are very professional. Ask experts using their website or head to a travel agent to ensure you find a trip to suit you.

👿👿: Mr. Grumpy says, "As magnificent as it all is—and it does give you an occasion to dress up—I don't like opera. It is one step up from ballet and I detest that. You're on your own with this choice."

Orienteering is a popular sport—there are approximately one hundred and twenty orienteering clubs in the UK alone. It exercises both the mind and the body and is perfect for those, who like to be outside. When orienteering, you travel between specific control points marked on a special map. You have to work out the best course and route for your personal ability and then do it. An electronic card is used to confirm that you have visited all the controls in the correct order and to record your times.

Orienteering can take place anywhere from remote forest and countryside to urban parks. The easier routes follow footpaths and set tracks; the most challenging orienteering takes place in areas, which have demanding terrain and few paths.

With a range of opportunities, from half-day "tasters" to, whole-week courses available throughout Britain and increasingly further afield, why not consider an orienteering holiday?

There are number of centres in the UK and abroad—particularly in Spain and Portugal—that offer orienteering travel packages and training camps, which combine interesting and varied terrain with the chance to visit regions with a rich culture and good weather. The packages provide for all levels of fitness, ability and age, making them ideal for individual travellers, families, or friends.

If the idea of map reading appeals—but the thought of all that running around the countryside does not—you can still take pleasure from an orienteering holiday. Avid cyclists, for instance, can attempt bike orienteering (MTBO), while skiers can opt to navigate a route on cross-country skis at a number of centres throughout Scandinavia and there are even mounted holidays for horse riders too.

This is not all about kagools, maps and running about like a madman or mad woman. You can jog, walk, or amble your way around a course, unless you happen to be very competitive, like me. Last one to the finish line is a sissy!

a keen orienteer asked his vicar if there was orienteering in heaven and if so, what was it like? the vicar had a chat with saint peter and the next day, told the orienteer that there was indeed orienteering in heaven but that he had some good news and some bad news.

"what do you want to hear first?" asked the vicar.

"the good news please," replied the orienteer.

"well," said the vicar, "it's marvellous. the maps are perfect, there are no brambles, the sun's always shining, the women run in bikini tops and you never have to search for a control."

"that's great!" said the keen orienteer. "but what could possibly be the bad news then?"

the vicar looked at his watch as he replied, "your first start time is in ten minutes."

☺: Mr. Grumpy says, "Not a bad choice of holiday. However, I refuse to go with my wife. She will undoubtedly get us horribly lost."

P

P is for painting, paragliding, parasailing, picnicking, Pilates, photography, polar expeditions, polo, psychic break.

The artist Pablo Picasso said, "Every child is an artist. The problem is how to remain an artist once we grow up." I was the exception to the rule. I was hopeless at art at school. For my art mock GCSE examination I painted a cottage in the country. I was unhappy with the look of it so I whitewashed it then gave it another coat of colour—brown. My muse remained dissatisfied so I gave it another coat of colour—black. I attempted to draw a creeping ivy up the wall to hide the woeful sight and surrounded it with trees. Needless to say I failed miserably, gave up art and took Chemistry GSCE instead. I was watching the programme *Posh Pawn* a few weeks ago and, lo and behold, a picture just like mine came up for sale. It had been painted by the Kray Twins while in prison. I guess they did not pass GCSE Art either.

Undeterred, I took up **painting** four years ago and can now sketch and draw a reasonable picture. It depends on your inspiration and mine came from trips to the Italian lakes particularly Lake Orta surrounded by vibrant flowers, verdant gardens, ochre buildings, sparkling blue waters and lashings of colour everywhere I looked.

Find your inspiration, as so many artists do, by going on a residential painting course in the south of France, Italy, Spain, Greece, or wherever you fancy. From Amsterdam to Zambia you will find a course or a destination to inspire you.

There are many residential courses including those in picturesque

Skyros Village, Greece. Skyros Centre is set in a stunning location in the hillside village with panoramic view of the hills and the sea. It is home to the renowned Writers' Lab, Life Coaching programme and The Art Studio where you can sign up for a course to suit your level of expertise with one of their visiting artists.

Imagine yourself on a fifty-acre creative retreat of farmland nestled in the Parque Naturel Sierra María-Los Vélez, Andalucia, Spain, learning how to paint with watercolours. The area is perfect for any muse and to cap it all you stay in a luxury eco-chic guest house, which has been recommended by Alastair Sawday. The ambience is ideal for any artist.

What about painting Niagra Falls? Or stay and work on the magical, mystical island of Monhegan, Maine, USA, long known for creative, spiritual, and life-altering forces with like-minded individuals seeking the essence of oneness and serenity with nature.

Rather than stay in one place, take an art safari where your sketch book becomes your visual diary. Travel to Namibia, the Galapagos, Zambia, Northern Lights, Scotland, Malawi … you get the picture?

Become inspired and follow in Monet's brushstrokes at the *Normandie Impressionniste* festival that takes place across the two regions of Normandy. This innovative festival open to everyone will next be held from 16th April to 26th September 2016. Learn how to paint Rouen Cathedral—subject of a series of paintings by Monet in the 1890s—in the artist's distinctive manner, and devour a meal "inspired" by Claude's personal cookery repertoire.

Pablo Picasso's first spoken word was the Spanish word for pencil.

😑😑😑: Mr. Grumpy says, "I would prefer a photography course. Just saying!"

In my opinion, it would be a brave fool, who decided to go **paragliding** for their holidays though I am assured that those, who have the paragliding bug, love their sport.

One of our friends took up paragliding in his fifties, launching himself every weekend from the top of the gorges by the Aveyron River, France and floating down to fields below. I am not sure what he would have made of paragliding in India but those, who have taken a paragliding holiday there have written glowing testimonials.

Skylark Paragliding run a variety of trips throughout the year and if you want to soar over valleys like an eagle, this is an ideal opportunity for you.

Paragliding, like most of my suggestions can be taken up worldwide, from Argentina to Zambia. Choose your location, then check to see what is on offer. My ideal spot would be Cape Town, South Africa, where you can sign up with Birdmen Paragliding, owned and run by Barry Pedersen.

Barry is a qualified advanced pilot with well over 2,500 flights, a SAPHA Instructor for Paragliding and Powered Paragliding. Barry is a qualified TFI Tandems Pilot for both power and mountain flying.

If you have ever wanted to learn how to paraglide, or take a tandem flight near Table Mountain, here is your chance.

During a stay in Cape Town, I watched the paragliders spiralling and swirling over the sandy beaches outside Cape Town, in the shadow of the magnificent Table Mountain and almost convinced myself to have a go. I did not and to this day I regret it and keep promising myself that I will do it. Part of me wants that sense of freedom I am assured you experience when doing this activity. My older but not wiser part is aware I suffer from vertigo and would need throwing off the mountain. I know that once I get off the edge of the cliff or mountain, I shall love it. One day, I shall be courageous enough to have a go at this. I might have to be blindfolded for take-off though.

The biggest paragliding wing has a wingspan of 66 feet and can carry a load of 1300 pounds. It was used to drop an Audi A6 all-road vehicle from a Lama heavy-lift helicopter.

The origins of paragliding can be traced to David Barish, an American, who developed the Sailwing—the closest thing to a paragliding wing. He took the first Sailwing flight in 1965 launching from Hunter Mountain, New York. There is much speculation that he may be the paraglider's inventor but to this date the title has not been made official.

The world's oldest paraglider recorded in the Guinness World Book of Records is Baruch Gurwitz at seventy-seven years old.

Parasailing differs from paragliding in as much as you no longer soar completely free like a bird but are propelled by a motor and attached to the vehicle.

Parasailing is a recreational activity where a person is towed behind a vehicle (usually a boat) while attached to a specially designed parachute, known as a parasail. There are two types of parasailing: aquatic (over water where a motorboat is used) and terrestrial (over land towed by a jeep).

If you prefer a shorter "flight" then try out parasailing.

😩😩😩: Mr. Grumpy says, 'I wish you'd stop giving me holiday choices that involve an element of risk. I am beginning to think you have an ulterior motive."

The word **picnic** conjures up long car journeys punctuated by stops in laybys to grab a cup of lukewarm coffee and a soggy egg sandwich. Any place that is green and clean—or indeed, is a layby—can become a picnic spot. There are, however, some very sought after places, which should be added to your list of ultra-special picnic spots. Such picnic areas, which may qualify as the best in the world include:

Huayna Picchu, Peru. Located high above at 9,000 feet, this is probably the highest picnic spot in the world. It towers over Machu Picchu and gives you a spectacular view of these world famous ruins. You will certainly have an appetite after the strenuous hike to the top.

Jardin des Tuileries, Paris. Having lived in Paris, this has to be one of my favourite picnic spots. It maintains an aura of romance and an olde-worlde feel. I half expect ladies in long crinoline dresses to float by me every time I am there. Pick up a filled baguette and park yourself under any one of the magnificent trees for a perfect picnic.

Pansy Island, Mozambique. Famous for those pretty seashells with a pansy shape etched onto them, this is ideal for a secluded picnic spot. Pure white sands and azure waters contribute to make this a perfect spot for a picnic.

Makes those layby picnics seem pretty dull.

The French started the modern fashion for picnics when they opened their royal parks to the public after the revolution of 1789.

In the year 2000, a six hundred-mile-long picnic took place in France on July 14th to celebrate the first Bastille Day of the new millennium.

Our word "picnic" dates back to 1794, exactly one hundred years after "pique-nique" was first seen in French.

😠: Mr. Grumpy says, "No matter how wonderful the setting, nothing will help me swallow or digest Mrs. G's Scotch eggs and curled up sandwiches."

Come home from your holiday looking and feeling twenty years younger without any surgery. **Pilates** will tone your body to combat back problems and arthritis. It will relax your mind and make you feel well. It is suitable for any age or ability. Pilates courses will leave you feeling truly rejuvenated.

Having been a personal trainer for some of my working life and a sufferer of back pain, I can testify to the benefits of Pilates. Pilates focuses on your core postural muscles that are responsible for keeping the body balanced and the spine supported. It is a gentle non-aerobic exercise that strengthens the muscles and improves poor posture, which can often be the cause of back and shoulder pains.

Doing a course at home is one thing but combining it with a holiday away will amplify the effect and give you a new zest for life.

Try out Beach Pilates in Fuerteventura. The sound of the ocean crashing against the white sand beaches provides a perfect setting and combines Pilates' powerful core focus with nature's own energising elements. Or, choose from Pilates mat sessions overlooking the Tuscan hills to Pilates reformer machines in sunny Andalucia. Splash out and go to the Turks and Caicos, or Saint Lucia in the Caribbean or Mauritius in the Indian Ocean. Stay closer to home or head to Europe. Health and Fitness Travel offers courses to suit every taste and pocket.

😠😠😠😠😠: Mr. Grumpy says, "Harrumph!"

"Say cheese!" **Photography** holidays can be quite phenomenal depending where you go. It is one thing to take snapshots of your other half attempting to smile for an eternity while you set up the perfect shot or grab a quick selfie with your camera phone but a holiday where you can learn to photograph and then take some special pictures is unbeatable. On top of it all, you will have some stunning reminders of your holiday.

Head to the enchanted Galapagos Islands to photograph creatures from prehistoric times unique to the islands. Capture bears in the Alaskan wilderness or Rockhopper, Magellanic or King penguins in the Falklands. There are any number of websites or holiday operators, who will be able to help you decide where to go but to get some ideas, take a look at website Responsible Travel for a cornucopia of possible destinations and courses including the Northern Lights, Fire and Ice tour and a Hebridean photography cruise in Scotland.

☺: Mr. Grumpy says, "At last, a holiday beginning with the letter P that I fancy going on."

ᎴᎥᎴ ᎽᎾᏌ ᏂᎬᎯᏒ ᎯᏴᎾᏌᏖ ᏖᏂᎬ ᎷᎯᎴ-ᏦᎬᎬᏁ ᎮᏂᎾᏖᎾᎶᏒᎯᎮᏂᎬᏒ, ᎳᏂᎾ ᏴᎾᏌᎶᏂᏖ Ꭿ ᏞᎯᏴᏒᎯᎴᎾᏒ ᎯᏁᎴ ᏁᎯᎷᎬᎴ ᏂᎥᎷ ᏦᎾᎴᎯᏦ, ᏕᎾ ᏂᎬ ᏦᎾᏌᏞᎴ ᏕᎯᎽ ᏂᎬ ᎾᎳᏁᎬᎴ Ꭿ ᏦᎾᎴᎯᏦ ᏞᎯᏴ.

Wrap up warmly for this next idea—go on a **Polar expedition**. A Polar expedition will take you to places you have only seen on television and view creatures and sights only brought to you before by David Attenborough: Polar bears, walrus, penguins, seals, whales, not forgetting giant icebergs the size of housing estates.

Take jaw-dropping photographs of the wildlife, visit remote areas of captivating beauty and explore vast wildernesses.

Travel company Exodus offers Arctic and Antarctica expeditions on a number of dates and with group size and length of stay to suit you.

You can work on and from small ships crewed by committed and experienced staff. Be astounded by the beauty and wilderness of the Antarctic, Baffin Island, South Georgia, the Falklands, Spitzbergen, the Sea of Okhotsk or any of the incredible thirty-eight destinations offered by Exodus.

hERE YOU havE an incREδibLE OppORtunity to RELEaSE YOUR innER ExpLORER anδ tRavEL SOMEWhERE that not Many havE viSitEδ. what δO pOLaR bEaRS Eat fOR Lunch? icE bERG~ERS.

: Mr. Grumpy says, "This holiday is for true adventurers. If I want to get freezing cold fingers, I'll go and stick my hand in the chilled food cabinet at the supermarket.

The game of **polo** originated in Persia more than two millennia ago and is one of the oldest team sports ever recorded. It was brought to the East by the Mughals and was later known as the "game of kings." It was in Asia (in particular, India) that the English later picked up the sport.

Today, the game is played all over the planet. The dominant nations are Argentina, the USA, and Britain, each of, which has a thriving polo scene and industry. Other polo hotspots include New Zealand, Australia, South Africa, Dubai, China, Chile, and Spain.

You too can learn to play polo. Polo playing holidays can be taken in the UK or better still, in Argentina, home to some of the finest polo playing in the world.

Contact Carlitos' White Waltham Polo Club to find out about his specially designed polo playing holiday in Mar del Plata, four hundred kilometres south of Buenos Aires. There you can spend two weeks learning how to play polo and participate in a polo tournament. A typical day's itinerary taken from his website is as follows:

08:30 Breakfast
09:30 Pick up from hotel
10:00 Ride on the beach. This helps you get used to the polo ponies and teaches you how to control your pony, stopping and turning and fast transitions. It is fun way to get used to the speed of the polo tournaments.
11:30 Stick and ball session. Here you are taught how to hit the polo ball correctly from your pony, and all the different swings needed to play polo.

14:00 BBQ in the stables, (at the weekend, lunch in the polo club restaurant).

15:00 Siesta

16:00 Chukkas. During these sessions you will learn to play polo as part of a team, and cover defence and attack and the tactics and rules of the game of polo.

20:00 Return to the hotel for a chance to freshen up.

21:00 Evening meal with Carlitos to discuss the next day's training and how you have done that day.

On the final weekend you will be able to take part in the scheduled club tournament. The tournament matches take place in the afternoon, so the itinerary for the morning stays the same at weekends as on a weekday.

Other places in the world where you can saddle up and learn this sport include Dubai. The Desert Palm Dubai is the home of major international polo competition, the Royal Salute UAE Nations Cup, so it is a great place to learn to play polo, dressage, or just have riding lessons (beginners welcome). The Desert Palm Dubai by Per Aquum is also one of the most exclusive boutique hotels in the UAE, with twenty-six suites and apartments set in tropical gardens. Sit under palm trees sipping cool drinks then pop out for a quick chukka when you feel like it.

Most polo games are cheap to watch with some smaller clubs around the world having free entry so should watching the game be more appealing, check out the St Moritz Snow Polo World Cup, Switzerland, that takes place January/February, China International Polo Challenge, Tang, Beijing in October, Miami Beach Polo World Cup, Miami in April, Barbados Open, Lion Castle in March or any one of a number of matches taking place worldwide.

Do you think there's more to life than meets the eye? Do you see ghosts or sometimes feel you have a sixth sense? You should take a **psychic break** and discover more about the supernatural.

You might not have to travel far to find some psychic activities and if you only want to dabble briefly, a weekend away should be enough.

a Lonely frog, desperate for some form
of company telephones the psychic hotline
to find out what his future holds. his
personal psychic advisor tells him, "you
are going to meet a beautiful young girl,
who will want to know everything about
you."

the frog is thrilled and says, "this is
great! where will I meet her, at work, at
a party?"

"no," says the psychic. "In a biology
class."

😁😁😁😁😁: Mr. Grumpy says, "I'd love to go on this holiday. Bet
you didn't see that one coming. I am joking, of course."

camping is nature's way of promoting the motel business.

Q is for quad biking.

Quad bike in Morocco, Egypt, Highlands of Scotland, South Africa, Jamaica, Southern Spain... I could go on and on. If you have never tried quad biking you should. It is fun, easy and allows you to explore terrain and areas that otherwise would be impassable.

You do not need to take a course of lessons. A few minutes with an instructor and hey presto, you will be ready to travel in a small convoy and explore. It is considered unsafe, but follow the instructions and be sensible—no attempting wheelies or back flips—and you should have no problems at all.

Against my better judgement, I agreed to accompany my other half up a mountain in South Africa on a quad bike. We booked a day excursion with an instructor/guide that began with learning the basic workings of the quad bike. Once we could manoeuvre it around some cones and had mastered the controls, we set off to a lake only accessible by quad bike or hiking.

The ascent was rough in parts. We drove up gravel tracks punctuated by small mounds that required you to rev the engine and approach with a little speed. I managed to get stuck on almost every one of them and rocked my quad bike back and forth in an attempt to rock over them, much to the evident glee of my husband. Somehow I did not quite master that. It did not matter though because once we began the track that meanders through the foothills of the Drakensberg Mountains up to Lake William, this became an adventure.

We stopped for a halfway stop and a celebratory drink by Lake William ... nothing alcoholic, of course. The silence was deafening and there was not a soul to be seen. The air was intoxicating. For one mad moment, we considered leaping into the lake. The guide reminded us we needed to move on. We remounted our metal steeds and were treated to breathtaking views of Cathedral Peak, the Inner and Outer Horns, Cleft and Champagne Castle in the Central Drakensberg Mountains.

Quad safaris are becoming increasingly popular. You can swap jeeps for quad bikes and go on safari in remotest Botswana. On a five-day quad adventure, you learn about life inside Meerkat Manor, track hyena and wildebeest over the scorched, white earth and blaze across vast lunar expanses on your quad en route from Kubu to Kubu Island—a mystical place of ancient baobab trees and home to the largest flamingo colony in the world. Black Tomato, specialists in unusual holidays, offer you all this and more. Cost is about £4,299 per person so it does not come cheap.

Quad bikes are known as ATV (All-terrain vehicle) in the USA.

how do crazy quad bikers travel through
the forest?
they take the psychopath.

: Mr. Grumpy says, "Fun. Yes, fun. Give it a go."

R

no matter how many rooms there are
in the motel, the fellow, who starts up
his car at five o'clock in the morning is
always parked under your window.

R is for rafting, rambling, reindeer racing, renting unique homes, rodeo clown school, rodeos, running of the bulls, running holidays.

The beauty of **rafting** holidays is they can range from the tranquil to the extreme. Make sure you are both in agreement as to, which would suit you before you book. Rivers often pass through beautiful, remote areas that put you in touch with nature and we grumps love peaceful surroundings. Rafting is also one of the more accessible extreme sports so almost anyone can give it a go. Do not let that word "extreme" put you off.

Do your homework and you will surely find a destination that will appeal. How about these for starters:

Asia, the world's largest continent, is home to great rapids, an array of landscapes and ancient cultures From the Himalayas of Nepal to the jungles of Borneo and frozen tundra of Russia, the scale of Asia is incredible and you will find plenty of rafting trips to excite you.

The mighty Zambezi is Africa's fourth largest river and the biggest running into the Indian Ocean. The river was first commercially rafted back in 1981 and today there are many different kinds of Zambezi rafting holidays to try out, from the stretch below Victoria Falls that is the location for adrenaline-fuelled rafting adventures to more peaceful rafting safaris downstream.

Back in Europe, Lake Garda, Italy's largest lake, is fringed with beaches, forests, and attractive harbour towns. It is surrounded by Alpine mountains, covered in snow and ice in winter. When that snow melts, it feeds the fast-flowing mountain rivers that make a Lake Garda white water rafting trip one to remember. It is for those, who want high excitement as they paddle over boulders and crashing waves. Lake Garda has hosted the Rafting World Championships in the past, so it definitely has the credentials to thrill.

Water By Nature offers some fantastic rafting opportunities that might just tick your boxes. I fancy the Grand Canyon adventure or travelling through the Sierra Nevada Mountains. Their website claims, *"We take you on a different kind of rafting journey... there are no cars here, no stress and no cell phones. There is just the rhythm of the river, the soothing sound of the water to send you off to sleep, and the warm sun to kiss you awake in the morning. Be warned: Rafting with us may even change your life."*

😒😒😒: Mr. Grumpy says, "File this one under "holidays that don't interest me."

I have been accused many times of **rambling** but not in the sense intended here. I was unsure as to how rambling, walking, and hiking differed so I spoke to an expert, who assured me that hiking is for routes over fifteen to twenty miles, carrying full kit, either just for a day or maybe a weekend. Rambling is under fifteen miles, carrying a rucksack with some water and food, just around and about woods and hills and so on, while walking was going to work or shops or school and was generally along urban paths.

The Bradford CHA Rambling Club defines rambling as, "strolling about freely, nomadic; wandering." And states that walking is "travel on foot."

Whatever your definition, I am going to suggest a rambling holiday is similar to a walking one, so please refer to the chapter beginning with the letter W for more information about this.

😒: Mr. Grumpy says, "Ideal for getting away from it all and probably lost."

"Dashing through the snow..." Santa would deliver his presents in record time if he employed some of the reindeer that race in reindeer games in some of the chillier parts of the world, where the horned hoof stock are an integral part of everyday life. **Reindeer racing** is a popular and highly competitive sport in parts of Norway, Finland,

and Russia, where reindeer pull sleds or skiers, and sprint over the snow.

In Inari, Lapland local breeder cooperatives compete in the Reindeer Cup Championship Drives to determine, who owns the fastest and strongest reindeer for breeding in the coming spring. Reindeer are so beloved in Lapland that in the 2013 World Cup held at the nearby Levi Ski Resort, reindeer were awarded as prizes to the top skiers.

Book a trip to watch the intrepid skiers clinging to harnesses and travelling at breakneck speeds behind their reindeer, or, don your thermals and visit the Sami Easter Festival in Norway. Not only can you get up close and personal with the reindeer but there is a, whole array of activities that showcase Sami life and culture.

The festival now takes place in Tromsø in Norway, where the highlight is the reindeer races. These are reportedly the "fastest reindeer in Norway.» The races take place in the centre of the city as part of Sami National Day in February.

The reindeer is a source of fur, transportation, meat, and cultural pride for the Sami people, who are indigenous to Norway.

Reindeer sled racing also takes place in Naryan-Mar, Russia, where teams from reindeer herding communities travel from all over for the competition. The reindeer is so central to life and transportation that the 2014 Olympic flame even passed through the area on a reindeer sled.

Want to have a go yourself? The Reindeer Carnival in Oulu, Finland has less swift, but equally rambunctious, reindeer sled racing, and you can even get your own reindeer driving license at the event. That could be a talking point at the next dinner party.

how come you never hear anything about
santa's tenth reindeer "olive"?
you know, "olive the other reindeer, used
to laugh and call him names."

: Mr. Grumpy says, "Well, it's different."

You can put your thermals away now as we consider **renting unique homes.** Website One Off Places specialises in unique, individual holiday accommodation all over the world, including beachfront villas, eco-houses, lighthouses, windmills, chateaux, shepherd's cottages or even train carriages. Be daring and try somewhere different from your usual hotel room.

☺: Mr. Grumpy says, "Surely, "unique" just mean it's expensive? Some of these look quite interesting though."

"Wanted: Someone to attract, cajole and taunt a 2,000-pound bull. Must be willing to dress up, have fun and be a good sport." In a nutshell, that is what it takes to be a rodeo clown. You are right. It is not really a holiday, is it? Though some may be tempted to send a particularly grumpy person to **rodeo clown school**.

Academies and schools in the USA offer training in all areas of rodeo work, including how to become a rodeo clown. These schools will not only teach you the art of bullfighting, but will instruct you on safety while in the ring (, which is jolly important). Some bullfighting schools place emphasis on bullfighting technique, while others offer a curriculum that blends the entertainment aspects of clowning with traditional bullfighting.

You might prefer to go to a **rodeo** and watch the rodeo clowns in action. It will be much safer. Rodeo events across the USA reflect the talents and skills of working cowboys. They include a variety of events testing a, whole range of skills, from calf roping, steer wrestling, barrel racing, bareback riding, saddle bronco riding, to bull riding. Taking place across the country from spring to December, rodeo events have become one of the most popular sporting events in the USA.

One such rodeo event is the National Western Stock Show, which is over a hundred years old. It is spread out over sixteen days and one hundred acres. This is the second largest rodeo in the United States. With a preparation area open to the public, livestock buffs can see rows of cattle, horses, sheep, yaks, llamas, bison, and swine being preened for judging. Sporting more than 15,000 head of livestock, the competition for the best in class is tough.

Known as the *"Daddy of 'Em All"* to cowboys and fans alike, Cheyenne Frontier Days gives the most prized award buckles after the World Championship buckles given out at the NFR. This rodeo started in 1919 as a stock show and has grown into the most anticipated rodeo outside of the finals. There is over a week of rodeo action and related events, carnivals, dancing, music concerts (with major headliners), a western art show, behind the chutes tour, a chuck wagon cook off, and much more.

Outside of the USA, rodeos also take place in Canada and Australia. Website USA rodeos will give you links and information about these.

Learning to become a rodeo clown was not a serious suggestion so gloss over it and move on to my next one, which—oh dear—involves bulls again.

👹👹: Mr. Grumpy says, "Ouch! That looks sore. I fear I'll wince all the way through a rodeo."

What about being a participant in the **running of the bulls**? Somehow I am reluctant to agree that this should even be on your list of holidays. If you are signing your beloved up to this, you will most definitely need to take life insurance out before he has a go at outrunning the bulls. Three men were gored to death at the event in 2013.

This famous event takes place in Pamplona. Runners wait from seven-thirty in the morning and start somewhere between the Plaza del Ayuntamiento (City Hall Square) and the pink-slab Education building in the Cuesta of Santo Domingo. The "encierro" begins at the corral in Calle Santo Domingo when the clock on the church of San Cernin strikes eight o'clock. After the launching of two rockets, the bulls charge behind the runners for eight hundred and twenty-five metres, the distance between the corral and the bullring. The run usually lasts between three and four minutes.

I would not recommend you actually try and outrun the bulls but you might want to go and watch the frenzy from the balconies above the streets. There are tour operators, who will arrange either for you so if your man is desperate to test his speed against a few hefty bulls, look at website Running of the Bulls.

😩😩😩😩😩: Mr. Grumpy says, "I couldn't outrun a snail on Valium. Count me out."

Forget the bulls and choose to go on a **running** holiday. Somehow those two words "running" and "holiday" seem incongruous together. I am not keen on running. At school, I used to hang back from the other runners, dive off up a shortcut and hide behind the bushes near the finish during the obligatory cross-country runs, only reappearing as the first person raced by, so it looked as if I had kept up with the leaders. I got away with it—after all, I was the cross-country teacher.

Keen runners might like to consider a holiday where they can do what they love best—run.

Running Crazy are the running holiday specialists for individuals, clubs and groups with great races all over Europe and an expanding programme. You pay for your flight while they arrange everything else. Instead of pounding along your local paths or roads, consider joining a half-marathon at Budapest, an evening race at Prague, or a social running break in Mallorca.

The mega-fit among you might like to sign up with Embrace Sports, who offer training with like-minded people although be quick because places on the triathlon marathons in the Algarve are selling out fast. Embrace Sports offer novices the chance to train and take part in Triathlons too. Have fun getting fit in a beautiful location.

Other companies and operators offer similar events and the opportunity to improve you as an athlete. Of course, you can always take your trainers wherever you travel and just rejoice in running somewhere warm, sunny, and different to your usual route.

a man decided to take up jogging and went to purchase some appropriate running shoes. at the local sports store he was astounded by the vast selection of shoes in front of him. there were all sorts of colours and styles. eventually he chose a pair and tried them on. they fitted but he noticed an unusual feature on the shoes and asked the assistant, "what is this little pocket thing here on the side for?" the shop assistant replied, "oh, that's to carry spare change so you can call your wife to come pick you up when you've jogged too far."

😵😵😵😵😵: Mr. Grumpy says, "Bwah-ha-ha! Running? Bwah-ha-ha!"

S

S is for safari, sailing, salsa, Scrabble, scuba diving, sexy hotels, shark diving, singing, skiing, skijoring, sledding, snake catching, snorkelling, space ship holidays, snowballs, spy holidays, stalking jaguars, stand-up comedy courses, star gazing, storm chasing, surfing, survival skills, swimming with dolphins.

Going on a **safari** is top of most people's bucket lists. It was at the top of mine too. It is one of those "must-do" holidays. People, who have been on an African safari will tell you that it is life changing; that is why, despite the high costs, those, who have revelled in the experience invariably come back for more.

Whether you decide to go big cat hunting in the Maasai Mara or seek the Big Five in Kruger Park, South Africa I am positive you will have an exhilarating trip. Look at all the possibilities before choosing because there are parks elsewhere that might hold more appeal. I spoke to several couples, who had been on safari in Namibia and raved about it and another, who had been to the Kalahari and rated it as "the best holiday ever!"

A safari will do more that delight, it will remind you of the power of nature and make you appreciate the planet we live on.

The language of the African Bushmen depends as much on gestures and grimaces as on words. I'm guessing Bushmen don't talk after dark.

🗿: Mr. Grumpy says, "An excellent holiday for those of us, who hate the modern word with its materialistic nonsense. Life in the Bush is inspirational and refreshing. I almost volunteered to stay as a guide."

I really do not know where to begin with this topic—**sailing** holidays. There are numerous choices of vessel and destination so other than mention one sailing trip I thought would amaze you, I am going to be awkward here and send you scurrying to yachting for more about this topic. Sorry but I needed to fill the Y section up with some ideas.

Another World Adventures has an unbelievable range of sailing holidays that might turn you into a true adventurer. Of the many on offer, I fancied the idea of helping to crew on an 18th century Lugger.

The Cross Channel Cargo Delivery Adventure sails to and fro across the English Channel between the UK and France. Each voyage consists of fourteen nights on board the vessel, up to two complete channel sailings, night watches, and hand loading and unloading boxes of ale, wine, vegetables, oats, and buckwheat. You will be trained in many tasks from sailing handling, navigating, and steering to traditional ship maintenance, cooking, and deck scrubbing.

No previous sailing knowledge is required although they request a good level of fitness and a willingness to learn.

🗿: Mr. Grumpy says, "Oh lummee. Left hand down a bit. Once I get the hang of it, I might like this." (Only those, who remember *The Navy Lark* will have any idea what he is on about.)

Cuba and **salsa** go together like chilli and hotdogs. That is probably not the best analogy but there is no denying that Cubans love music and dance. Those of you, who would like to share that passion should really head to Havana and learn to salsa.

New York created the term "salsa," but it did not create the dance. Salsa music is a synthesis of European and African musical influences that was born in Cuba. The European part being mainly the melodies and harmony of the Andalucia region of Spain, while the African part in Salsa is mainly from the western coast of Africa where the slave trade was most prevalent.

If you want to pick up a few steps, drop by one of the many Havana dance schools but better still, drop into one of the clubs where you will be blown away by the ability and skill on the dance floor. It makes our efforts to do the *Birdy Dance* or *Macarena* at the annual Christmas party look shameful.

Club Dance Holidays have courses in Havana. Here you will learn how to dance, have dance tuition every day and go to clubs with the professional dancers on an evening. This island is alive with a vibrant and heady salsa scene. And, if your partner proves to be no good at dancing find another and send him or her to learn to play big band salsa in Havana.

😀😀😀: Mr. Grumpy says, "Isn't salsa what you have on your Fajitas?"

What about a **Scrabble** holiday? Addicts can play this game on cruises or indeed book a Scrabble holiday in a hotel. It is ideal for single travellers and those, who want to exercise their brain, meet new people, who share their passion and play the game. The internet will provide you with a range of holidays in the UK and abroad.

Famous Scrabble-playing enthusiasts include Barak Obama, Kylie Minogue, Eddie Izzard, Mel Gibson, and HRH Elizabeth II. I would like to see them all play each other.

my dog ate all the scrabble tiles. he keeps leaving little messages around the house.

😀😀😀: Mr. Grumpy says, "N.O.W.A.Y. I don't like games."

Scuba diving is exciting yet simultaneously relaxing. Package holidays to popular dive sites can include Mauritius, Malta, Corfu, and the Costa del Sol in Spain. Diving holidays will include all lessons, accommodation, and dive excursions by qualified PADI instructors. Again, diving is a skill that can be practised well into later life. This is not an expensive activity and the range of diving locations around the world is endless.

I could not get Mr. Grumpy to take it up with me. He refused outright to submerge himself completely underwater, however, I succeeded in getting him to snorkel. Should you prefer snorkelling to scuba diving, you can have the same experience as divers by hopping onto a snorkel/dive boat. While those suited up will plunge below you, you can still delight in the clear waters, watch dazzling coloured fish unperturbed by how little air is remaining in your tank.

☺☺☺☺: Mr. Grumpy says, "I have trouble with my ears. Count me out but the underwater world is marvellous."

Best **snorkelling** sights for us included seas around the Bazaruto Archipelago where we observed some of the largest parrot fish I have ever seen, Stingray City, Grand Cayman where we stroked underbellies of friendly stingray (in truth, my other half refused to get in the water on that occasion), Ras Mohamed National Park, Sharm El Sheikh, Egypt where crystal clear waters allowed perfect viewing of coral reefs and the marine life there, and in Barbados where we hovered over turtles feeding below us. For a grumpy guts, who hates swimming, loathes the sea in his ears, and dislikes wearing masks and snorkels, the results were surprising. He was infused with enthusiasm and somewhat excited. Such a transformation. I must try and cajole him to the sea again.

☺: Mr. Grumpy says, "See above problem with ears. I am willing to stick my head underwater long enough to see the marine life and to blow bubbles. It is worth all the pain afterwards. No, I did not make 'an enormous fuss,' Mrs. G. My ears really were full of water."

I read an article a while ago in *The Times* about the sexiest hotel rooms in Europe. The list of twenty properties included the Soho House in Berlin, L'Hotel Particulier in Arles, France, and the Buddha Bar Hotel, Klotild Palace in Budapest.

It appears *The Times* is not alone in choosing its top **sexy hotel rooms**. In November 2014, Water Villa number 5 at the Six Senses Hotel, Ninh Van Bay in Nha Trang, Vietnam was awarded the title of sexiest hotel room after being honoured in the Smith Hotel Awards.

The hotel is perched on the edge of, and overlooks a coral reef, faces the sunset and can only be accessed by a hillside staircase to ensure total privacy.

Villa number 5 comes with its own plunge pool, split level layout, private sunbathing deck, handcrafted bathtub and dedicated 24-hour butler service. It also has its own mini wine cellar. (Based on that fact alone, I would vote for it.)

What makes a room sexy? According to the Smith Hotel Awards they look for a super-comfortable bed that is dressed for the occasion with quality bedding. The décor must be luxurious. It needs to be a place where you can feel truly alone with attention to details like a thoughtfully stocked minibar and a bath big enough for two. There should be an element of surprise, like a television hidden at the end of your bed that rises when you click a button or an astonishing view when you open your blinds with your remote control. The best rooms all possessed a little "wow" factor.

Should you, like the judges for the Smith Hotel Awards be looking for a place to delight, excite, and surprise then I would like to add some of my favourites including the Hotel du Palais, Biarritz—a majestic hotel perched on a cliff overlooking the Grand Plage.

To say you have stepped back in time is not an understatement. You most certainly will feel like royalty as you waft up the magnificent staircase to your room or languish in your exquisite marble bathroom, while imaging you are Empress Eugenie. This is her former residence boasting one hundred and thirty-two rooms and twenty suites including the Imperial Sissi Suite, Imperial Léopold II Suite, Royal Edouard VII Suite, and the Royal Alphonse XIII Suite.

The hotel has retained all its period charm and you will be treated royally. Sexy in a bygone era sort of way.

Sexy? Most definitely. A honeymoon villa at Cathedral Peak Hotel, Drakensberg Mountains, South Africa will ensure romance is on your holiday agenda. Thatched cottages with beds in the middle of a huge circular room and views that will take your breath away are only the start of what you can expect from your stay here.

Each executive suite, a thatched cottage, is set apart from other rooms in secluded gardens. All boast a king-size bed, LCD television, telephone, stocked mini bar fridge, electric fireplace, under floor heating, spa bath, and private veranda with breath-taking mountain views and … no children are permitted.

Les Trois Rois, Basel, Switzerland is beside the mighty river Rhine. The Trois Rois website claims that the hotel "turns the 'Tales from 101 Nights' into reality" and indeed it does that. Each room is individually furnished with its own colour scheme and style. Our suite had some of the most generous wardrobe space I have come across, which was great given that Hubby had brought his entire wardrobe for the three-day visit. He also fell for the Bang & Olufsen flat screen television, the Bang & Olufsen DVD/CD player with superb slim speakers and the minibar with free soft drinks and chocolate that was replenished every day without fail. He even managed to cajole room service into giving him extra chocolate.

The hotel has won many awards including several from Condé Nast, and will make you feel like a king or queen.

Les Trois Rois is related to Le Grand Bellevue, Gstaad, Switzerland and oh boy, if you want to have an unforgettable romantic break away then book the Panorama Suite at this hotel.

This very special duplex suite has awesome (a word I rarely use) views that stretch all the way to Glacier 3,000. The upper level—which can be used as an additional sleeping area—offers extensive sitting and dining space, and brims with character thanks to one-hundred-year-old ceiling beams. Below, there's a large bedroom/living area with a king-size bed, extensive lounge and a separate dressing room.

Our finances could not stretch to that particular suite but our room was equally romantic, trendy, and smart. It also had some of the best mountain views imaginable from our balcony.

Go in season to get that added magical feel you find in Alpine resorts during winter or visit out of season to appreciate this stunning location without the hordes of skiers or the cold weather.

My most recent discovery was at the Gran Melia Don Pepe Hotel, Marbella, Spain. We stayed in a Red Level Ocean Suite with views over the Mediterranean, along the coast to Marbella and along the Golden Mile to Puerto Banus. I had difficulty leaving the bathroom where I languished in the huge bubble-filled tub staring out at the sea. However, the three suites on the top floor have the most exceptional terraces. The Moët & Chandon Penthouse Suite obviously piqued my interest as I am rather fond of the fizzy stuff.

Designed by the luxury French champagne makers themselves, this is an elegant suite designed in striking black, white and the signature Moët & Chandon gold. The first guest to stay there was actress Eva Longoria and she is a lady with taste so need I continue?

The spacious and stylish rooms lead out to a terrace that actually took my breath away. I was not too distracted by the stunning Moët & Chandon bar filled with my favourite tipple, nor by the large Bali beds next to what looks like a small river. I trotted across the wooden slat bridge and gazed at the vista beyond—in the distance the lights of Puerto Banus with its glamorous yachts were twinkling while the deep red sunset revealed Gibraltar and the coastline of North Africa. Behind us sat the large darkening Sierra Nevada. I almost did not notice the large whirlpool bubbling merrily and beyond that a putting green—what more could you want? Champagne, magnificent views, a warm Jacuzzi and for the man (or woman) in your life, an unsurpassable golfing opportunity all make for a super sexy room.

There are three Penthouse suites in total—the Presidential Suite and the RocheBoBois, along with the Moët & Chandon Suite—that link together should you wish to book all three.

In fact, why not treat yourselves? Book all the mountain facing rooms as well for members of your family or staff, hire the entire top floor, and celebrate a special birthday or event? I make a great party guest, especially when champagne is involved so feel free to send me an invite.

Slightly cheaper master suites can be booked in the adults only Club at the Hotel Volcan, Lanzarote. Not only will you get your own dining room, music system complete with classical music, sumptuous furnishings, a bed big enough to lose your other half in but you will discover a Jacuzzi large enough to host a small party. It can easily accommodate two of you. More if you want to invite the neighbours around.

The Tao Suite has a Balinese bed outside on its private balcony for added pleasure. From there you have a view of the Marina Rubicon, Fuerteventura, and a fabulous sea vista. No music, no noise, no children—grumpy paradise.

: Mr. Grumpy says, "There's no doubt that a sexy room can really make your holiday, especially when there is an enormous bathroom, and Mrs. Grumpy spends hours sitting quietly in the bath tub, leaving you free to check out the offerings in the minibar."

I harp on all the time about seizing the day and grabbing opportunities yet when I was invited to dive with **sharks** at Blue Planet Aquarium near Chester, I politely declined. Sitting in a very large aquarium with toothy creatures from the deep was not on my personal carpe diem list. After further cogitation, I changed my mind. Here was an opportunity to do something incredibly exciting. I was foolish to disregard it.

The entire team at the Blue Planet Aquarium are enthusiastic, knowledgeable, friendly, and highly professional. If you have never dived you *must* try this as an introduction to the sport.

Everyone starts their shark encounter adventure in a classroom where they learn the basics of diving. Next, they move off to get kitted out in diving suits and boots before entering the small training pool. The emphasis is always on safety so you need have no fear. There is a professional team of three to deal with needs in the pool and all equipment is to a very high standard. Only when the instructor is completely satisfied you are well prepared for your underwater adventure, safe to dive, and comfortable, does your dive begin. You are told you can come out of the aquarium at any time should you suddenly develop a nervousness ... trust me, you will not.

I have dived in some wonderful places and seen pretty fish and turtles but I have never dived anywhere that is a) so comfortably warm b) not difficult to navigate (normally tides and waves move you about) c) seen so many fish and variety of species in one dive, and d) seen or been in immediate proximity to some of the most magnificent sharks.

Two safety divers are with you as well as your instructor. They block and protect you, should you manage to get in the path of one of the sharks.

Diving with sharks has become hugely popular at this venue. I now know why. It is, how can I put it? Amazing? Awesome? Fantastic? Just wow? Yes, all of those. I urge you to put it on your "book it" list.

Of course, you can take this to the next level and do a cage dive.

My partner on the aforementioned dive had done just that. On a trip to South Africa she had been secured in a cage and lowered into the sea where she waited for sharks to come and investigate her. She said she felt like bait and it was a terrifying when they finally circled ever closer to her yet at the same time she recommended it highly. "It is one of those moments you will never forget," she added. I relayed this information to my other half, who suggested maybe I would like to try it myself and possibly even take my mother with me.

If you do a shark encounter dive like the one above, it counts towards your PADI diving licence. If sharks are definitely not your thing then have a go at doing the course online, sign up to do an open water dive locally or head off on holiday to a resort like those in Egypt.

😁😁😁😁😁: Mr. Grumpy says, "I still think she should have taken her mother with her."

When I was younger, I was a member of the local choir. They accepted me only because their numbers were down at the time and I was only allowed to stay as long as I promised to mime. I was great at miming. Time has not improved my voice and although I love singing along to songs on the radio, those around me do not rejoice in my efforts.

Singing is excellent for mind, body and soul. It's uplifting, stress relieving, a thorough body workout and great for mental ability. Recent studies prove that singing rhythmically as a group is excellent for your health.

If your voice is better than mine and you fancy a break during, which you can work your lungs and improve your vocal range, look up "singing holidays."

The aptly named Singing Holidays is run by Temi and Alex professional singers, who studied singing in the Guildhall School of Music, London. They now live in Umbria, Italy and host an array of courses in various locations including: a singing retreat in Sicily, a vintage pop holiday culminating in an open-air extravaganza in Borgo della Marmotta, Umbria, and a Viennese break.

😊😊😊: Mr. Grumpy says, "Singing is not one of my talents. It would be best for everyone concerned if I do not attempt this. Even better if I keep the wife away too."

Skiing is a skill that can be learnt at any age and only requires a moderate level of fitness. The beauty of skiing holidays is that they combine an active sport with stunning locations and great nightlife options—unless you are very grumpy and prefer early nights. Skiing is not only a winter holiday option. Locations such as the Stelvio Glacier in Italy are open during the summer months. There are even ski holiday packages designed specifically for the over fifties.

Neither of us is any good at skiing. We both tried it and decided we preferred watching others tumbling over or sliding backwards down slopes, while we sipped hot chocolate drinks at the café beside the slopes.

😊: Mr. Grumpy says, "I hung up my furry skiing hat with flaps that covered my ears, after I collided with a snow mound and left an imprint that resembled the outline of Deputy Dawg. Some people are better without skis attached to their feet, and I am one of them. I enjoyed it while I did it. I enjoyed the après-ski even more. Recommend it to those who have better balance than me."

Here is a slightly crazy idea—**skijoring**. Skijoring is best described as horse-drawn water-skiing on snow. This form of cross-country skiing originated in Scandinavia over seven hundred years ago and is now popular in the Alps, the Pyrenees and North America. The World Skijoring Championships in Whitefish, Montana attract huge crowds with participants performing incredible times and feats on their skis while being pulled along. With such a following, maybe it is not quite as crazy an idea as I first thought. "Gee up Neddy!"

what do you get when you cross a snake
and a plane?
a boeing constrictor.

😇😇😇😇😇: Mr. Grumpy says, "I am astounded. Who comes up with these crazy ideas? Obviously people who are determined to injure themselves in new and novel ways."

Catching **snakes** is possibly one of the quirkiest holiday ideas I came across. If you book a stay Taj Fisherman's Cove at the old Dutch fort overlooking the Bay of Bengal in Chennai, you can take part in snake catching. Accompany Irula tribesmen, who are specialists in snake catching, into the forests for a close and insightful encounter with snakes. Poison will be deftly collected from the snakes for medicinal use, after, which the unharmed creatures are set free.

I am not sure how well this would go down with you or your other half. I almost passed out when a large snake was draped around my shoulders at the Djemma El-Fna in Marrakech. Consequently this would be far from my ideal holiday although my other half would delight in watching me shriek and squeal as he caught the slithering things.

I accept some folk are interested in the reptiles and if you are one of them visit Kenya and pop by the Bio Ken Snake Farm. Most of the fork-tongued inmates at Bio Ken Snake Farm were removed from local people's homes and farms. Excuse me while I pause to let the shivers pass. Bio Ken is also a fully functioning research and treatment centre, giving out anti-venom to snake bite victims. On tours of the farm you can meet pythons, mambas, and cobras, and handle the less deadly ones.

what does an exhibitionistic snake wear to the beach?
a pythong.

😇😇😇: Mr. Grumpy says, "I have had a couple of run-ins with grass snakes. The last one which was huge, hissed at me and sent a shiver up my spine but don't tell the wife."

A more gentle holiday involves **Saint Bernards**, that most iconic of rescue-dog breeds, first bred at a monastery at the Great St Bernard Pass in Switzerland. Named after the patron saint of Alpine mountaineers, Saint Bernards were intended to be guide dogs but their strength in heavy snow and strong scent-tracking abilities led to them being used as rescue dogs from the early eighteenth century. According to the legend, Barry, the most famous of them all, saved the lives of more than forty people. There is a monument to Barry in the Cimetière des Chiens, and his body was preserved in the Natural History Museum in Bern.

Try a few days **snowshoe trekking** with an overnight stay at the monastery, which is still run by monks. There are nineteen trails for you to follow or explore further with a guide. You do not need a great level of fitness for this activity, however, if you are able, there are some more advanced trails to explore.

Be it snowshoeing or simply on foot, you will discover beautiful panoramas in winter that are virtually unmarked by human beings. Ideal for an injection of oxygen and peace.

Saint Bernard dogs have long since retired from rescuing but they are still a big part of the region's heritage and you can visit them in their kennels and even go on snowshoe walks accompanied by them.

🙂: Mr. Grumpy says, "Sounds idyllic. Those dogs do still carry casks of brandy, don't they? I might need a sip to keep the cold out."

You might be forgiven for thinking I am making this up but believe me, you can actually go on a **space holiday**. At the moment, I understand it is only available for Asian clients. Customers from Singapore and Hong Kong are able to book for the first flight, which should be ready to leave late 2016 or early 2017.

Called Bloon, it is set to rival Richard Branson's Virgin Galactic space tourism programme. Bloon differs from Virgin Galactic in as much as travellers ascend slowly over the course of two hours to around 118,000 feet in a four-man pod powered by helium. They then descend very slowly during, which time they will be able to eat dinner, sip a glass of wine and relax while observing the Earth's curvature.

Prices start from 111,000 Euros, nearly half the price of a Virgin Galactic flight, which is around 200,000 US dollars.

The company behind Bloon, zero2infinity, is based in Spain, which is also where the pod takes off from and lands.

😠😠😠😠😠: Mr. Grumpy says, "If I want to see what the planet looks like from space I can zoom into an area very fast using Google Earth. It's much cheaper. The cost alone makes me want to scowl."

Equally bizarre is this offering—spend a night in a **snowball**. I do not mean one of those icy missiles that children hurl at each other (or grumps). These epic creations are the work of a snow sculptor and are fixed to flat ground so no one is likely to roll you down a hill and put the footage of it on YouTube.

Inside each snowball bedroom there is an insulating reindeer skin topped with a thermal sleeping bag with a polar fleece liner to endure you stay snug and warm.

The town of Jokkmokk in Sweden is home to an annual winter market that has taken place for over four hundred years and is a delightful celebration of the indigenous Sámi people, their culture, traditions and history. Pay a call to the market, then nip back to your snowball for a snug night in.

Artisan Travel offers this strange but intriguing holiday along with other incredible opportunities involving snow.

😠😠😠😠: Mr. Grumpy says, "Snowballs are for shoving down the back of the necks of wives and children. No to this, thank you."

"Your mission, should you choose to accept it, is to use all the survival and espionage techniques you learn throughout the week to complete your task. This is a top secret assignment and you will have to take part in a range of activities, which will test your skills." I was ridiculously excited when I discovered this holiday from Mission Spies at PGL holidays.

Years ago, I was invited to interview for the Military Intelligence Corps but turned down the opportunity. I wonder what might have happened had I gone to that interview. I was disappointed to find out that the holiday mentioned above was only for children.

The best I could come up with was a **spy** experience incorporating a variety of spy challenges, contact drills, unarmed combat, and quick draw competition.

Several companies offer the chance to be an undercover agent for the day and many of them are run by ex-members of the police and the Special Forces, so they talk with authority, and whatever the espionage situation, they have been there, done that, and no doubt got the T-shirt.

Expect plenty of standard secret agent stuff like deciphering codes, using listening bugs, concealed surveillance, and so on, but the emphasis is very much on all-action adventure. If you fancy in-car shooting, movie-style shoot outs with the bad guys and weapons training (axe-throwing was my favourite) then you will be in spy heaven.

In 2012, to celebrate the fiftieth anniversary of the first Bond film and the release of the film *Skyfall*, the Charles Hotel, Munich offered the chance for guests to be the famous secret agent for a day. Lucky winners (paying approximately 60,000 Euros per package) enjoyed a tailor-made experience and the choice to do whatever they liked— from helicopter rides to the Alps to bungee jumping to jet skiing. They were expected to complete a mission too. The new Bond-for-a-day had to rescue a hostage or fight somebody. It took four months to plan, and those, who became Bond were treated to rides in a fully equipped control room/black van to the heliport, from where they could fly to the German-Swiss border, secret messages on USBs, fighting with the bad guys on trikes and flying dragons and more.

To cap it all, the lucky winners were followed by a professional filming crew, who recorded the entire day, edited it, and supplied the finished result so they had their very own personal James Bond movie. I wish I had known about this sooner. I would have made a wonderful Pussy Galore to Mr. Grumpy's Bond.

The above may no longer be offered but all is not lost because Superstars Memorabilia offers a James Bond package for £995. Pick up the keys to an Aston Martin DBS Volante (yours to drive for twenty-four hours) and head to Stoke Park Country Club and Spa and Hotel in Buckinghamshire for an overnight stay. The hotel was the setting for James Bond's golfing duel in the 1964 movie *Goldfinger*. On arrival, you will be greeted with either a glass of champagne or a vodka martini (shaken not stirred, of course.)

😑😑: Mr. Grumpy says, "After watching the television drama series *Spooks*, I am less inclined to try this. Spying can be dangerous and seriously bad for your health."

I am not certain if my next option is any less scary than hunting for snakes but **stalking jaguars**—the animal variety rather than the luxury car—is an option you might like to think about. I considered it for all of five seconds and then decided to take my curmudgeon to a Jaguar car showroom instead.

The jaguar is the third largest feline behind the tiger and lion and is the largest cat in the western hemisphere. It is known as a stalk and ambush predator catching anything from frogs and mice up to deer, anacondas and even caimans—small, alligator-like animals. Today significant numbers of jaguars are found only in remote regions of South and Central America—particularly in the Amazon Basin.

Similar to a leopard, this stealthy cat is a loner, who prefers hunting near water. These beautiful and powerful beasts were prominent in ancient Native American cultures. In some traditions the Jaguar God of the Night was the formidable lord of the underworld. The name jaguar is derived from the Native American word *yaguar*, which means "he, who kills with one leap." A jaguar safari can therefore be exhilarating, as long as you are observing from a safe distance.

Sadly, the numbers of jaguars are in decline but you can still find some excellent tours in Brazil where you will be able to see these stealthy felines in their natural habitat.

😑: Mr. Grumpy says, "This is similar to being on safari. Count me in."

Did you hear the one about the grumpy pants, who did a **stand-up comedy** course? Well, this grumpy old woman did one with surprising results. She now tours the UK encouraging people to laugh and doing a gig called, "Smile While You Still Have Teeth."

You will find one-week courses in the UK but if you fancy going abroad and combining a course with travel, take a deep breath and get signed up. It is probably something that will terrify you but rest assured that it will give you a tremendous buzz when you make people titter. It will also improve your self-confidence at a time in our lives when it is taking a dip. Go on. Give it a go. There are so many older people, who would love to hear your jokes. You will not be thrown in the deep end. You will be taught how to think up and write material that will make others laugh.

Most comedians are concerned that the audience will not laugh at their jokes or will kick their teeth out. At our age that is no longer a problem. We are at the ideal age to take up comedy. You can neither see the audience clearly nor hear them booing and as for knocking out teeth ... they probably only need to tip over the glass where we keep our teeth at night. Boom, boom!

If you do not want to face a proper audience after taking your course, then you do not have to. You can always break out your routine for family and friends. Bet you want to do more though. Laughter is infectious.

I discovered courses in London, Manchester, Brighton and Edinburgh. I think the Brits are great at comedy and would take a course here in the UK, yet there are courses elsewhere so I leave the choice to you.

😆😆😆😆: Mr. Grumpy says, "I'm funny enough. The wife gets all her material and best lines from me."

"Twinkle, twinkle, little star ..."One of the most sublime sights on planet Earth is the night sky with brightest stars from the billions in our Milky Way, the streak of meteors, planetary neighbours such as Venus and Jupiter, and the glow of other galaxies such as Andromeda. It is without doubt a spectacle.

Stargazing require no or little light pollution. It might surprise you to learn that some of the darkest skies on the continent can be found in Scotland making it one of the best destinations in Europe for stargazing. The Northern Lights are even visible occasionally, a phenomenon that usually requires a trip closer to the Arctic Circle.

If you want to appreciate the full extent of how small our planet is in relation to the universe, travel to Chile's Atacama Desert—the highest desert on Earth. It mixes high altitude, dry air, and an absence of light pollution to create a perfect recipe for some of the world's best stargazing. Join a public tour at the observation centre—the Observatorio Cerro Mamalluca at Vicuña—where tourists have the chance to stay overnight and carry out various activities with the same equipment used by researchers.

Hawaii is also a highly regarded destination for viewing the stars. In the middle of the Pacific Ocean, it's relatively untouched by light pollution. The best spot in the island chain is the volcano of Mauna Kea on the Big Island. At an altitude of nine thousand feet, it is home to the Keck Observatory and one of the world's largest optical telescopes.

The Blue Mountains—a two-million-acre UNESCO World Heritage Site in New South Wales, Australia—are quite a backdrop for a twinkly night sky. Group tours with overnight stays camping under the stars are available from tour operators.

But where is the best place in the world to see the firmament in all its glory? In 2013 the Starlight Foundation, which aims to preserve clear skies, awarded Teide National Park on the Canary Island of Tenerife the title of "Starlight Tourist Destination" and "Starlight Reserve" thanks to its clear, dark skies, high altitude and proximity to the Equator.

Tenerife is accustomed to hosting "astro tourists", who flock to the island for the Starmus Festival. The unique event first held in 2011 features astronomy talks, documentary screenings, astrophotography exhibitions and 'star parties'.

We have often seen spectacular displays of shooting stars in clear skies while abroad but it was only more recently that we signed up to an organised stargazing event. We did not expect it to be more spectacular than skies we had witnessed in the past. How wrong we were. The skies over the Canary Islands were an inky black and without doubt every star was visible. Attempting to count the millions—no, make that billions—of stars that studded the sky made me heady. Then, to observe some of them through a state-of-the-art telescope was one of those extra special pure-magic moments.

😑😑😑😑😑: Mr. Grumpy says, "Seeing Venus, other galaxies, and the moon through a serious telescope was stupendous. It reminds you of how large the universe is and how microscopic we all are. Your problems fade away into insignificance in face of such an incredible sight. Lots of smiley faces. Do it."

Storm chasing is hugely popular in the States and Storm Chasing Adventure Tours are almost completely booked for next year at the time of writing this. These guys have been chasing tornadoes for over a decade in Tornado Valley and been seen on National Geographic Television & Film, CBS 48 Hours, NBC Nightly News, the Discovery Channel, BBC World TV, CNN News, the Weather Channel, FOX News, the Travel Channel and many other media outlets around the world. News crews and filmmakers regularly travel with them.

This is sure to be an incredible adventure and most operators will even give you a DVD of the, whole event for you to share with those back home. It will be like watching a disaster movie without the disaster and you as the heroes.

what did the hurricane say to the other hurricane?
I have my eye on you.

☺☺: Mr. Grumpy says, "Electrifying."

"We all live on a yellow **submarine**," not so much live, as travel on. I realise it is not a holiday as such but if you happen to be on Lanzarote then go to Puerto Calero, book a trip on this yellow submarine and view life under the ocean without the hassle of putting on a wetsuit. The operators also have a submarine on Tenerife in Marina San Miguel, situated in the south of the island.

Climb aboard this specially fitted out submarine with viewing portholes and you will be able to see the creatures of the sea in comfort.

For a proper holiday on board a submarine that could well float your boat, book a trip on *Lovers Deep*—a leisure submarine intended for couples, who want to have a private night together submerged beneath the ocean waves. The vessel comes fully staffed with the Captain, chef, and personal butler (, who share separate accommodation to ensure guest privacy).

The submarines have wide-screen windows and can dive to depths of around one hundred metres, so you can glide by shipwrecks or just cruise along looking at the fish. You even get to choose where you would like to go or moor whether that be a stunning coral reef or a sunken wreck.

Private speedboat transfers come as standard and optional extras include helicopter transfers with a beach landing, free rose petal scattering service or champagne breakfast in bed.

The only snag with this suggestion is it will set you back about £175,000. Still, holidays do not get quirkier than this. Forget joining the Mile High Club. What about joining the very exclusive Mile Low Club?

☻: Mr. Grumpy says, "Good way to see the world underwater. Up periscope."

I do not need to say much about **surfing** other than it is a hoot! Once you get the idea of how to stand up on a board it is not as difficult as you may first think. You do not need to call everyone, "Dude," nor wear a bandana and strut about with a surfboard under your arm. This is an activity for any person and is sure to keep you fit and active on holiday.

There are plenty of excellent surfing sites and beaches where you can learn to surf and although there are more famous surfing beaches consider a trip to Taghazout, Morocco's leading surfing beach, just north of Agadir to be exact—and sample the waves there.

Taghazout has approximately three hundred and twenty days of sunshine, perfect sea conditions and a team of ex-pro surfers on hand, who will be able to coax the grumpiest of grumps onto a surfboard and teach them how to surf. It does not matter how old you are. You will soon be triumphantly punching the air having cruised your first wave.

☻☻: Mr. Grumpy says, "Do I look like a surfer dude? This is not really for me, is it? I can't even swim. What do you mean, Mrs. G, you know I can't?"

Mr. G is determined to go on a **survival skills** holiday. I blame Ray Mears. We watched all his shows on television and marvelled at his ability to survive on only what nature provides. When I happened upon an article about survival holidays where you too could learn survival skills from Ray Mears himself, my other half steamed up to the attic to hunt out his old penknife and tent and was ready to go before I could say, "Kindling."

Woodlore, the UK's premier school of bushcraft, was founded in 1983 by Ray Mears. It offers different courses, from expeditions in Namibia and Canada to wilderness first aid courses. But closer to home—near Ukfield in Sussex—the Family Bushcraft three-day/two-night course offers families the chance to get closer to nature. You learn how to build campfires, make shelters, track animals, and understand the flora and fauna of England's forests. Survival one-week courses with Ray Mears are snapped up by keen folk wanting to get to grips with nature. Book well in advance. All places his courses for this year were taken when I last looked.

For enthusiasts of the outdoors, who want to test living rough in the desert, endure survival in the highlands, UK, or survival in the Sierras, USA television personality, Bear Gryllis, also offers challenging survival courses. Bear Grylls has become known around the world as the most recognized face of survival and outdoor adventure. He has been offering courses since 2012 and now offers a survival in the desert course.

The Hajar Mountains of the Musandam peninsula in the UAE is the location for the new 24hr Adult Desert Survival Course. In this unforgiving terrain participants will find themselves tested to the maximum.

Techniques taught will include surviving the desert sun, how to build and light a fire, finding and purifying water, dealing with snakes and scorpions, using a survival knife, and crossing difficult terrain.

The second day of the course is action packed. You will have to climb, abseil, scramble, crawl, and run back to civilisation.

I doubt my other half would survive that particular challenge. It seems a far cry from rubbing two sticks together to create a spark or making a tent out of leaves.

There are other survival holidays that might appeal to those, who want to live in the wild including a Swedish expedition that combines snowmobiling, cross-country skiing, snowshoeing, and dogsledding. The first three days are spent in and around a traditional log cabin acclimatising and learning the necessary survival skills.

The following three days are spent in the wilderness living in self-built wooden shelters and snow holes.

Or, you might fancy two weeks in the Amazonian bush of Guyana in South America. The first week is spent finding and setting up camp, wildlife tracking and bow hunting, locating drinkable water, catching and eating piranha, and lighting fires without matches, all done under the watch of two local Amerindian guides. Week two is the isolation phase. With no more than the clothes you are wearing, your machete, bow and arrow, and belt kit, you will have to put all your new skills to the test.

I shall let my husband go alone on this one. I manage to burn ready-made meals, so heaven help us if I have to light the wood, catch, and prepare the food. It would turn into a weight-loss holiday.

🐾: Mr. Grumpy says, "Maybe Ray Mears can teach me how to survive living with Mrs. Grumpy."

If you **swim** laps at the local baths every week, you might want to stock up on some Sanatogen vitamin pills before diving into the world's biggest pool at the San Alfonso del Mar Resort at Algarrobo on Chile's southern coast. It is more than one thousand yards long, covers twenty acres, has a one hundred and fifteen-foot deep end, and holds sixty-six million gallons of water.

It may have taken five years and over one billion pounds to build but it is an astonishing sight and its turquoise waters are so crystal clear you can see the bottom even in the deep end.

It dwarfs the world's second biggest pool, the Orthlieb—nicknamed the Big Splash—in Morocco, which is a mere one hundred and fifty yards long and one hundred yards wide. An Olympic-size pool measures some fifty yards by twenty-five yards and my local pool is considerably smaller than that.

Don your swimming hat and attempt a length with no risk of children bombing or splashing you as doggy paddle to the far end.

Swimming comes into my next suggestion too—swimming with dolphins. You do not so much swim with them but propel yourself along with one of those fantastic underwater scooter machines as seen and used by James Bond in *Thunderball*. They allow you to swim at speed, keep up with and "play" with the dolphins, who splash merrily beside you as you whizz about. You also use a surfboard and are pushed along by the playful creatures at a phenomenal speed. It is heart-warming.

Many prefer to swim with these intelligent creatures in their natural habitat and for that you can find tour operators in Fiji, Antilles, Mexico, Australia and in other resorts.

Take a trip to Bimini, Bahamas where you can join Dolphin Expeditions for an eco-friendly trip on board Indigo.

Dolphin Expeditions' focus is to protect and respect the dolphins in their home environment and to do their best to give their guests the experience of a lifetime in a safe and unique environment.

They are listed in *Frommers Travel Guides* as one of the six best "eco-friendly" wild dolphin swim companies in the world and have been number one in the Bahamas since 2004, while Tripadvisor has listed Dolphin Expeditions in their popularity index as the number one attraction in Bimini, Bahamas.

Although swimming with wild dolphins is magical and a dream for many, you should take look at Right Tourism website listed at the back of this book to learn more about the pros and cons of swimming with dolphins and find ethical tour operators.

The "killer whale," or Orca, is actually a dolphin.

☻☻☻☻: Mr. Grumpy says, "I am not a watergrumpy."

T

T is for table tennis, T'ai Chi, tall ships, tank adventure, tennis, tiger hunting, touring the outback in Australia, trampolining, travel agents, tree planting, trekking holidays, trains, truffle hunting, tubing.

Table tennis, also known as ping pong, is one of those activities that is superb for us ageing folk. It requires skill and dexterity, but little running around. It also enhances brain fitness.

A 2010 documentary entitled *Ping Pong* followed the story of pensioners, who compete in the 2010 world over-eighties table tennis championships.

One of them, ninety-year-old Inge Hermann, a retired teacher from Berlin, stopped eating and drinking after her husband's death. She became "confused," and it appeared that she might end her years in a fog of dementia in an old people's home. However, she discovered table tennis in her early eighties and her life transformed. She was shown happily involved in the game and beating her opponents at this sport.

Many hotels offer table tennis facilities and even mini ping pong tournaments. This might be too tame for you so search for somewhere where you can really have fun and practise with others, who are equally enthusiastic about this sport.

Fly to China, home to some excellent table tennis players, and try out at the table training base in Zhengding, Hebei. It is vast with over sixteen ping pong tables, and as many as thirty to fifty players playing at any one time. Although there are many young people playing—some to an exceptional standard—you will be able to play and improve your game.

You will need to look into this carefully so check the reviews on Tripadvisor before racing off, bat in hand.

For an alternative choice of active holiday that is less strenuous, consider a retreat where you can sample **T'ai Chi**, a form of exercise, which combines spirituality with slow, yet powerful physical activity. Deeply rooted in both Taoist and Confucian philosophy T'ai Chi helps restore the balance between your Yin and Yang, and it will help you to channel the Chi, or life energy, to give you a healthy mind. You are taught to focus on your breathing, whilst holding different positions to help you concentrate and achieve inner peace. It is normal for T'ai Chi to be practised outside in the open so you feel more at one with nature.

The movements, in spite of being slow and deliberate will tone your muscles and improve your fitness greatly. See, you do not need go to the gym and work out every day to be healthy and fit. I can testify to both this and the fact that T'ai Chi is a mighty stress buster. Give it a go at and you will come home feeling renewed and far from grumpy.

There is a majesty to **tall ships** that captivates the individual regardless of age. The idea of escaping from the pressure of daily life and being in a different environment altogether is a romantic notion. Both Mr. G and I were enchanted by one tall ship that, due to appalling weather conditions, was forced to dock at the Marina Rubicon in Lanzarote. It was huge by comparison to the other vessels and as it manoeuvred into position we all held our collective breath. The crew were hearty individuals—all young scientists and students—who were sailing around the world as part of their studies.

On our return to the UK, we searched for adventures on tall ships for adults and came up with some tall ship holidays designed specifically for adults up to the age of eighty. You need not have sailed before. You need only turn up with an enthusiasm to sail and a desire to learn.

Tall Ship Pelican sails on various dates throughout the year but my choice would be to join the crew at the beginning of July and sail from Liverpool to Belfast for the start of the celebrated Tall Ships Races. Look out for two grumpy individuals waving at you from the crow's nest shouting "Yo-ho-ho and a bottle of rum!" It will be me and my curmudgeon.

For adventures in other seas take a look at website Classic Sailing where you can learn about brigs, barques, barquentines, brigantines, large gaff-rigged ketches and schooners and choose trips from two day tasters to ocean journeys of several legs following the trade winds around the globe.

: Mr. Grumpy says, ""Hoist the mainbrace, me hearties and let's set sail!"

Should your sea legs be too wobbly and you prefer land-based activities, explore the possibilities surrounding the idea of a **tank holiday**.

There is a surprising abundance of choice for those, who are passionate about these military vehicles. Travel to Russia where you can embark on a military tour that includes tank rides, a military heritage tour, a Second World War tour, and a visit to Kubinka Russian Tank Museum—the largest armed vehicle collection in the world, and even sample some Russian army experience. (Although I have no idea what experience that might be.)

Book on a tank driving weekend in Wales where you learn to drive a tank, work on them behind the scenes, sample life as tank crew, learn to strip machine guns, learn basic field craft and stay in a tank school's barracks.

Driving your family car down country lanes will seem very tame after one of these holidays. You may have to upgrade to a small Sherpa van.

In 1995, a man named Shawn Nelson stole a tank from the US Army and took it for a joyride on a highway in California.

: Mr. Grumpy says, "I must admit there is something macho and entertaining about driving a tank, or an amphibious landing craft. Worth exploring."

Do you need to improve your backhand or your overhead smash? Get lessons and learn to play a mean game of **tennis** at Europe's premier tennis centre—La Manga Resort in Spain. This 1,400-acre sporting complex near Alicante caters for any tennis enthusiast or indeed reluctant beginner.

Boasting twenty clay courts, four hard courts and four artificial courts, the Tennis Centre employs the very highest of standards throughout, whether for amateurs playing for fun or more professional players looking to train or improve their game. First-class tuition is available, using advanced video analysis and the latest in digital training aids. Off season, La Manga is the headquarters for the Lawn Tennis Association.

The tennis-bonkers among you ought to sign up for the Gold Academy course. This is an intensive thirty-two-hour tennis course lasting five days. It also provides an in-depth analysis of the mental and tactical aspects of the game.

For non-devotees of tennis, there is much to sample including golf, football, beauty spa, boat trips, canoeing, casino, climbing, crazy golf, pitch and putt golf, fishing, fitness classes, go-karting, hang-gliding, horse riding, hot-air ballooning, Jacuzzis, jogging, dance academy, diving, snorkelling, kite surfing, lawn bowls, shopping, markets, mountain bikes, paddle tennis, play areas, quad biking, saunas, squash, walking, and water sports to name just a few.

For one of the best places to learn tennis, it has to be game, set and match to La Manga.

For an extensive list of best venues to learn tennis and to find out more about tennis resorts, look at website Tennis Resorts Online. Tennis Resorts Online solicits the opinions of racquet-wielding vacationers worldwide and compiles their collective experience into their annual ranking of the Top 100 Tennis Resorts and Camps.

Last year's winners included venues in California, Austria, Florida, and the Virgin Islands.

tom, a management executive, is advised by his doctor to take part in some form of sporting activity so he decides to play tennis.
after a few of weeks, sarah, his secretary asks him how he's doing.

"It's going very well, thanks," Tom replies. "When I'm on the court and I see the ball speeding towards me, my brain immediately says, 'To the corner! Back hand! To the net! Smash! Go back!'"

"Really? What happens then?" Sarah asks, in awe.

"Then my body says, 'Who? Me? You must be kidding!'"

👶👶: Mr. Grumpy says, "Sound a bit exhausting."

Whether you do this by boat, by jeep, on elephant, or on foot, a hunt to discover the endangered Royal Bengal tiger in India is without doubt thrilling. Wanderlust Magazine states that the top five places to go to see **tigers** are:

- Ranthambore National Park, Rajasthan where **tiger** numbers—once around forty—have tumbled due to poaching, but you still stand a fairly good chance of spotting the big cat. This is, however, a popular park where the jeeps run wild.
- Tadoba-Andhari Tiger Reserve, Maharashtra. An estimated forty tigers live in this reserve, so you should get good sightings.
- Pench National Park, Madhya Pradesh & Maharashtra. With perennial springs, the meandering seasonal river, open hilly terrain and teak forests, Pench is a beautiful national park that lies at the foot of the Satpura range of hills.
- Corbett National Park, Uttarakhand. Head out to the dense vegetation by jeep or on elephant-back and you might spot a tiger lurking in Corbett National Park. Encounters are hit-and-miss though so you need to stay vigilant.
- Bandhavgarh National Park, Madhya Pradesh. Bandhavgarh, once the hunting preserve of the maharajas of Rewa, the reserve's open terrain features large grassland meadows, which offer good chances of tiger sightings. It has one of India's highest tiger densities so you stand a good chance of spotting one here.

🙂: Mr. Grumpy says, "I spotted a tiger yesterday. It was on the front of my cereal box. Any of these trips would be a worth taking."

Have you ever imagined **touring the outback** in Australia? If so, did you realise you could do it a number of ways? Cross it on horseback, camel back, by push bike, motorbike or in a four-wheel-drive, or you can even sail the remote coastlines.

Australia's outback is the vast, remote, arid area of Australia. It is a large section of remote and wild Australia, which has been the subject of myths, legends, and fascination ever since Europeans arrived on this interesting and incredibly diverse continent. In addition to hosting a rich and ancient native culture, the Outback also is home to a number of small settlements. Visitors to Australia often try to make time to visit the Outback, since it has become such a cultural icon, and numerous companies lead tours of the region for people, who are interested.

You may also hear the Australian Outback referred to as the "back of beyond" or "beyond the black stump." It is a dangerous place so ensure you are well prepared for your adventure. Research and plan your trip ahead so you have a clear idea of what you want to see and ensure you have sufficient water, food supplies, and gas should you decide to go it alone.

No trip to the Outback would be complete without a visit to Uluru (Ayers Rock) the single most famous tourist attraction in Australia. Other attractions that are part of the same national park include Kata Tjuta—the Olgas. These thirty-six steep sided monoliths, like Uluru, look most impressive at sunrise and sunset. And just like Ayers Rock, the Olgas also have an official sunset viewing area that you have to use if you want to see the spectacle.

Organised tours of the Australian Outback are increasingly popular with us older tourists. As a consequence you will find quite a few operators and tour companies willing to accompany you, or happy to plan your agenda for you.

Australian slang words:

- *Bush telly – Campfire*
- *Dunny - Outside lavatory*
- *Galah - Fool, silly person*

- *Hooroo - Goodbye*
- *Joey - Baby kangaroo*
- *Tucker – Food*
- *Ute - Utility vehicle, pickup truck*

Now try and make a sentence using all of the above. Done it? Bonzer, you are definitely ready for a trip down under.

😑😑😑: Mr. Grumpy says, "It's a very, very long way. Has Mrs. Grumpy checked her facts? It is miles and miles and miles and miles."

Adult **trampolining** sessions and holidays are not silly. Stop sniggering at the prospect of all your wobbly bits bouncing up and down and look at the options. Trampolining is fantastic for fitness and having fun. Still shaking you head? Okay, let me try harder to persuade you. It is after all, an aerobic exercise that strengthens every part of the body and is safe and gentle enough for everyone— old and young.

Trampolining—also called rebounding in the USA—reduces body fat, increases the muscle to fat ratio and increases the efficiency with, which the body burns carbohydrates. The upward force of the bounce improves body tone and exercises a, whole range of muscles in the body, not just the legs and heart.

Aerobic exercise is good for improving blood circulation by pumping more blood through the body and to the heart where it is enriched with oxygen. Trampolining is particularly effective because jumping results in contractions in the muscles such as the calf muscles. These contractions act like pumps circulating more blood back into the heart to be replenished with oxygen, thus improving circulation and reducing clogging of the arteries. It also, as with all aerobic exercise, strengthens heart muscles.

Bouncing about on a trampoline decreases stress hormones such as cortisol, and increases endorphins—your body's feel-good chemicals. An added bonus is that the physical activity of bouncing can take your mind off your problems. Not only that, but the physical improvements that come about through exercise, like weight loss and increased health, can increase your feel-good factor, which itself can reduce stress and depression over the long term.

Trampolining is ideal for those of an older age as it provides a safe, gentle, no-impact exercise. Unlike other exercises it does not damage the knees or back. In fact, this exercise can reduce pain in some arthritic joints and can strengthen bone density as well as muscles. Increased bone density helps to prevent broken or fractured bones and osteoporosis.

There should be no stopping you now. Book a trampolining holiday or one where there are trampolining classes and you will be performing somersaults or back flips in no time at all and feeling like a youngster once more. Search for rebounder courses and you will find an array of appropriate exercise courses that use smaller trampolines.

For a short break, head to the largest indoor trampoline park in Europe in East Kilbride, Scotland. *Air Space* is 35,000 square feet, boasts three trampoline dodgeball courts, a football area, two bouncy basketball lanes, high performance trampolines, and a free-style area with more than sixty interconnecting trampolines wall to wall.

There are even trampolines set at forty-five degree angles, so jumpers can bounce off the walls, and instructors of all ages, including one, who is seventy-four, and can throw some shapes better than most young folk.

😑😑😑😑😑: Mr. Grumpy says, "I'm not going to waste my breath making a comment."

In truth, I added **travel agents** here so I could tell you a joke about them but it is worth pointing out that travel agents really can help make your holiday special. They have a wealth of knowledge and are extremely helpful in determining what would be the best holiday for you. Some of the smaller, independent agents are able to meet all your demands and will help you with visas and much more. Companies like Travelbag, and Kuoni offer tailor-made trips worldwide. They have a breadth of knowledge about places and have often visited countries themselves to see what is on offer. If you cannot find what you want in the brochure be sure to ask one of their experts.

Always ask travel agents for a discount, especially if your trip is an expensive one. It is better if you regularly use the same travel agents for all your bookings as you will accrue a loyal status. Some tour operators recognise that and after a few trips will give you VIP status thus allowing you to receive complimentary wine or fruit in your room and upgrades. Most travel agents are able to shift on price so do not be afraid to ask. If you don't ask...

a travel agent looked up from his desk to see an older lady and an older gentleman peering in the shop window at the posters showing the glamorous destinations around the world. the agent had had a good week and the dejected couple looking in the window gave him a rare feeling of generosity.

he called them into his shop and said, "I know that on your pension you could never hope to have a holiday, so I am sending you off to a fabulous resort at my expense, and I won't take no for an answer."

he took them inside and asked his secretary to write two flight tickets and book a room in a five-star hotel. they, as can be expected, gladly accepted, and were on their way.

about a month later, the little lady came in to his shop. "and how did you like your holiday?" he asked eagerly.

"the flight was exciting and the room was lovely," she answered. "I've come to thank you. but, one thing puzzled me., who was that old guy I had to share the room with?"

~ will and guy

Help conserve the planet. Combine a trip away with something worthwhile by going on a **tree planting** holiday. I was astounded at how many locations offer this type of holiday. You can travel to Israel, Canada, Scotland, or Gambia to mention only a few of the destinations where you will be able to help reforest an area.

This is a golden opportunity to work with other like-minded volunteers and do something positive and empowering for our planet.

: Mr. Grumpy says, "I like the idea of giving something back to nature. I'm also fond of trees. They are ideal for shade and for hiding behind when I want to get away from the wife."

My next suggestion ought to appeal, unless you spent most of your working life commuting on the seven-thirty to London—**train trips**. I mentioned a few under "luxury train holidays" in an earlier chapter but here are a few more to consider. Unlike your usual city commute these trains will whisk you through some astonishing countryside and allow you to travel through the country in comfort:

The first—the Ghan—takes you through the Australian Outback. Starting at Adelaide, this train will transport you the one thousand, eight hundred and forty-five miles through the vastness of the Australian Outback, stopping along the way at Alice Springs and Katherine to allow for leg-stretching and sightseeing. A tad easier than trekking through the wilderness.

Should you prefer cooler climes, travel along the twenty-kilometre Flamsbana route that weaves through a majestic Norwegian fjord landscape, considered by National Geographic magazine to be one of the most beautiful routes in the world.

Flamsbana is also an engineering triumph. It is one of the steepest tracks in the world, where almost eighty percent of the journey has a gradient of five-point-five percent.

Along the way, passengers are treated to a series of spectacular sights, from natural wonders such as the many breath-taking waterfalls and awe-inspiring mountains to the man-made tunnels.

The Visit Flam website adds: "In the span of a single hour, the train takes you from the ocean level at the Sognefjord in Flam, to the mountaintop at Myrdal mountain station on Hardangervidda, 863 metres over the ocean."

Switzerland is renowned for the quality and punctuality of its trains but some journeys are more special than others.

The GoldenPass panoramic train journeys between the Swiss cities of Monteux and Lucerne, passing through a dazzling variety of Switzerland's most spectacular lakeside and mountain scenery. Sit back in comfortable armchair-style seating beside vast panoramic windows and gasp in awe at the captivating views of pristine forests of pine and fir, alpine valley meadows, clusters of traditional chalets dotting green hillsides and dramatic peaks.

A trip on the Glacier Express from Zermatt to St Moritz is another visual feast. The train races through ninety-one tunnels and crosses two hundred and ninety-one bridges on its seven-hour journey through picture perfect chalet-and-cow-dotted green valleys and the awe-inspiring craggy Alps.

There are some spectacular routes in the USA too. Consider a scenic day trip from Williams to the South Rim of the Grand Canyon on the Grand Canyon Railway in Arizona where coach class cars are vintage 1923 Pullmans, the café car dates to 1952, and first class cars are all from the 1950s era, as are most of the observation/dome cars.

For those, who love nostalgia, jump on board the Durango and Silverton Narrow Gauge Railroad, a circa-1882, coal-fired, steam-operated train in Colorado. You can travel through the steep mountain passes between Durango and Silverton and convince yourself you have gone back in time one hundred and thirty years. By the way, the train is featured in the 1969 movie *Butch Cassidy and the Sundance Kid*, starring Paul Newman and Robert Redford.

I cannot leave this subject without mentioning the Talyllyn Railway in Wales. It may only be a fourteen and a half mile round trip and you may only travel at nine miles an hour but this train journey will charm you. It certainly charmed and inspired the Reverend W.V. Awdry to write the *Thomas the Tank Engine* books.

Staffed by volunteers, the historic train (locomotives and carriages date to 1865) steams its way through the verdant Fathew Valley from Tywyn on a route originally used to carry slate from the area's many mines.

Trains are ideal for viewing scenery and travelling distances. Nevertheless if you want to get into the heart of any country, entertain the idea of **trekking**. Check out picks from the difficult and challenging Silk Road to the more relaxed Japanese and Thai terrains. Here are a few ideas to get you thinking but there are many, many more:

The historic, four-day Inca Trail to the ancient Lost City of Macchu Picchu, Peru is one of the world's greatest hikes.

Expect steep, high altitude sections, camping en route and varied terrain before being rewarded with sunrise views of the ancient ruins. You will be required to have a reasonable level of fitness but I know elderly ladies in their seventies, who have trekked this route and one, who intends tackling it again.

Serious trekkers, who want a thrill should entertain the idea of Nepal, which offers some of the world's most spectacular scenery but you need at least three weeks for the popular base of Everest or Annapurna trek. You can trek independently but there are plenty of good tour operators offering guided walks too.

Morocco offers some great trekking country. Head for either the Rif Mountains in the north or the spectacular High Atlas mountains close to Marrakesh. The scenery is as the youth of today like to say, "Amazeballs!"

Chefchaouen is a large city where most of the tours start for the Rif Mountain area, especially if you are interested in a day or multi-day hike. The Rif Mountains combine a number of ranges, peaks, gorges, and valleys. Cedar and fir forests spread throughout, providing a wonderful place for the Barbary Apes to live. Stop and listen and you will hear them calling in the valleys. You might also encounter wild boar on your trek through the forests or indeed, as we did, a pack of wild dogs, who were actually not very wild especially when they discovered we had food.

My favourite trekking is in the Atlas Mountains. These mountains are a magnet for trekkers, mountain bikers, enthusiasts of Berber culture and anyone in search of solitude. There are three ranges: the Middle Atlas, with its cedar forests and birdlife, the seldom-visited Anti-Atlas and the soaring heights of the High Atlas, culminating in 4,167-metre Jebel Toubkal.

The dramatic scenery is incredible, the people exceptionally friendly, and you will fall in love with the place. I did.

The Pyrenees, which divide France and Spain also offer spectacular sightseeing. There are high peaks, coastal walks, sub-tropical valleys, vineyards, lakes and waterfalls, and medieval villages as well as rare wildlife including golden eagles.

Mallorca, one of the Balearic Islands, attracts quite a few walkers and hikers. The northwest coast of Mallorca has moderate to fairly challenging trekking in the Serra de Tramuntana range of mountains, a world away from the busier resorts. There are various routes, many offering great coastal views. Mountain tops are bare, but lower slopes are thickly forested with holm oak and Aleppo pine. In the settled valleys there are ancient terraces of olive, orange and almond groves. A protected length of coastline includes an important bird sanctuary and you may see the rare European black vulture near Puig Roig.

There are other treks in this vicinity and you may be surprised by the number of older people marching off up tracks with rucksacks and water bottles ready for an active day. Makes a change from sea, sun, and sangria.

☺: Mr. Grumpy says, "A thumbs up from me. If you are fit enough you really should go on at least one trekking holiday and I vote for the Atlas Mountains. There is something rather magical about them."

Truffle hunting is a must for all discerning gastronomists. You will find excellent truffles all over the world including the UK, USA, and Australia but for those, who live near Europe, I recommend considering the Dordogne or Provence in France where you can accompany truffle-hunting dogs on their trips.

Trained dogs have replaced pigs that used to hunt for truffles. Dogs tend not to devour the find. Imagine trying to wrestle a hundred pound pig off a truffle. Must have been difficult.

France is the largest producer of truffles, harvesting up to thirty tonnes a year. There are two varieties of truffles—white (tuber magnatum) or black (tuber melanosporum). Tricastin in southwest France is one of the main places for production of the black truffle otherwise known as the "black diamond." Should you have no luck in finding your own truffle, shop at one of the truffle markets such as the one in St Paul-Trois-Châteaux to purchase this prestigious delight.

You may prefer the Piemonte region of Italy at the foot of the Alps—home to the world's most famous truffle, the "tartufo bianco." If possible, combine your truffle hunting with a visit to the world-famous white truffle festival "Fiera del Tartufo Bianco d'Alba" in Alba. This annual event attracts chefs and foodies from the world over to celebrate their love of all things to do with truffles. You can join in and celebrate each weekend throughout October and November.

I found a specialist in truffle tours in Italy and liked the look of a wine and truffle tour that was offered, however it reminded me of an occasion in France:

My husband is not a big drinker; the odd beer, an occasional glass of wine but he never imbibes from "the top shelf." He used to drink more. We both did. I can remember nights when I could put away an entire bottle of vodka and not feel the effects but, as you get older, you slow down. You have a glass or two of wine and feel sleepy. In Hubby's case a glass of white wine will send him to his chair where he will sit and snore for a good hour. No, as we have become older our bodies are less able to cope with the alcohol and we don't party like we used to.

A couple of years ago we met up with friends, who lived in France. They were delighted to see us. We were thrilled to see them. Of course, it being France, no sooner had we arrived than the beer and champagne was dragged out to celebrate our arrival. We had been travelling since five o'clock that morning and only consumed a sandwich and a small pot of porridge each. Therefore, it was not long before we were both a little drunk.

After much wine, many laughs and a light supper made from home-grown produce, our friend Greg pulled out his pièce de resistance—home-made sloe gin lovingly made with berries gathered from local bushes. Hubby was too pickled to care what he was drinking, so Greg poured a generous glass for him.

"Mmm, that tastes nice and fruity," mumbled Hubby, which for some reason made us all laugh even more.

"Should be good stuff," replied Greg, who went onto describe the process of making sloe gin. I was sitting in a nice warm fuzz by now and my lips were becoming pleasantly numb so I didn't quite comprehend the sloe gin making techniques (apologies to those of you, who were planning to take notes). My sole recollection was when Greg announced that it had matured nicely and was probably sixty-per-cent proof by now or maybe even eighty-per-cent proof. I think I spluttered in amazement and looked at Hubby's face. Too late.

"S-s-sixty-per-cent proof," he slurred and took a large glug.

Night turned into morning. The "munchies" set in and in the absence of a doner kebab shop we ate a large plate of cheese. The conversation turned to life in France again and Greg told he had recently been truffle hunting.

"Snuffle trunting?" I queried. Everyone hooted with laughter and guffawed for what seemed like two hours.

"You should write about that," they giggled. "You could call your next book 'Snuffle Trunting in France.'" More guffaws. Anyway, my recollection of the rest of the night is somewhat hazy but it seemed that Greg had discovered that he, like truffle-hunting pigs and dogs, could smell out a truffle. While out with an expert, he had found several truffles when the dog could not.

"They smell of beetroot," he explained and filled up Hubby's glass again. I am unclear about what happened next, but as dawn was breaking, Hubby and Greg disappeared. After a few minutes, when we could finally get our legs to work, Sarah and I followed, weaving down the lane to the edge of the hamlet where we collapsed into each other's arms with laughter. For there, in a clearing beside a group of trees were two grown men scuffling about on their knees, bums in the air and with noses to the ground attempting to sniff out truffles. I only wish I had been sober enough to video the entire episode and put it on YouTube. Needless to say, not only did they not find truffles but Hubby has not let another drop of gin pass his lips since.

Many people think of truffles as a fungus, but they're actually a cross between that and a tuber, so a truffle is more closely related to a carrot than it is to a fungus.

A rare Italian white truffle sold for £28,000 at a charity auction in 2004.

A truffle tree is any tree that's related to the oak tree family.

Truffles form in the summer months and they look like a white fungus. Then, as the months get cooler, they ripen and produce a chemical almost identical to a sex pheromone found in male pig's saliva. This attracts the female pig to go and eat it, subsequently passing on the spores through the forest.

You have not heard of **tubing** before? No, it is nothing to do with the Underground or Metro. There are various types of tubing, all of, which involve a large inflatable ring that you sit in. First of all, there is the form of tubing that resembles water skiing. This is a fast-paced, action-packed, adventurous pastime. Then, there's what is commonly referred to as river tubing. This is the act of floating down a river on a giant inflatable ring and having a leisurely, relaxing time. And finally, there is version of tubing where you descend winter slopes at speed—fun for all the family.

River tubing was once famous in Laos and a must-do for all backpackers. Now, after many accidents, the infamous tubing bars, slides, zip-lines, and rope-swings on the bank of the Nam Song River just north of Vang Vieng have been closed down, torn down, and destroyed. You can still visit Vang Vieng and physically float down the river on a tube if you like, but there is no party going on., which is just as well, because I for one am far too old to consume large amounts of alcohol while floating down the river on a giant inflatable ring. In fact, I am too old to consume large amounts of alcohol at all without dozing off.

There is an abundance of destinations where you can attempt tubing once you start searching. You might like to float lazily down the river Sok and explore Khao Sok Park with Khao Sok River Tubing, Thailand. On this two-hour trip will be accompanied by guides, who will point out wildlife as you drift quietly past sleeping snakes and monkeys.

You may prefer the lure of South Africa with its abundance of rivers, lakes, dams as well as the awesome Indian Ocean, which provides an excellent platform for some fun South African tubing.

South African tubing experiences include being towed behind a jetski or a speed boat, or down river rapids and not suitable for all grumpy guts so make sure before you book.

Other areas offering tubing adventures include Grenada, Texas, Missouri, and Jamaica among many others.

Winter tubing holds more appeal for me and is fun for all ages. Sit down, hang on and enjoy the exhilaration of whizzing down a slope.

I can cope with that. Tubing parks can be found all over the USA. Visit Snow Tubing Source for details of the ten largest tube parks.

😠😠😠😠😠: Mr. Grumpy say, "No. Not doing it. The last time I saw a ring like that it was to help someone who had piles."

U

there was an old lady, who lived in a shoe ... and also had a time share in hawaii.

U is for underwater rooms, undiscovered destinations, unique places to stay, upgrades.

Bet you thought I would not find anything appropriate for the letter "U." I confess, neither did I until I came across an incredible collection of rooms that are **underwater**. You have already read about Lovers Deep, the luxurious underwater submarine I now want to live on but here are some other ace contenders for those, who are fascinated by marine life:

The aptly named Atlantis, The Palm, Dubai has two astonishing underwater suites: Poseidon and Neptune. Both the bedroom and the bathroom have floor-to-ceiling windows, so that you can wonder at the views of the marine life in the Ambassador Lagoon.

Those, who cannot afford the price tag of this jaw-dropping suite should admire the photos and videos of the rooms online, then place a goldfish bowl complete with fish in your bedroom—almost the same thing!

Get away as far as is possible from civilisation and stay at the Manta Resort in Zanzibar. This is the ultimate in hideaway retreats. It is a private floating island with your bedroom four meters below the surface.

The floating structure is Swedish engineered and consists of three levels, those above water clad in hardwood.

The landing deck, at sea level, has a lounge area and bathroom facility. A ladder leads up to the roof, which has a lounging area for sunbathing by day and stargazing by night accompanied by the soft murmurings of the sea.

Descend to the lower deck for a night to remember. (Now then, not *that* sort of night.) Your double bed is surrounded by panes of glass affording almost 360-degree viewing. Watch the shoals of reef fish visiting your windows. There are even some regulars, who float by; one is a trumpet fish called Nick.

Those, who can dive ought to try Jules' Undersea Lodge, Key Largo, Florida. Visitors can stay for lunch or spend a night here.

To enter the Lodge, you must actually scuba dive twenty-one feet beneath the surface of the sea, through the tropical mangrove habitat of the Emerald Lagoon and into an opening at the bottom. Inside what used to be a research laboratory you will find comfortable accommodation and forty-two inch round windows allowing visitors to look out to the underwater world.

Book a night there and not only can you expect hot showers, books, videos and the ultimate in aquatic entertainment outside your window, you can also expect a pizza delivery dinner, included in the price. I wonder how the pizza delivery person gets his scooter down there.

If a room underwater is not impressive enough then what about an entire resort? Poseidon Mystery Island is still at the planning stage but they are inviting people to register for bookings so if you want be one of the first to live underwater, in a resort that will have luxury facilities, a spa, an underwater chapel, a golf course, and underwater activities including zooming about in submersibles, then get your name down.

The resort will cover some two hundred and twenty-five acres and is about a mile long. It is surrounded by a five thousand acre lagoon with an abundance of marine life. You can watch a virtual tour of the resort on their website. Details at the end of this book.

Should the thought of a night with octopuses and fish staring in your bedroom window be off-putting then compromise and dine in style while the marine world swims over your head. The Ithaa Undersea restaurant at the Conrad Maldives Rangali Island, is sixteen feet below sea level. Sample Maldivian and Western cuisine while watching beautiful reef and marine life. No mask or dive suit required.

☻☻: Mr. Grumpy says, "I prefer the fish tank in the corner of the room idea. It's a much cheaper option and there is no chance of a Jacques Cousteau-a-like swimming past your bedroom window."

Bored of the same offerings in the travel agent's window? Bet you have not thought about visiting any of the following destinations. While many, more popular places get swamped or spoiled by tourism there are always places that are less discovered. Break out and look at these (almost) **undiscovered destinations** for a holiday your friends most definitely will not have taken:

Transylvania, home to legends about vampires, is a beautiful and historic region in central-western Romania. Visit the city of Cluj-Napoca, once the capital of Transylvania and one of the most important academic, cultural, and industrial centres in Romania today. From the Middle Ages onwards, the city of Cluj has been a multicultural city with a diverse cultural and religious life.

Though many have heard of Tasmania, its remoteness means that few actually visit. Off the southern coast of Australia, the island is the only place in the world where you can find the famous Tasmanian devil in the wild. The island's many wildlife refuges are also home to wombats, wallabies, and a dizzying array of birds. Do not miss the opportunity to eat fresh Tasmanian Rock Lobster, at the Sea Life Center in Bicheno.

Backed by mountains and tucked away in a one of Montenegro's most beautiful secluded bays, Kotor exudes picturesque scenery and natural beauty. Visitors can walk through a maze of winding, cobblestoned streets, and tour buildings that date back to medieval times. For unparalleled views of the mountains and water, climb 1,350 steps to the town's ancient fortifications. Adventurous souls can also opt to paraglide from atop the surrounding cliffs. It is however, beginning to get on the radar and recent visitors include actors Michael Douglas and Catherine Zeta-Jones.

It may be overshadowed by the more famous Machu Picchu but Colca Canyon is worth seeing on any trip to Peru. Located about one hundred miles outside of Arequipa, it is more than twice as deep as the Grand Canyon. Keep an eye out for the Andean condor, a native bird that makes its home in and around the canyon.

Take a horse trek across the steppes in Mongolia, following the same paths that generations of nomadic tribes have taken, or across the desert. The Gobi Steppe Ride is supported by camel carts and ventures south through treeless steppes and semi-arid areas towards the desert. Both rides take you into areas where there are no fences, no tracks and no telegraph poles; the only sign of human activity are the nomadic herders you meet along the way. This is a truly unspoilt land and it is almost unbeatable as a holiday destination for those, who love the great outdoors.

Blue Spring State Park is a designated manatee refuge located near Orange City, Florida, some forty-five minutes away from popular Orlando. Visitors can get a close-up glimpse of these gentle creatures. Take a two-hour boat tour on the St. Johns River to learn about the local ecology.

Tibet is becoming a much more popular tourist destination now that the Communist government of China is promoting tourism; nevertheless, it is still a place worth visiting because of the fascinating history of turmoil that has beset the nation. This is the home of the unique form of Buddhism known as Tibetan Buddhism (headed by the Dalai Lama).

Or, if none of those suggestions are for you, stick a pin in a map. Make it best of three though because I tried that and am still looking for holidays to Oymyakon in Siberia.

Hang out at some of the most **unusual places** in the world. How unusual? Pretty unusual. Take Spitbank Fort, in the Solent, off Portsmouth, in the UK. A former sea fortress and home to hundreds of soldiers guarding the approaches to Portsmouth it has since been transformed into a nine-bedroom hotel with three bars, a hot pool, sauna and three restaurant areas. Or, what about the Palacio de Sal Hotel & Spa in Bolivia, which is built entirely of salt. Yes, walls, floors, ceilings, and most of the furniture too including chairs, tables and beds, are all made of salt. The hotel overlooks the incredible landscape of Salar de Uyuni, the world's largest salt flat, located in Bolivia that attracts photographers from all over the world, who wish to capture this unique landscape. Just do not lick any of the furniture. You know too much salt is bad for your health.

For a little monkeying around, stay in a tropical forest treehouse overlooking the Caribbean. Nature Observatorio is a two-storey treehouse, suspended twenty-five metres in the rainforest canopy.

Situated in Manzanillo, Costa Rica it is the ultimate in eco-friendly accommodation, with modern conveniences and comforts, powered by solar energy and using collected rainwater. Not one screw or nail was used to build it and in a few years' time it will be dismantled and rebuilt on another tree.

Chocks away! Or not, if you spend the night in the cockpit of the Jumbo Stay jet at Stockholm Arlanda Airport, Sweden. This is not any old cockpit, nor will you have to share it with the captain because this is a luxury bedroom suite in a converted cockpit with a panoramic view of the airport. Other room categories are available but do not expect any in-flight service.

Remember the nursery rhyme about the old lady, who lived in a shoe? You can see what life might have been like for her by staying at The Boot, located in the heart of the Ruby Coast on New Zealand's South Island. I am sure it is more luxurious than the old lady's accommodation as this piece of footwear has a mini bar, an upstairs bedroom, an open fire and opens onto a private courtyard surrounded by a fragrant garden.

The aptly named V8 hotel in Böblingen, near Stuttgart, Germany offers thirty-four car-themed rooms with cars made into beds, plus car wash, mechanic's workshop and petrol station-style rooms. Book the Tower Suite and spend the night in a Mercedes-Benz bed— appropriate, given that Porsche and Mercedes-Benz factories are nearby. Book a tour to visit them while you are here. Mr. Grumpy says it is a "must-do!"

Finally, spend the night with your loved one in a whisky barrel. The eco village of Findhorn in Inverness-shire is built from recycled whisky barrels and you can stay in one from fifty-five pound per night. I really do not need to add a comment here, do I?

🗿: Mr. Grumpy says, "Unusual indeed. Do they have beer barrel rooms as well as whisky ones?"

It seems relevant to add a piece about **upgrades** here. Getting an upgrade on an airplane or at a hotel adds a certain extra spice to your trip. If aircraft are full or some folk need moving around so they can sit together, crew will seek out suitable candidates to bump up into business class. Similarly, should the extra legroom seat next to the exit be vacant, staff will be looking for a responsible, polite, agreeable person to fill it for safety reasons. Follow the tips below and there is a possibility you will be upgraded and join those behind the little curtain at the front of the airplane or bag yourself an extra legroom seat:

- Travel at the weekend as it will increase your chances of an upgrade because there are fewer business travellers around at then.
- When you add your details to the flight information (API) ensure you have booked using your title, so if you are a doctor, a professor or a judge then you can use that status to your advantage.
- If possible book a flight for earlier in the day as staff will be feeling fresher, less pressured and more amenable.
- Closer to the date of departure, check to see if there any offers of cheaper business class seats.
- On the day *of departure wear smart clothes and look like a business traveller. (No need to take a briefcase and bowler hat.) Act like you deserve to be in first or business class.*
- Let the staff know if you are celebrating a special occasion.
- Sign up for frequent flyer programmes. Get enough points and you can use them to upgrade.
- If the flight is full and you are not in a hurry to get to your destination, offer to get bumped to a later flight. If you are fortunate they might upgrade you.
- Be polite, grateful and nice. It might not get you an upgrade but a little courtesy does not go amiss.

As for hotels, I always email the hotel ahead of my trip and let them know I am looking forward to staying with them. If we are celebrating an anniversary or birthday I include that in the email too, stating we are looking forward to celebrating our 155th (some days it feels that long) wedding anniversary at their hotel or resort. If the hotel is not too busy, you might fall lucky and be granted an upgraded room. Do not, however, ask for one—instead, cross your fingers and hope.

You might also be upgraded if you have a legitimate complaint about the room you are offered. If it is noisy, overlooks the bins or is unsuitable, let reception know immediately. After a bad night listening to the lift next to my room creak up and down every fifteen minutes, I complained to reception and was moved to a quiet suite on the top floor, well away from any lifts. It is worth mentioning any gripes. Hotels will do their utmost to please guests whenever possible.

As with airlines, many hotels have loyalty programmes or will send you newsletters. Sign up for them to discover their offers. As with any loyalty programme, should you accrue sufficient points, you will be entitled to benefits such as late check out or upgraded rooms.

If you are on Tripadvisor, ensure you write helpful reviews. Hotels check them and if you are an active member they may feel inclined to upgrade you so you have an even better time.

V

It's entirely possible to spend your whole vacation on a winding mountain road behind a large motor home.

V is for Vespa, vintage cars, volcanoes, voodoo

My first ride on a **Vespa** was in my youth when, clinging onto the waist of a handsome young Italian waiter I buzzed along the stunning Amalfi coast to Positano. It was heady combination and endeared me to the Vespa scooter.

Vespa scooters are easy to ride and hold a certain nostalgic appeal, even to those of us, who never owned one but would have liked the glamour of riding over cobbled Italian streets, basking in the warmth of an Italian late summer. This little Italian scooter has been romanticized for decades through countless movies such as *Roman Holiday*, advertisements, and postcards and holds appeal for many of us of a certain age.

Google "Vespa tours worldwide" and you will have plenty to look at. There are tours in Bali, Sardinia, Ibiza, New Zealand and of course, Rome.

Be a tad different and try an unconventional, fun and exciting panoramic tour of Palermo, Sicily as a passenger on this iconic Italian Vespa scooter. These scooters are everywhere in Palermo. A Palermo Vespa Tour offered by Personal Guide Sicily is the perfect Italian experience, ideal for stopping to snap photos and for those keen to see sights not found on the tourist map. With an expert private guide, you will ride through Palermo's bustling old city centre to admire the city from an insider's perspective. By his own admission, he is not licensed to do this so bear that in mind should you book.

Hustling, bustling dynamic Saigon is even more exciting on a Vespa.

Experience Travel Group will provide a guide to navigate you around this vibrant city at evening, stopping to take in food stalls of eels and frogs, restaurants and ending at the well-hidden "The Secret Garden," a jazz club filled with charm and authenticity.

This tour allows you to ride alongside locals and feel like part of the city rather than a mere tourist. Please try to keep your eyes open rather than shutting them in fear. You will miss out otherwise.

Vespa means "wasp" in Italian. Looking at the MP 6 prototype with its wide central part where the rider sat and the narrow "waist", its founder exclaimed, "It looks like a wasp!" And so the Vespa was born.

Being a pillion passenger is great if you do not want to attempt zipping in and out of heavy traffic in cities alone, however, Vespas are not difficult to drive. Even I, who have terrible balance can manage to handle a 125 cc scooter with no gears. It is huge fun. It gives you a sense of freedom. It is not difficult to learn to drive. They are comfortable and make you feel younger. Now might be a nice time to include a Vespa experience in your holiday or, have a proper Vespa holiday.

Scooter Tours Spain offer four-day or seven-day scooter excursions through idyllic Segovia countryside, the wine region of Ribera del Duero, or historic cities around Madrid. Accommodation and price of hiring the Vespa is included.

: Mr. Grumpy says, "Excellent entry level for non-bikers. Next stop—a Harley Davidson."

I suppose I should have put this under "c" for cars but that section was rather full and **vintage cars** are quite different to supercars. This holiday suggestion is quite different too—book a stay at the Schloss Fuschl in Salzburg.

Situated in western Austria's Salzkammergut region, just a short drive from the city of Salzburg, the resort is surrounded by Austria's well-known mountains, abundant forests, emerald fields, pure lakes, and mysterious valleys. Scenic and peaceful, it has inspired famous painters, composers, and poets since 1450.

It is not only in a beautiful situation but the hotel has one of the largest private collections of vintage cars in Europe.

The hotel's event team can organise to have you transferred to and from the airport in a vintage Rolls Royce, or a limousine, or be chauffeured for the day around the region. Better still, allow them to arrange a private rally including a road guide in one of their exquisite cars.

I came across a, whole host of vintage car events including the Classic Car Rally of Mallorca that has been held every March since its inception in 2005. It starts at Puerto Portals on Mallorca's south coast and covers four hundred kilometres of beautiful Mallorcan countryside. It attracts drivers from all over Europe. There are two categories in this popular event – one for the die-hard, race-ready and another for the casual—but proud—classic car owner.

You should find Citroen, Porches, Alfa-Romeo, Triumphs, Jaguars, Saabs, and other pampered cars rest all from a bygone age when cars were more a work of art than a life necessity.

Whether you want to go on a tour with other enthusiasts or travel alone, Classic Travelling will craft you a tour that takes in stunning scenery, charming hotels and allows you to drive some of the prettiest routes in the UK or take a three-week New England Falls Colour route, to be astounded by the rich autumn colours for, which this region is famous. Other suggestions include: a scenic route through Croatia and Slovenia, a two-week tour of the Alps and mountain regions of France, Germany, Austria, Italy and Switzerland on a journey through historical, cultural and scenic delights, or a spectacular Cape Town Safari route where you will be able to see the migration of the whales at Hermanus, the elephants at Addo National Elephant Park and the winelands of Stellenbosch, Franschhoek, Robertson, and Constantia before returning to Cape Town.

This is one of the best ways to really appreciate a country. You see much more and can take time out to visit parts that interest you. Take one of their escorted tours and you can expect their mechanics to join you to assist should anything befall your car. Do it alone and Classic Travelling will ensure they plan your route, send you a book of the tour and give you all the information you require to make the most of your trip. They will even provide the car.

🗣: Mr. Grumpy says, "For anyone, who loves cars and wants to see the country, this is a great way to do it. You need to enjoy driving. Those routes are long and some require concentration but I still recommend giving it a go."

As improbable as it might seem there are a variety of holidays for those interested in volcanology or the study of **volcanoes**. (Not, as my grumpy suggested, anything to do with Mr. Spock and *Star Trek*.)

For a taster, you can hang out on the Canary Islands—islands created by volcanoes—take a trip to the national parks and learn more about how the islands came about, or for a more informative trip go on volcano tours.

Several companies offer such opportunities. You might like to consider the following:

The Cascade Range—a chain of volcanoes in the Pacific North West region of North America. The range extends along the coastal range from British Columbia in Canada in an arc for around seven hundred miles as far as northern California. There are thirteen major volcanoes in the range. Most are located in the states of Washington and Oregon. Lying on a destructive plate margin, part of the Pacific "Ring of Fire", the volcanoes have been responsible for some spectacular eruptions over many thousands of years.

Visit Haleakala National Park in Maui, Hawaii. The East Maui volcano is referred to as the Haleakala, meaning "house of the sun." Early Hawaiians named it this because they believed it was where the demigod Maui captured the sun and forced it to slow down its journey across the sky.

El Salvador is the location of twenty-two volcanoes but only six are considered to be active. A popular destination for tourists is the Cerro Verde National Park, which is home to the volcanoes Santa Ana, Cerro Verde, and Izalco. These volcanoes can be hiked and climbed. Other volcanoes in the country include San Diego, Conchagua, and San Vicente.

Big Island of Hawaii and Honolulu where you can see lava flowing from Kilauea.

Santorini in Greece is the site of Southern Europe's only active volcano outside Italy. It last erupted in 1950. The island is believed to have given rise to the legend of the "lost" continent of Atlantis in Ancient Greek mythology.

The volcanoes and other landscape features of the North Island, New Zealand on, which all current volcanic activity occurs.

Get up, close and personal with some of the twenty-two volcanoes to be found in Guatemala. In fact, a few, such as Pacaya, can be climbed. As such, these tend to be popular destinations for adventurous tourists and hikers.

Sicily and the Aeolian Islands where you can walk on Mount Etna, Europe's highest active volcano.

Costa Rica where you can trek the slopes of the Arenal Volcano or many of the eleven volcanoes here. These include the volcanoes Poas and Rincon de la Vieja. Poas is one of largest active volcanoes in the world, reaching a mile in width.

Travel to southern Italy, home to Vesuvius, and see the effects on the surrounding area, especially the results of the eruption, which devastated the Roman town of Pompeii in 79 AD.

Tours and hikes up volcanoes are very interesting but for a truly explosive trip, visit the Þríhnúkagígur Volcano in Iceland to "see exactly what this geological behemoth is all about." This is the only holiday to date that actually takes visitors inside a volcano.

Black Tomato holidays, known for extraordinary holidays, are offering a trip to explore Iceland's lunar landscape by super jeep and helicopter, look into the vast crater left by the eruption of Eyjafjallajokull Volcano in 2010 then, accompanied by a scientist specialising in volcanology, head off to Þríhnúkagígur Volcano. Here you take a lift to descend the one hundred and twenty metres under the surface of the earth into the giant magma chamber of the dormant volcano.

The holiday is advertised as luxurious so expect some surprises and delights—including a culinary experience like none other in the vast chamber of the volcano. Your holiday will culminate in a trip to the famous Blue Lagoon for a dip in the therapeutic azure waters. Ideal if you have got hot under the collar.

: Mr. Grumpy says, "A volcano erupting is not as frightening as your other half when she is cross about you forgetting your wedding anniversary."

Fancy something edgy and different that, according to Dan Austin director of Austin-Lehman Adventures "appeals to teenagers and teen backpackers to sixty-year-old grandmothers"? Then try **volcano boarding** in South America.

Volcano boarding involves climbing up an active volcano, donning a protective orange suit and goggles then plunging down the rough and rocky forty-one-degree slope on homemade toboggans.

It may sound utterly ridiculous, but this sport has attracted a massive following. It was developed in the mid-2000s by Darryn Webb, an Australian, who founded the Big Foot tourist hostel in the Nicaraguan city of Leon. Webb had climbed the nearby Cerro Negro but was looking for a faster way to get to the bottom. He tried sliding down on surfboards, snowboards, mattresses and even a refrigerator door before inventing a sit-down sled made of plywood with a Formica strip on the bottom.

The hot spot for this activity is Nicaragua's Cerro Negro volcano, which has become a magnet for volcano boarders even though it has erupted twenty-three times in the past one hundred years, burying homes, crops and people in lava and ashes.

☺☺☺☺: Mr. Grumpy says, "Is what angry wives send their husbands to do when they forget their wedding anniversary two years in a row."

Take part in a **Voodoo** tour. Yes, you read that correctly. Since its founding, New Orleans has suffered more disease, disasters, destruction, and death than any other American city. Spirits are taken for granted there. The influence of voodoo has been profound and it seems that almost every building has its own haunting story. Even the sidewalks and rooftops have their resident ghosts and spirits.

Join a tour for an historical, fun-filled, and chilling after-dark walk around the Quarter's edges in search of the living dead. The tours are not spooky or supernatural. Rather, they are historical, informative and educational. They allow you to explore the mystical world of voodoo in New Orleans. You will hear stories about practitioners, visit real voodoo altars and an authentic New Orleans Voodoo shop. You can tour one of the city's most haunted cemeteries, St Louis

Cemetery No. 1, and visit the tomb of the Voodoo Queen of New Orleans, Marie Laveau where you can make a wish or cast a spell depending on what you fancy. Grumpy folk will love it because it is not appropriate for children!

Other voodoo tours or holidays are available. Journey across Togo and Benin in West Africa where you can witness traditional rituals, ancient voodoo traditions and colonial architecture. The tour helps you to learn about daily life and voodoo traditions of communities in southern Benin and Togo. Or, travel to Haiti where the Haitian government declared Voodoo an official religion in 2003, granting voodoo priests the authority to perform weddings and baptisms.

"When preparing to travel, lay out all your clothes and all your money, then take half the clothes and twice the money."
~ Susan Heller

W is for walking holidays, water park, whale watching, White Desert, white water rafting, wildlife, wine tasting, windsurfing, winter sun, wisteria tunnels, the World, wrestling, writing courses.

"I love to go a-wandering..." Please feel free to join me as I sing about knapsacks on backs. I like **walking** and am lucky enough to live near the Peak District National Park where there are some superb paths and trails. For those of you, who prefer the outdoors and are relatively fit, this is a great way to see the true countryside and get close to nature.

Some of the best trails we discovered were in Gstaad, Switzerland. Famous for its skiing, we found it to be an ideal spring, summer, or autumn destination. Gstaad is not just a single village, but a region collectively called Saanenland with a total of ten small mountain villages and some excellent summer walking. The region is predominantly German speaking, but being located on one of Switzerland's linguistic borders, some of the walking extends into the French speaking part of the country. The locality benefits from nearly two hundred miles of walking paths offering the walker an immense choice with diverse mountain scenery. Each walk is signposted and while some take you into the mountains others lead you past pretty wooden chalets and alpine flower-filled fields where cow bells ring out in musical harmony as the animals graze in peace.

Travel to your start point by rail on the railway line that links many of the villages or use the post bus. Post buses and trains will also transport you to the many cable cars and chairlifts on, which you can rise swiftly into the mountains to be impressed by the incredible scenery before disembarking on the descent to the nearest bar for a welcome meal and drink.

There is walking for everyone here whatever your ability, whether you like alpine meadows, mountainous scenery or glaciers. Worth investing in new walking boots.

For such a small country Switzerland has four official languages – French, Italian, German and Romansch.

I RANG THE RAMBLERS ASSOCIATION TODAY AND THE BLOKE JUST WENT ON AND ON AND ON ...

: Mr. Grumpy says, "I'm good at walking. I do it every day. I think I've got the hang of it now."

Pop those speedos on and join other adults at the first ever adults-only **water park** on Mallorca. This might not be to everyone's taste but if you have a longing to hurtle down high-adrenaline slides including Aqualoop—a 360-degree human rollercoaster—book in at the BH Mallorca resort in Magaluf. Only for those, who are children at heart.

Note: I have not written much about water parks on the basis that Mr. Grumpy made a derisive noise when I flagged it up to him.

Are you fascinated by wildlife, marine ecology, photography, or sailing?

Do you want to contribute to whale conservation?

Would you like to go somewhere remote?

Would you like to learn more about whales and their behaviour?

Whale watching may be just the trip for you. Many whale-watching trips will take you to far-flung islands and isolated bays (Greenland, Tonga, Nova Scotia...) so be prepared to get out of your comfort zone. You are often accompanied by marine biologists, who will give talks and presentations, and guide you on the trips. Numerous research and monitoring trips are also available so why not consider a whale-watching trip that will give you huge satisfaction and makes other trips pale into insignificance?

There is something mysterious and almost mystical about these great mammals of the sea. Due perhaps to their immense intelligence, their strong social bonds and their gentle nature despite their mammoth size, many people feel a strange connection to whales, and seeing them in the wild can be almost spiritual. The best place to see whales is in their own, natural home, whether that be the poles or the tropics. You may not always get as close to them as on other trips, but you should feel a much stronger connection.

Whale-watching tours take place all over the world so go online or ask your travel agent for some recommendations or check the website at the end of the book.

Should you wish to get up close and personal with whales, such as orca or humpback whales, you will be able to do so in Tonga and at the Silver Bank—part of the much larger Sanctuary for the Marine Mammals of the Dominican Republic—where you will be able to swim with these magnificent mammals. Do your research and you will have a truly exceptional holiday.

: Mr. Grumpy says, "Tempting though it is to make a rude comment about my wife in the bath at this point, I'll restrain myself and say that this is a magnificent spectacle and one that should be considered."

It is not just whales that excite animal lovers. We love **wildlife**. The thrill of getting up close to wild animals in their natural environment is incredibly rewarding. You will find lots of travel companies offer safari trips to Kenya, Zambia and South Africa where local guides will take you to see lions, rhinos, tigers, elephants, and a host of other animals in their natural habitat. (We even got to chase after and see an aardvark!)

The famous barrier reef in Australia as well as other destinations offers you the chance to view marine life like sharks, colourful tropical fish, turtles, and a host of other sea creatures. You can swim, scuba dive or snorkel in the reef and see first-hand all the beautiful coral in clear blue water.

Companies run cruises to the reef and some of the islands, and non-swimmers do not miss out on the underwater adventure either, as many of the boats have glass bottoms to view the marine life on the bay from the comfort of the boat. A few of the tour operators also offer trips in submersibles where you can view the reef from beneath the waves.

No matter what your interest, there are specialist travel companies, who will have a tour of some kind that will be suitable for you.

⊜: Mr. Grumpy says, "Top choice of holiday. Wildlife watching is very rewarding."

This one is for those real adventurers—Antarctica's first luxury camp and your only access to the world's final frontier—the **White Desert**. Sleep next to a 200-foot icefall, walk amongst a colony of 6,000 emperor penguins, and stand at the lowest point on earth.

", whichaway Camp" sits on the edge of a frozen lake overlooking a magnificent icefall, and features solar-powered heating, private spacious domed tents, and cuisine from an award-winning chef.

Run by Patrick Woodhead, this is a holiday for those with money to burn. It costs £48,000 for an eight-day stay but so what? This is a, wholly unique adventure.

After your private chartered jet from Cape Town lands on the ice runway, White Desert's aim is to help you do "as much or as little" as you like. Try your hand at an expedition led by guides like world-record pole trekker Paul Landry, or kite-skiing, ice-caving and scaling the "Wolf's Fang" peak. The less adrenaline-inclined can take scenic flights in the private DC-3 turbo-prop, spend the night in an igloo or visit the incredible 6,000-strong colony of emperor penguins

The camp has played host to billionaires, Bear Grylls and Prince Harry, has attracted huge attention from the media and is always fully booked. If you want to snuggle up with a penguin and see nature at its most incredible, make sure you book now. Life is short and those kids, well, they will be fine without any inheritance.

⊜: Mr. Grumpy says, "Where's my chequebook? I am keeping it well away from you. I recognise that gleam in your eyes. You want to go on this, Mrs. G, don't you? Why don't I buy you a wildlife DVD instead? It is a sublime experience but the cost is prohibitive."

Ah! We are onto another of my favourite holidays—**wine tasting**. Wine tasting is so enjoyable, it has become a vacation in itself. Wine tourism has increased in the past ten years and many wineries around the globe now provide exquisite tasting rooms with scenic vineyard views, wine-tasting dinners, and tours of the vineyards and cellars.

Imagine lingering over a glass while watching the sun dip below rolling hills of vineyards. Now imagine doing it every day for a week or longer.

Wine regions like Napa and Sonoma counties in California and Bordeaux and Burgundy in France are well-known tasting destinations. More recently, however, areas around the States, South Africa, Canada and Australia have come into their own as wine-tasting destinations.

Top hotels for wine lovers include Château l'Hospitalet in the Languedoc-Roussillon region France. There are some very pretty walks around the estate surrounded by tranquil landscape of vines, pines, and scrubland. You might like to take a dip in the swimming pool or visit their organic vegetable and aromatic herb gardens. You may delight in trundling through their truffle fields or wandering through the olive groves or, you may want to find out more about the wine that is produced here. This is a working estate that offers the opportunity to learn more about the wine-making process. Guests can join guided tours, tasting workshops or masterclasses. The estate has thirty-eight rooms and on an evening you can head to the wine buffet where there are twenty-four wines to choose from. I would not recommend you try to drink them all in one go even though they are all delicious.

By the way, the Château l'Hospitalet site has a landing strip suitable for helicopters. Well, you never know, you may want to bring in your own chopper to carry off caseloads of the latest Gérard Bertrand vintage from the shop.

This is not the only chateau in France and you really must take time to learn about some of the wonderful places you can visit and stay before embarking on a wine trip. Much will depend on the sort of wine you like drinking. Similar wine-tasting visits are to be found in Italy, South Africa, Spain, Portugal, United States or anywhere that has vineyards.

Here are some more unusual wine-tasting destinations that you might not have thought about:

Morocco has a thriving wine culture—surprising, perhaps, for a Muslim country. Its Val d'Argan winery uses grapes similar to those grown in the south of France.

Thailand's where grapes are cleverly being grown in "floating vineyards." Canals of water run between the vines keeping the grapes alive in the intense heat. Siam Winery, Thailand's leading wine producer of Thai premium wine, and importer of quality wine makes over 300,000 bottles of the Monsoon Valley label a year.

Wine has been produced in Egypt since the time of mummies and tombs, the pyramids and Pharaohs. These days Egypt mostly imports wines for tourists and there are quite a few varieties. Try Obelisk, considered by many to be one of the best; Aida, a sparkling wine, Abarka (warning: it is sixteen percent proof); Omar Khayyam, produced for the poet, philosopher, and mathematician or Cru des, Ptolémées, successor to a brand founded under the Ptolemic dynasty and you might soon be able to "walk like an Egyptian."

I usually associate the Ukraine with bitterly cold winters and lashings of vodka, however, monks in the north of Ukraine have been churning out wine since the fourth Century BC. Ukraine was the Soviet Union's largest supplier, until 1986 when Mikhail Gorbachev decided to put a stop to the "drunken Russian" stereotype and set fire to over eight hundred square kilometres of vineyards in a bid to reduce the country's intake of alcohol. Political events changed and the Ukraine resumed its wine making.

According to Wikipedia "Lebanon is among the oldest sites of wine production in the world. The Israelite prophet Hosea (780–725 BC) is said to have urged his followers to return to Yahweh so that 'they will blossom as the vine, [and] their fragrance will be like the wine of Lebanon.' The Phonenicians of its coastal strip were instrumental in spreading wine and viticulture throughout the Mediterranean in ancient times. Despite the many conflicts of the region, the country has an annual production of about 600,000 cases of wine."

Nowadays, many of Lebanon's wines can be purchased in UK supermarkets however, one of the finest comes from Chateau Musar run by the Hochar family. This winery won international acclaim and led the way in popularizing Lebanese wines overseas. If you are travelling in this area, make a detour and go and visit.

An oenophile is a person, who enjoys wines, usually as a connoisseur.

Wine is not merely produced by families, who have long been involved in the process of cultivating grapes. Celebrities, who have bought vineyards include: Sir Cliff Richard, who owns a vineyard in Portugal's Algarve region and Brad Pitt and Angelina Jolie, who splashed out on a sprawling vineyard estate on the French Riviera in 2008. Director of Oscar-winning films, Francis Ford Coppola's private passion is also wine. His estate in California's Napa Valley produces over forty wines. Sting now produces his own organic and biodynamic wine, as well as olive oil and honey at his Italian estate. He says that he often wanders into the cellar to practice songs in front of the wine. Maybe he will write a new song and call it *Message in a Wine Bottle*. French actor Gérard Depardieu owns vineyards in several countries including France, Spain, Morocco and Argentina. Well, he is French and the French love wine.

If wine really is your tipple in a big sense, invest in your own vineyard. At the time of writing this, I discovered a few for sale including one in Provence. The secluded eighteenth-century Provençal Bastide comprises one hundred and seventy-two hectares of landscaped parks, ornamental lakes, forests, olive groves and vineyards. The principal villa is arranged over three floors and comprises six en suite bedrooms, the main reception rooms and a south-facing family dining room. Within the grounds is an olive grove of 1,000 trees and dense indigenous woodland. Price tag: a mere 7.9 million Euros.

You may not be able to afford a vineyard but many offer you the chance of owning a row of vines. You will be sent information on how your grapes are ripening or details of when they are being harvested. (We were invited along to harvest ours.) You can then watch or join in the production and when the time is right, take home your very own bottle of wine from your very own grapes.

A little bit closer to home, you could book a Scottish whisky trail tour, which will take you to distilleries in the highlands and islands of Scotland for tastings of the various malt whiskies.

Romania is one of the largest producers of wine in Europe with an annual production of 5 to 6 million hectolitres. Taste some of the finest wines of Romania, Murfatlar and Zarea being the finest ones.

☻: Mr. Grumpy says, "It seems such a shame to spit wine out when you are tasting it. If you swallow it instead, be prepared for the mother of all hangovers after several stops at various chateaux."

Those long dark **winter** nights are bad for us all and if you are a grump, they can have an extremely negative effect on you. Book a trip away and head to brighter climes.

Many Brits and Europeans head to Egypt, Thailand, Spain, Australia, Florida, or the Canary Islands for some winter sunshine but there are other gems where you can bask in sunshine and forget all about the nasty cold winds that are howling back home.

My top five destinations for Grumpies include Dubai, which is not only warm at this time of year but is a shopper's paradise. Now that may seem a dreadful choice given that a certain Mr. G detests shopping. However, shopping in Dubai is not like nipping to your supermarket or going to your local town. The city has more than forty malls with some classy goods for sale. Ideal for window shopping at least.

The temperature is perfect for those who hate humidity or despise getting too hot under the collar with temperatures in the mid- to high twenties degrees Celsius. It is invariably sunny with the occasional shower and light wind.

Dubai has more to offer than shops. For starters it has the Burj Khalifa—the world's tallest building. Check out the exhibit on the building's history, then take the fastest lift in the world. Hold on to your hat—it only takes a few seconds. It is not for the faint-hearted but is well worth it, as the views will blow your mind.

For a less heady activity take a simple *abra* ride on Dubai Creek. The creek is one of Dubai's oldest and most beautiful areas. Cross the creek for just one dirham or charter a private abra for ten pounds an hour. Once on the other side, revel in the smells of the spice market or visit the gold market and maybe pick up a little gift—well, a girl can hope.

You cannot visit Dubai without admiring or visiting the iconic Burj Al Arab, a seven-star hotel (the only seven-star hotel in existence) that looks like a billowing sail and is the most photographed structures in the world. If you can afford to stay there, then wallow in the luxury it offers and send me a postcard please.

Once you have enough of soaking up the sights, drive a jeep across the desert and through wadis (dry valleys or dry riverbeds), or go skiing at the Ski Dubai snow park, situated in the Mall of the Emirates. Spend a night in the desert in a Bedouin tent or just walk along the beach. And, most of all, be thankful you are not back home in the cold and wet.

Mr. Grumpy's top destination for the cold season is South Africa. Choose to drive the famous Garden Route, head to Cape Town, take the cable car up Table Mountain or join the beautiful people at Camps Bay, travel inland for spectacular wines and Michelin-starred meals surrounded by the rugged peaks of the Winelands. Hike through the vast and impressive Drakensberg mountain region, stay in Durban to sample beach life and play golf, head to Kwa-Zulu-Natal and gen up on the Battlefields, or take a trip to the iSimangaliso Wetland Park one of the jewels of South Africa›s coastline, with a unique mosaic of ecosystems—swamps, lakes, beaches, coral reefs, wetlands, woodlands, coastal forests and grasslands—supporting an astounding diversity of animal, bird, and marine life. The list of places to visit is exhaustive. South Africa is a diverse, stunning, and fascinating country with an equally fascinating history.

🐵: Mr. Grumpy says, "I never tire of South Africa. I would live here if I could. It has everything you could possibly want in terms of wildlife, scenery, food, and activities, and the people are very friendly."

The length of flights often dictates how far you are willing to travel. We are getting too old to sit on airplanes for hours on end and prefer to take short-haul journeys. A shorter flights of under five hours from the UK will take you to the Canary Islands for some brighter weather. Do not underestimate these islands. There is far more to see and do than you might first think. There are also some terrific bargains to be had if you travel the early part of December or the second week in January. One gentleman, who queued behind us at check-in was delighted to tell us that his ten-day trip, all inclusive at a five-star hotel, including flights had only cost him three hundred pounds.

Top activities for grumps include visiting the Loro Parque on Tenerife. Regardless of age, this park will leave you wanting to return. Be prepared to cheer and clap at the various shows. We took friends in their sixties, who were reluctant to leave and insisted on watching every show including the dolphin show. For me the highlights are the parrots and the penguins, which live on icebergs in polar conditions in Planet Penguin and are viewed from a moving platform.

The park was initially conceived as a paradise for parrots and has developed over the years into one of the biggest attractions of the Canary Islands. It houses the largest collection of parrots in the world.

Yet it is not all about attracting or entertaining tourists. The Loro Parque Fundación, was set up to highlight the need for conservation of nature and the environment. The foundation is particularly active in conserving the most endangered parrot species in the world, both with captive breeding and field projects.

I am fairly certain a visit to the park will put a smile on your face. If it can do that to us, it will do it to you.

"Loro" is Spanish for parrot.

Lanzarote has much to offer its visitors including the Timanfaya Park with a natural geyser but for me its pièce de résistance is a visit to Jameos del Agua. The Jameos is a striking combination of geology, architecture, and design. The island's most famous architect, César Manrique, built a visitor centre complete with a restaurant, bar, one of the most amazing auditoriums I have ever seen, and a museum inside what used to be a gigantic lava tube.

Visitors descend a stone staircase into an open cavern called the Jameo Chico. (The word "jameo" is used in this context to refer to the large openings in the tube, which formed when parts of the roof collapsed due to a pressure build up caused by the volcanic gases.) This houses a restaurant that overlooks a large lava tube with a crystal-clear lake—regulated by the Atlantic Ocean—and is home to a species of blind albino crabs known as "jameitos", which are only found on Lanzarote. These crabs have been adopted as the symbol of the Jameos del Agua.

Cross the lake along a narrow pathway and emerge from the darkness into the Jameo Grande where you will be struck by the sparkling white surfaces and the shimmering water of a stunning turquoise pool surrounded by palm trees and tropical shrubs. Reputedly, only the King of Spain is allowed to swim here. The Jameo Grande is often used for parties. César Manrique dubbed this incredible place as "the most beautiful nightclub in the world" while Rita Heyworth, the legendary Hollywood movie star described it as "the eighth wonder of the world." It is hard to disagree.

At the far end of the Jameo Grande, another wonder awaits—the auditorium. This concert hall, built in a cave, can house six hundred spectators and boasts excellent acoustics. Clap your hands to get an idea of the quality of the acoustics but whatever you do, do not let your other half sing the title track from Disney's *Frozen*.

Fuerteventura has some of the most impressive beaches in Europe. There is a vast expanse of sand here—from the golden sand dunes of Corralejo in the north to the miles of flat beaches in Jandia in the south—which makes Fuerteventura an ideal destination for the beach lover.

However, the best time to visit is during the International Kite Festival. It started in 1989 and is held over three days in November, usually on the second weekend of the month at the Playa del Burro sand dunes, south of Corralejo.

It attracts visitors from all over the world and a spectacular array of kites. Sunday is a key day when over one hundred and fifty kites are handed out to children, who help paint the sky with colours.

Gran Canaria is famous for its sand dunes but my tip is to head to the north of the island and walk up Roque Nublo, which is the highest point on the island. (Top tip from travel agent Matt Barley: "remember to take good foot wear if you do, I ended up trying to climb it in flip flops!")

The Roque Nublo Walking Route runs through some of the most impressive landscapes of the Gran Canaria Biosphere Reserve with spectacular views over the valleys and mountains of the west side of the island.

This unique scenery that you can see from this route was named "The Petrified Storm" in reference to its violent and spectacular shapes. Miguel de Unamuno, a famous Spanish philosopher, wrote:

"a tremendous upheaval of the entrails of the earth; it all seems like a petrified storm, but a storm of fire, of lava, rather than of water."

The Roque Nublo Walking Route starts in Cruz de Tejeda and runs through the border of the "Caldera de Tejeda" (the cauldron of Tejeda), a result of numerous volcanic eruptions in times past. The majority of the time you are shaded by pine trees and from the viewpoint at La Fogalera the views impress and then get even better.

From Roque Nublo you have far reaching views and can even see the dunes at Maspalomas.

Getting back is a lot easier. Promise yourselves a nice meal and a drink at the end of the walk and you will be back before you can say, "Roque ..."

The Canary Islands are made up of other less visited islands that might hold more allure for you especially if you are adverse to late nights, bars, tourists and crowds; islands such as La Gomera, a nature reserve island close to Tenerife, and second smallest of the Canary Islands. This largely unexplored gem features a wealth of traditional culture and history.

It may be small, but it is perfectly formed and even has a large-scale golf course at quaint Playa de Santiago. Hikers and walkers can explore the lush Laurisilva forest as La Gomera is blessed with ancient subtropical forests.

With only a small tourist industry this island will appeal to those, who crave tranquillity and a laid back, slower pace of life.

El Hierro is the most westward island and the smallest of the seven with approximately ten thousand inhabitants. The nearest land to it is the east coast of America. It is a biosphere reserve island with a spectacular rainforest. It has very little tourist industry and can only be reached by sea via Tenerife. Ideal for diving, snorkelling, whale watching, and getting away from it all, El Hierro could be your ideal island in the sun.

La Palma is superb if you love exploring nature and walks in the woods. It is verdant and very peaceful with no night life. With untouched natural resources and outstanding landscapes, La Palma makes an ideal alternative to the more established Canary Islands. The lush green island attracts eco-travellers, and the clear skies, free of light pollution, attract astronomers from across the world. In fact the astrophysics observatory here is said to be the most important in the northern hemisphere.

There are other smaller islands including La Graciosa, Isla de Lobos, Montaña Clara, Roque del Este and Roque del Oeste but some of these are uninhabited. I do, however, know of a special retreat to stay on one of them. I might part with that information for a ludicrous amount of money.

La Palma in the Canaries is often called "la isla bonita" (the beautiful island)—remember the Madonna song that was a huge hit in the 1987?

If you have the winter blues, jet off to any of my suggestions or to Thailand, Morocco, Tunisia, Egypt, Doha, California, Cuba, the Caribbean, Maldives, Australia, New Zealand, Goa, Dominican Republic or Cape Verde. I am sure I left a few out. Suffice it to say, you do not need to stay at home and suffer from cold noses, chapped lips, and SAD. Buy some sun cream and get away for a while. It will do wonders for your mental and physical health.

I cannot begin to describe the beauty of my next suggestion. The colours are beyond words. The Kawachi Fuji Garden, located in the city of Kitakyushu, Japan is home to an incredible one hundred and fifty **wisteria** flowering plants spanning twenty different species. The garden's main attraction is the pastel-coloured fairy tale tunnel created by the wisteria. The best time to visit is from late April to mid-May, typically peaking at the end of April. The garden is private so there is an entry fee.

😠😠: Mr. Grumpy says, "I have wisteria in the garden. I ought to charge people to come and look at it. That would help fund my next holiday. I should have thought of this before."

What about looking at different scenery from your veranda every single day? That is the case for the one hundred and sixty-five residences on board **The World**, the largest cruise ship in the…yes … the world.

You can wallow in supreme luxury where thought has been given to your every desire or needs. It has world-class restaurants and The World Spa & Wellness Centre with personal trainers and physiotherapists to help you burn off the excesses of the day before. There is also a 12,000-bottle wine cellar (and sommeliers, who know each resident's personal wine preferences). I am curious as to how long it would take to drink all 12,000 bottles?

The World's one hundred and thirty residents vote each year on the ship's itinerary, which could take them anywhere from the cliffs of Antarctica to the east coast of Madagascar, with varied fascinating expeditions guided by a team of experts. The programme for 2015 starts with a voyage from Southeast Asia, diving into the Maldives, Seychelles, and West Africa, and visiting one hundred and four ports in total, with fifteen new ports such as Colombo, Sri Lanka, and Bazaruto Island, Mozambique.

Your every whim is catered for on board The World, but should you want some quiet time, you can snuggle down on an evening with one of the four thousand books that are in the library. (I wonder if any of mine are in it.)

Prices range from a mere one million US dollars to thirteen million US dollars, from two hundred and ninety square foot studios to a four thousand square foot, six-bedroom ensuite penthouse that accommodates up to twelve people and come up for sale regularly. Here is a case of The World could be your oyster. You will never be stuck for choosing holiday destinations again.

🙂🙂🙂: Mr. Grumpy says, "I can hardly manage to read one book let alone four thousand!" (I think he missed the point of this suggestion.)

If you remember Big Daddy, Giant Haystacks, Ken Walton's over-excited commentary and chanting, "Easy, easy!" you might fancy going on a **wrestling** holiday. I do not expect you to grapple with a stranger in a ring or team tag with your partner in a local bout. I was thinking more about looking at other forms of this popular sport by visiting a sumo wrestling match in Japan, or WWF in the USA.

Sumo is a Japanese style of wrestling and Japan's national sport. It originated in ancient times as a performance to entertain the Shinto deities (gods). Many rituals with religious background, such as the symbolic purification of the ring with salt, are still followed today. In line with tradition, only men practice the sport professionally in Japan.

The rules are simple: the wrestler, who first exits the ring or touches the ground with any part of his body besides the soles of his feet loses. Matches take place on an elevated ring (dohyo), which is made of clay and covered in a layer of sand. A contest usually lasts only a few seconds, but in rare cases can take a minute or more. There are no weight restrictions or classes in sumo, meaning that wrestlers can easily find themselves matched off against someone many times their size. As a result, weight gain is an essential part of sumo training.

The best way to see sumo is to attend a sumo tournament or visit a sumo stable to witness a morning practice session. Sumo stables are where the wrestlers live and train together and where all aspects of life, from sleeping and eating to training and free time, are strictly regimented by the stable master. Only a few stables accept tourists and they must be part of an organised group.

If you are interested in this sport, visit Tokyo where you will also be able to see the Tomioka Hachimangu Shrine and treasure house displaying some sumo-related items, the Sumo Museum and chanko nabe—the staple food of sumo wrestlers—restaurants.

For those, who want to be more "hands on" in a literal sense, discover more about the national sport of *la lutte* (wrestling) from villagers in Senegal, in excursions run by Les Paletuviers resort located on the outskirts of Toubacouta. Learn the art of *lutte*, where wrestling meets dancing, and attend a tournament accompanied by a chorus of monotone singing and djembé beats.

I bet Mick McManus would not have managed those moves.

Less energetic and more creative types might prefer **writing** holidays. Writing retreats and courses are available in the UK and throughout Europe, including Spain, Greece and France. There are creative courses on various genres of writing and are mainly for small groups of individuals. Tutors on some of these courses are quite well known authors and poets.

Other crafts and creative courses available include: painting, pottery, song-writing, sculpture, learning to write comedy or stand-up comedy, and photography, to name just a few.

why did the watch go on holiday?
to unwind.

X is for Xanadu.

Xanadu is the noun for a place of great beauty, luxury, and
contentment. (Originated from Samuel Taylor Coleridge's Poem
Kubla Khan written in 1797.) Therefore, it allows me to add a few
stunning places worth a visit. It is no mean feat to choose the most
beautiful destinations in the world. One of those chosen by Forbes
is the Lau archipelago—a remote collection of fifty-plus atolls and
islands located two hundred miles from the mainland of Fiji. The
region sees few tourists, but those, who make it are rewarded with
a mind-blowing array of marine life and a gentle, carefree vibe from
the community settled there.

Forbes rates Fjordland National Park on New Zealand's South
Island, claimed by Rudyard Kipling as the "Eighth Wonder of the
World." Both North and South Islands stood in for Middle Earth
during the filming of Tolkien's *Lord of the Ring* series and greatly
impressed cinema goers, who were astonished by the magnificent
landscape.

Your Amazing Places includes Aogashima in Japan in its list of one
hundred beautiful places. Aogashima is a submarine volcano that has
emerged from the sea and is part of a large crater, whose outer rim
height ranges from two hundred metres to four hundred and twenty
metres. Located in the Kuroshio region of open seas and known for
tidal wave generation, the island is barely reachable except by boat.
With a population of about two hundred people, there is little to do
on the island than bask in the serenity of a tropical paradise.

Daddu website lists Manhattan as one of the most beautiful—
"from the lush greenery and openness of Central Park to the awe-
inspiring and breath-taking view from the top of the Rockefeller
Centre, to the iconic Statue of Liberty and the world famous yellow

cabs, it would be difficult for anyone to visit Manhattan and not find part of it stunning."

Bryce Canyon National Park in Utah is one of Lonely Planet's choices. Millions of years of wind, water, and geologic mayhem have shaped and etched the pink cliffs at Bryce, resulting in thousands of delicately carved spires that rise from the amphitheatres of Bryce. It is a dramatic landscape and one that changes colour at dawn and sunset leaving you in wonder at the beauty of nature.

It is not possible to list all the beautiful places in the world. They are in abundance. Find one for yourselves, then marvel at what a truly magnificent world this is.

💀: Mr. Grumpy says, "Always on the search for the perfect escape. My Xanadu is also called my shed."

I don't make enough money to go on holiday so I'm going to get so drunk this weekend, I don't know where I am.

Y is for yachting, yaking, yodelling, yoga retreats

I suppose **yachting** is the same as sailing thus I am combining the two here. If you were not tempted to take up sailing with my earlier suggestion these might tempt you to try it out.

Where to begin? How about on a tall ship? Star Clippers offer voyages on board one of their three spectacular tall ships. With their white sails billowing majestically as they cruise the waves, these magnificent four and five-mast boats will leave you feeling nostalgic for the days when these kinds of vessels ruled the oceans. Do not be fooled by the exterior though. You have not gone back in time once you descend below decks. The stylish interiors are up-to-date with luxurious state rooms for travellers all with modern facilities, and some even have verandas. This is sailing (or cruising to be more exact) for those, who want comfort, glamour and the thrill of being on board a beautiful reminder of a bygone era.

Sail in comfort and luxury to the Caribbean, Cuba, and the Panama Canal, or cruise the Mediterranean to some of the most picturesque locations in the world.

Now that is what I call yachting—yachting for those, who do not want to actually sail the craft.

True sailors like to be "hands on" and there are some spectacular destinations that can be best explored by yacht. You might want to start by taking a holiday where you learn to sail. Sailing is a super activity for us older folk. It keeps us active but more than that it is one we can appreciate. We can connect with nature. How could we not when the wind drives us along with minimal sound and zero pollution. Nature is more powerful than we are. Harnessing it as you do in sailing is a wild and exhilarating ride. Sailing also has those quiet moments that etch themselves into our memory, where the sea and skies provide moments of pure beauty. Grumps of both sexes will gain more than a new level of fitness on this holiday.

Once you have learned the basics at least, charter a yacht and discover towering cliffs, secret coves, deserted bays, and sandy beaches on a sailing holiday in Turkey. Located in the south-east of Europe and the south-west of Asia it is a popular sailing destination. The coastline is beautiful and the scenery is magnificent. Keen sailors will enjoy the reliable winds and choice of sailing itineraries, those with less experience will appreciate the many sheltered bays along the Turkish coast, which encourage you to stop for swimming and snorkelling in clear turquoise water. Turkey has over eight thousand, three hundred kilometres of coastline with a multitude of coves, inlets, bays, and beaches, as well as a large number of marinas.

One of Mediterranean's hidden gems, Croatia with more than a thousand islands, is a sailor's paradise and an excellent destination to charter a yacht. A sailing holiday in Croatia is the best way to discover a string of offshore islands, which provide stunning scenery and quaint towns. Fortified castles and Byzantine palaces reflect Croatia's great trading history and the towns come alive at night with harbour-side restaurants and street cafes.

The Dalmatian Coast boasts the barren and isolated Kornati—an archipelago of almost one hundred and fifty islands. The Kornati are a truly unique must-see in north Dalmatia. A large part of this beautiful island group was declared a national park in 1980. With their many islets and reefs the Kornati Islands are an excellent destination for enthusiasts sailing in the Adriatic.

There are many other islands with centuries of history, such as Korcula, Hvar or Brac, with the "Golden Horn" beach that many consider to be the most beautiful in the, whole country.

The medieval and beautifully restored city of Dubrovnik is beguiling and is justly named the pearl of the Adriatic. You must stop here. I consider it one of the most romantic cities in the world. Try to avoid it in the morning. All the cruise ships dock and the place is flooded with hundreds of tourists. Most of those depart at about two o'clock to return to their ships.

South of Dubrovnik lies a string of islands in sparkling clear waters waiting for you to explore. Believe me—they are magical.

Work colleagues, who cruised the one hundred and fifteen Seychelles Islands claimed it was the best sailing holiday they had undertaken. High recommendation as they sailed a different location every year.

When I asked them why it had been so special, they replied, "Incredible weather, idyllic white sandy beaches, calm waters, sparkling lagoons, brilliant coral reefs, and amazing giant tortoises."

The tortoises clinched it for me. I am fascinated by these wrinkled-neck, prehistoric creatures. These are not your ordinary pet tortoises though. They are extremely large. Giant tortoises are part of everyday life in Seychelles—they even feature on the 100 Seychelles Rupee bank note. Free-roaming giant tortoise populations are found on many islands including Silhouette, Curieuse, Cousin, Bird, Desroches, and Assumption but by far the biggest population—one hundred and fifty thousand giant tortoises—live on Aldabra Island, the world's largest atoll (twenty-two miles long and eight miles wide) and a Unesco world reserve since 1982. You can also see some in an enclosure on La Digue, on Union and in Victoria's National Botanical Garden, on Mahé.

A group of tortoises is called a creep.

The Seychelles archipelago consists of hundreds of islands and inlets scattered over an area of 400,000 square kilometres, northeast of Madagascar. Surrounded by clear warm seas of the Indian Ocean and blessed with gentle weather conditions, the Seychelles Islands are perfect for those wanting a holiday that is a little special, a holiday where one can relax, re-charge the batteries and return home feeling revived and refreshed.

Bird Island is home to Esmeralda, the oldest tortoise in the world. Born in 1771 and weighing nearly sixty-three stone, she has a place in the Guinness Book of World Records.

Again, there are many destinations where you can glide through azure waters, be smitten by tropical scenery or glamorous backdrops of outstanding beauty. There are top ten lists of places to sail in abundance. You will find some links to a few of these at the end of this book.

Bon voyage!

I hope I have painted an appealing picture for you. Now you only need to learn to sail. Or, recruit a crew to do it for you.

"my husband went on a sailing course in poole." "in dorset?" "yes, he'd recommend it to anyone."

: Mr. Grumpy says, "I actually want to do this. I know I don't like boats but somehow this sounds different and exciting."

Ever thought of traversing wild life sanctuaries with five-thousand-metre high passes, through alpine pastures, rolling meadows, turquoise lakes, gazing at rare and endangered flora and fauna and vast open spaces that stretch into infinity? Then consider crossing the Himalayas on a guided yak safari in India, Nepal, or Bhutan.

The **yak** is indigenous to the high altitude regions of this part of the world. Yak safaris provide the locals with an additional source of income and an incentive to preserve the animal and promote its numbers in the region.

Yaks are found throughout the Himalaya region of south central Asia, the Tibetan Plateau and as far north as Mongolia and Russia. They are bovine mammals similar to an ox in build, with short thick legs, humped shoulders, large curved horns, and a thick coat that hangs down to the hooves. They live in herds of as few as ten to up to hundreds of animals. These herds consist mostly of females and youngsters led by a few old bulls. Males prefer solitude (much like my husband after listening to me chatter away for hours).

At around six feet in height and one thousand kilos in weight, with a coat of thick black hair, the yak is capable of surviving a temperature of minus forty degrees centigrade and the extremities of the Himalayan climate. They have also adapted themselves quite well to snowstorms and blizzards. During winters, they live on moss and dried grass. Yaks are generally found at an altitude of around three thousand, two hundred metres. They are good climbers as well.

All of this makes them ideal for transporting travellers to the more hidden places of mesmerising beauty, wandering near glacial lakes, climbing through rugged peaks, and allowing visitors to be part of local culture in areas that otherwise would not be reached.

Take a yak safari into the Himalayas, or head into other mountainous areas of India and Pakistan. Talk to a travel agent about the best places to go and best times of the year.

When I mentioned going on a safari with yaks Mr. Grumpy made a rude comment about having to put up with me 'yakking' on. I assume he would not fancy going on it.

what do you call a yak that drinks too
much coffee?
an insomni~yak.

what do you call a nauseous yak on a 70's
dance floor?
an afro~dizzy~yak.

what do you call a yak exposing himself on
a trampoline?
a jumpin' yak flash.

what do you call a yak in a crate?
a yak~in~the~box.

what's a yak's favourite liquor?
cogn~yak.

If you are a fan of *The Sound of Music* and fancy alpine walking, cycling, mountain biking, horse riding or golf, then join a **yodelling** trail hike in the Alps and feel like one of the cast.

The trail, first unveiled in autumn 2012, on Wald-Königsleiten can be reached by cable cars leaving from the nearby Zillertal or Salzachtal valleys. Located in the province of Salzburg, around 300 miles southwest of Vienna, the area is near to where Julie Andrews launched into song in *The Sound of Music.*

There are currently five interactive stations (eight are planned) to visit as you hike through the mountains delighting in sights of edelweiss and gentle-faced cows munching, their bells tinkling melodic tunes. At each station, wannabe yodel-meisters can press a button, blasting a song from the speakers. Then it is your turn to copy it. Excursions start from the Tyrolean resort town of Mayrhofen and hikes are led by founder, Christian Eder or his sister Ursi.

If you want to do it without a guide, it is easy to locate the yodelling stations. Each is marked by a massive plastic sculpture, such as giant lederhosen, a round of cheese with a slide, a walk-in cowbell, and one with the largest alpine horn in Europe.

Yodelling originated as a way of communicating between the mountain valleys, before developing into a popular form of music and entertainment in Alpine regions across Austria and Switzerland.

The Tarzan yell used by Johnny Weissmuller in the early *Tarzan* films is a yodel-like call. Ladies, should you not be able to cajole your grumpy old man into a yodel, try plying him with Schnapps, attach him to a bungee jump and listen to his Tarzan call. Failing that, sing *The Lion Sleeps* at full volume until he promises to take you on an expensive Caribbean holiday.

knock, knock.
who's there?
Little old Lady.
Little old Lady, who?
hey! I didn't know you could yodel.

: Mr. Grumpy says, "I've never seen *The Sound of Music*. Let's keep it that way."

No matter what I say I cannot persuade my other half to go on a **yoga** holiday. He did at one point have a lesson in how to do a salutation to the sun and managed to hurt his back. That put him off for good. I fared better and went to yoga classes for a while. It is one of those exercises that is ideal for over fifties of both sexes as it does not put pressure on joints or cause damage (unless you are my husband attempting to do a sun salutation.) The NHS website states that, *"Dozens of scientific trials of varying quality have been published on yoga. While there's scope for more rigorous studies on yoga's health benefits, most studies suggest that yoga is a safe and effective way to increase physical activity, especially strength, flexibility and balance. There's some evidence that regular yoga practice is beneficial for people with high blood pressure, heart disease, aches and pains—including lower back pain—depression and stress."*

It is difficult to suggest where to go for the best retreat as there are so many to choose from. Seek advice and do some research before choosing. Health and Fitness Travel have picked the following among their favourite ten places:

Paradis Plage, Morocco. Set on a private beach the beachfront yoga pavilion sets the scene for this healthy holiday with three scheduled daily group classes from sunrise to sunset yoga. Unwind with a traditional Moroccan hammam treatment and relaxing massage, and try out a variety of group fitness classes and activities from mountain walks to beach circuit training.

Absolute Sanctuary, Thailand is famous for their world-class spa amenities and indulgent therapies along with healing treatments. It offers a range a range of disciplines from Ashtanga to vinyasa, and Hatha yoga to Pranayama.

The Farm, San Benito, Philippines is a sensational Asian spa holiday retreat and perfect for seasoned yogis and newcomers alike. It is easy to completely immerse yourself in the tranquil rainforest setting of The Farm at San Benito where you will soon get a sense of inner peace.

The Farm rests on one hundred and nineteen acres in the foothills of Mount Malarayat, one thousand and twenty-five feet above sea level. Consistently recognized as one of the few truly integrated medical and wellness resorts in the world by leading publications and sophisticated travellers, this multi award-winning resort, offers a complete immersion into healthy and mindful living. Reviews claim it is a "healing escape" that will change the way you live life.

Book a specialist yoga holiday at the luxurious Samahita Retreat in Thailand described by many as a "hidden gem" where optional evening activities include meditation. You can come away with instructional videos so you can continue your learning and practice even after you return home.

The retreat can tailor a programme to suit you or you can take up a detox, a candida detox, healthy weight, de-stress or even a wellness programme to help you feel fitter and well. With luck you will continue your activities back home.

The Parrot Cay Yoga and Pilates Retreat on Turks and Caicos is an exclusive private island. It is reached by boat from the private marina on the main island of Providenciales. Boasting a multitude of awards this slice of paradise is set in 1,000 acres of preserved nature with a mile of soft, white beach, turquoise waters and rich wetlands.

Yoga classes are held daily and "Wellness packages" are offered along with treatments to all guests. The emphasis in not merely on holistic treatments and yoga or meditation classes. The retreat promotes other activities including diving and kayaking and has a well-equipped gym. With attentive service, renowned cuisine, and one of the very best spas in the Caribbean this is the place to come to be pampered.

😒😒😒😒😒: Mr. Grumpy says, "We've been through this before. I am not going to attempt a downward facing duck or whatever it is. I am not flexible and I refuse to try this again. Last time it took three of us to remove my foot from behind my head."

Z

"the WORLD IS a BOOK and those, who do not
tRaveL Read only a page."
~ saint augustine

Z is for Zen, zero gravity, zip wire.

In a nutshell, **Zen** is about finding out about yourself—an
enlightenment if you like. Zen is a school of Mahayana Buddhism
that emerged in China about fifteen centuries ago. From China,
Zen spread southwards to Japan. To discover more about it and
practise it try a Buddhist "beginner" retreat or try a spiritual holiday
or become a Zen master in Tibet and get away from the hustle and
bustle of life.

I would love to go to Tibet and meditate on life but you-know-,
who is not into this at all. I shall have to go this one alone.

😵😵😵😵: Mr. Grumpy says, "I grumble therefore I am. How could
you get to old age and not know, who you are? Beats me."

One of my blogging friends, Fran Fischer decided at the age of
seventy-four that she would go on a **zero gravity flight**. She flew
in the same anti-gravity plane as the astronauts train in. As she says,
"I walk with a cane, but I did one-handed push ups and flew like
Superman—what a blast."

With space travel about to take off (forgive the pun) this could
be considered the entry level to it. Indeed, Virgin Galactic space
tourists are already preparing for their first flight into space with
ZERO-G.

If you are able to get to America, this is the ultimate voyage. You
can take off from many cities in the States. Check the official website
for dates and locations.

ZERO-G has a modified Boeing 727-200, G-FORCE ONE that

performs parabolic arcs to create a weightless environment allowing you to float, flip, and soar as if you were in space.

It is not cheap. A ZERO-G Experience starts at $4,950 per person. However, for that, your ZERO-G Experience includes fifteen parabolas, your own ZERO-G flight suit, ZERO-G merchandise, a Regravitation Celebration, certificate of weightless completion, photos and video of your unique trip. And indeed, that is what it will be—unique.

Famous people apart from my by now famous blogging buddy, who have taken a zero gravity flight include Doctor Buzz Aldrin, Martha Stewart, Ron Howard, who directed the film *Apollo 13*, and Professor Stephen Hawking:

"It was amazing. The zero-g part was wonderful. I could have gone on and on. Space here I come."—Professor Stephen Hawking, Astrophysicist

Shout, "To infinity and beyond!" and add this to your "book it" list. This one will ensure you and your Grumpy smile happily for weeks to come.

☻☻: Mr. Grumpy says, "It's certainly an unusual choice of holiday. I quite like gravity. It hasn't let me down so far."

If you had asked me about **zip wire** holidays a year ago I would have told you to forget it. Such craziness was for people, who had clearly gone bonkers. Ask me today and I will squeal with excitement and start gushing about all the incredible zip wires you can try. Yes, I have joined that group of crazy people.

I was cajoled into doing a zip wire challenge by my publishers. In truth, I am terrified of heights and really could think of nothing I would like to do less than speed down a zip wire. However, I had written about zip wires and other crazy activities in my novel, *Three Little Birds* and as part of the book promotion I was proving that you are never too old to try out new adventures by taking on some of those challenges set out in the novel. My publishers thought doing a zip wire would be great fun. Kim Maya Sutton joined me in a show of solidarity (and make sure I completed the challenge.)

Once I had opened my eyes, stopped my legs from trembling

and been talked into letting go of the tree trunk, the zip itself was incredible. So much so, I could not wait to travel down the next zip wire. The sense of freedom as you speed over a canopy of treetops is overwhelming.

It was only after I had completed two zips, my publisher told me a tale about being trapped on a broken-down ski lift in freezing cold temperatures and having to be rescued by zipping down the cable. Her father, paralysed by fear, was unable to be coaxed down so she had to return up the cable and zip down again, this time with her father. It made my effort seem somewhat feeble.

Anyhow, the rush from the zip wire was so great that I researched other zip wires in the world and have found the following. I am trying to decide, which one I shall tackle next. Even though I know I shall be petrified going up to the launch, I also know that the reward will be worth every second of fear.

Try a small zip wire like me to understand why this could make for an outstanding holiday, then consider visiting these destinations and trying out these formidable zip wires:

The Eden Project's Skywire, Cornwall, is, at six hundred and sixty metres, the longest zip wire in England. It is also eye-wateringly fast with test pilots having been clocked speeding along at sixty miles per hour. It offers visitors an exhilarating ride over iconic rainforest and Mediterranean biome structures and the huge outdoor gardens. If you want to see what a thrill this is, look at their website when you can watch a video of the ride.

The world's highest zip wire ride—La Tyrolienne—is located in the French Alps and offers intrepid skiers the chance to fly over snowy mountains at 10,000ft. The ride only lasts one minute and forty-five seconds and has been dubbed "a route through the skies mimicking the journey of an eagle in flight."

Gravity Canyon in New Zealand is the fastest zip wire in the world, reaching speeds of around one hundred miles per hour. It has been operating since 2004 and surprising even hardened thrill-seekers all over the world. Fly solo or with up to two friends. At one point, you actually pass under a bridge. Not sure if my spatial awareness is good enough for this one.

In Mexico, soar over iconic Copper Canyon on a series of zip wires measuring 8,350ft. The Copper Canyon ZipRider consists of seven zip lines and visitors take two hanging bridges down to the ground before catching the cable car back up—all with heart-stopping views of the canyons and beyond. This is suitable only for those people, who are fit and able to hike the steep and rocky terrain between zips. It is fair to say I shall not be attempting this ride. I almost passed out with fear just watching the video on the website.

Zip 2000 in Sun City, South Africa claims to be the original zip wire ride. Riders can expect average speeds of seventy-five miles per hour along the one and quarter-mile line and hang two-by-two from the cable with a fin between their legs for extra speed. Heights vary between 10 and 1,000ft and the South African grasslands below offer pretty awesome views.

For those folk, who really cannot get enough of an adrenaline rush head to ZipFlyer in the Himalayas, considered to be the "world's most extreme zip wire." It has a vertical drop of almost two thousand feet (gulp!) an incline measured at a sheer fifty-six percent, and is one of the tallest and steepest zip-slides in the world, according to operators High Ground Adventures.

Costa Rica is actually the birthplace of the zip wire, so if you are a true enthusiast, this is the place to go. Head to Arenal Volcano Park for a zip wire flight that will take you through the Costa Rican jungle. You not only zoom over the jungle but for added spice you fly past a live volcano, which last erupted in 1984. If you take a night flight you will see eruptions from the volcano as it bursts into life, as well as nocturnal animals in the rainforest.

The longest zip wire in the northern hemisphere is at Zip World in North Wales. The attraction, located in the world's largest old slate quarry in Gwynedd, sees visitors travelling at speeds of one hundred miles per hour on a zip line that takes them five hundred feet over a mountain lake and boasts views across Snowdonia, to the Isle of Anglesey and even the Isle of Man on a clear day. I am planning on taking Mr. G there as a birthday treat. I am sure he will be thrilled with the idea.

Australia and New Zealand zip wires are known as Flying Foxes and in South Africa as Foefie Slides. In the United Kingdom as in the rest of the world, they are now referred to as Zip Wires, Zip Lines, Zip Slides or occasionally Aerial Runways.

☺☺☺☺☺: Mr. Grumpy says, "To do these you need to be several sandwiches short of a picnic. Oh dear! My wife appears to be giving me a dirty look. I don't care. She's off her rocker if she intends doing one of these."

By now, I am hoping you have collected some ideas for your next holiday or to add to your "book it" list. Please send me some photographs of where you go and what you do. I really would like to know how you get on. Life should be an adventure even at our age, so book a trip to remember. After all, your dreams and plans today will be your happy memories and achievements of the future. YOLO!

"None are so old as those, who have outlived enthusiasm." - *Henry David Thoreau.*

APPENDIX

Aircraft
- Fun Random Aircraft Trivia www.sooperarticles.com/travel-articles/aviation-airplanes-articles/fun-random-aircraft-trivia-107650.html#ixzz3HF872c4B
- www.airbus.com/aircraftfamilies/passengeraircraft/a380family/specificatieons
- confessionsofatrolleydolly.com/2013/05/31/top-50-useless-aviation-facts
- Abseiling
- informationnow.org.uk/organisations/130/foreign-and-commonwealth-offices-travel-advice-unit
- www.fiftyplusnorthantsadventureclub.org.uk/index.html
- www.aspireadventureactivities.co.uk/activities/abseiling.php

Adults only hotels
- www.h10hotels.com/en/index.html
- www.inspiredluxuryescapes.com/luxury-holidays/adult-only
- www.luxury-resort-bliss.com/adult-only-resorts.html
- www.spoilyourself.co.uk/Destinations.aspx?HolidayTypeID=8

Arctic boot camp
- www.discover-the-world.co.uk/destinations/sweden-holidays/wellbeing-escape-at-the-icehotel

Art
- www.coxandkings.co.uk/royalacademyofarts

Art tours
- www.kirkerholidays.com/holiday-search/ctmh/0/0/0/2

Art courses
- www.cntraveller.com/recommended/itineraries/the-best-learning-holidays/page/art-holidays
- www.worldretreats.co.uk/art-holidays

Ayurveda
- https://www.wellbeingescapes.com/wellbeing-short-breaks-html

Bananas

- www.tenerife-holiday-home-insider.com/banana-plantation.html
- www.i-escape.com/hotel-el-patio/overview#overview

Base jumping

- www.teletextholidays.co.uk/Holidays/More-Types/Advice-Types/Travel-Advice/Friday-Feature/Five-great-BASE-jumping-locations

Bees

- www.humblebynature.com
- Bobsleigh
- www.exodus.co.uk/norway-holidays/winter/lillehammer-bobsled-weekend/cnl-0

Buddhist retreat

- www.gvi.co.uk.

Butterfly spotting

- www.macedoniaexperience.com/our-services/tours-in-macedonia/143-butterflies-of-macedonia
- www.naturetrek.co.uk/butterfly_watching_holidays.aspx

Camping

- www.moabundercanvas.com/glamping.html

Cars

- www.firenzeinferrari.com/index.php
- www.greatescapecars.co.uk
- Castles
- www.ltr.co.uk/featured-properties/contemporary-scottish-castle
- Canoeing
- iberianature.com/wildworld/best-places-to-go-canoeing-in-europe
- Caravan and camping cars
- www.rv-trips.com/rv-trips

Caravans with a difference

- www.underthethatch.co.uk
- www.uniqueholidaycottages.co.uk/locations/the-lake-district-and-cumbria/wild-in-style-gypsy-caravan
- www.ramblingrosecaravan.co.uk
- Celeb spotting
- losangeles.m.allsightseeingtours.com/tour/los-angeles/tmz-celebrity-hot-spots-tour-bus/0-3638TMZ/info.htm

- www.starlinetours.com/los-angeles-tour-1.asp

Chocolate
- www.chocolatetourism.com
- Circus skills
- trapezearts.com
- https://secure.sydneytrapezeschool.com/indexUser.html

Coaststeering
- www.coasteeringni.co.uk/the-oldest-person-to-ever-go-coasteering
- Cookery
- www.responsibletravel.com/holidays/cooking

Curling
- www.stantonamarlberg.com/de

Cycling
- www.imaginative-traveller.com/activities/active/tours
- Diamond tours
- www.costerdiamonds.com/book-tour
- www.gassan.com/en

Diamond mine tour
- www.africansky.com/tours/1daypretoriaandcullinan.html
- www.thebighole.co.za
- www.southafrica.net/za/en/articles/entry/article-southafrica.net-the-diamond-works

Drumming
- www.african-drumming.co.uk

Extra terrestial Highway
- www.rachel-nevada.com/ethighway.html

Elephants
- www.responsibletravel.com/holidays/elephant-conservation
- www.holidaystosouthafrica.co.uk/the-elephant-sanctuary
- Gaming tour
- www.game.co.uk/en/epic-gaming-adventure-212890?cm_mmc=Affiliate-_-Tradedoubler-_-Skimlinks-_-Deep_link

Gaps years for grumpies
- www.gapsforgrumpies.com

- Gliding
- www.cotswoldgliding.co.uk/holiday_courses
- soaringcenter.net
- Golf
- www.kauricliffs.com/PicsHotel/CapeKidnappers/Brochure/2014/Tiger%20Tour,%20March%2013-22,%202015%20Itinerary.pdf

Gourmet
- www.holidaysplease.co.uk/news/gourmet-holiday
- Grizzly bear watching
- www.grizzlytours.com/bear-watching-tours-bc.php
- greatbeartours.com
- Grizzly bear reviews and ratings
- www.hellobc.com/british-columbia/things-to-do/parks-wildlife/bear-watching.aspx.

Haunted house
- www.hauntedrooms.co.uk
- Healing hotels
- healinghotelsoftheworld.com
- Heli-skiing
- www.canadianmountainholidays.com/heli-skiing.aspx

Helicopter trips
- chelipeacock.com/flying-safaris
- Hiking
- adventure.nationalgeographic.com/adventure/trips/best-trails/worlds-best-hikes-dream-trails
- Horse riding
- www.farandride.com/riding-holidays/usa/bitterroot_ranch_(wyoming)
- mustangmonument.com
- www.wildfrontierstravel.com/en_GB/experience/horses

Ice blokarting
- balticadventure.com/en/tours/199/ice-blokart-in-nida-lithuania.html

Ice climbing
- www.ice-factor.co.uk
- www.kelsotravel.com/activities/outdooradventures/iceclimbing

- www.responsibletravel.com/holiday/3415/ice-climbing-holiday-in-the-french-alps

Igloo resort
- www.kakslauttanen.fi
- Igloo hotel
- www.grandvalira.com/en/igloo-hotel-andorra

Islands
- denisisland.com/accommodation-2
- Jungle trekking
- www.eldertreks.com/style/rainforest_jungle&fontup=2

Kangaroo Island
- www.tourkangarooisland.com.au
- Kangaroo Island trips and holidays
- www.responsibletravel.com/holidays/kangaroo-island

Kangaroo safaris and marsupial safaris
- www.royle-safaris.co.uk/wildlife-tours/marsupials
- Kayaking
- www.exodus.co.uk/cultural-holidays/europe

Kite surfing
- www.arizonaloukiteboarder.com/about.html

Komodo Dragons
- www.beautifulworld.com/asia/indonesia/komodo-national-park

Laughter Yoga
- www.laughteryoga.org/english/home

Log cabins
- loghouseholidays.co.uk
- Luxury trains
- www.trans-siberian.co.uk/Golden-Eagle-from-Moscow.html
- www.goldeneagleluxurytrains.com/journeys/trans-siberian-express
- Meditation
- www.travel-quest.co.uk/tqmeditation.htm
- www.theretreatcompany.com/spiritual-retreats
- Model airplanes
- www.rchotel.com/.

Motor shows

- www.topmarquesmonaco.com/en/actualites/just-100-days-to-go.html,026

Movie tour
- veryfirstto.com/never-done-before/the-worlds-most-famous-film-locations-in-one-blockbuster-trip
- www.ramojifilmcity.com/category/film-city
- www.universalstudioshollywood.com
- vipstudiotour.warnerbros.com
- britmovietours.com
- Nature
- www.naturetrek.co.uk
- www.natureholiday.co.uk
- Naturist holidays
- travel.aol.co.uk/2011/10/28/dare-to-bare-all-naturist-holidays-around-the-world/#!slide=aol_1247932
- www.naturist.co.nz
- ewaterways.co.uk

Ninja
- www.blacktomato.com/country/japan/tokyo-learn-the-way-of-the-ninja
- Ocean rafting
- www.oceanrafting.com.au
- www.cruiseinbali.com/3-island-ocean-rafting-cruise-bali-hai-cruises
- Opera
- www.kirkerholidays.com/events-opera

Painting
- artsafari.co.uk
- www.authenticadventures.co.uk/painting-holidays
- artworkshops.homestead.com
- Paragliding
- www.skylarkparagliding.co.uk/trips.html
- www.birdmen.co.za
- Pilates
- www.healthandfitnesstravel.com/pilates-holidays

Photography
- www.responsibletravel.com/holidays/photography

Polar expedition
- www.exodus.co.uk/polar-holidays

Polo playing holidays
- www.brettpolo.com/polo-holidays
- www.playpolo.co.uk/argentina/polo-holidays
- Rafting
- www.waterbynature.com
- Renting unique homes
- www.oneoffplaces.co.uk
- Rodeo
- nationalwestern.com
- rodeosusa.com
- www.cfdrodeo.com
- Running of the bulls
- running-of-the-bulls.com
- Running
- www.runningcrazy.co.uk
- www.embracesports.co.uk
- Sailing
- www.anotherworldadventures.com/adventure-type/ interests/all-sailing-trips
- Scrabble
- www.travel-quest.co.uk/scrabble.htm

Shark dive
- www.blueplanetaquarium.com
- Skijorking
- winter.adventuresinthealps.com/skijoring
- Snowball hotel
- www.artisantravel.co.uk/holidays/lulea-jokkmokk-winter-market

Snowshoe
- www.icicle-mountaineering.ltd.uk/snowshoe.htm
- www.saint-bernard.ch/en/winter/being-active/leisure-and-relaxation/snow-shoes

Space travel
- www.countryholidays.com.hk/space
- Spy holidays
- www.virginexperiencedays.co.uk/spy-academy
- www.viewlondon.co.uk/experiences/spy-academy-info-255.html

- www.superstarsmemorabilia.co.uk/proddetail. asp?prod=Jamesbondday

Stalking Jaguars
- www.wildlifeworldwide.com/discover/wildlife/jaguar-watching

Stand-up comedy
- www.eventbrite.co.uk/e/jill-edwards-summer-holiday-stand-up-comedy-course-1-week-tickets-12500305751
- www.laughinghorsecomedy.co.uk/comedy/courses.asp

Star gazing
- www.darkskydiscovery.org.uk
- www.welcomechile.com/vicuna/mamalluca-astronomical-observatory.html

Storm chasing
- www.stormchasing.com
- www.silverliningtours.com
- Submarine safaris
- www.submarinesafaris.com
- Submarine Lovers Deep
- www.oliverstravels.com/caribbean/anywhere/lovers-deep
- Surfing
- www.surftaghazout.com
- Survival courses
- www.raymears.com/Bushcraft_Courses
- Swim with dolphins
- www.dolphinexpeditions.com
- right-tourism.com/issues/marine-activities/swimming-with-wild-animals/#sthash.ISJJviyx.dpbs

Table tennis
- www.tripadvisor.co.uk/Attraction_Review-g1726792-d1805869-Reviews-html

Tall ships
- www.adventureundersail.com/tall-ship-holidays.html
- www.classic-sailing.co.uk/tall-ships

Tennis
- www.tennisholiday.co.uk/news/suggested-accommodation-for-your-tennis-holiday-at-la-manga-club-26.html

- www.tennisresortsonline.com/trofiles/top-100-tennis-resorts-and-camps.cfm

Tiger hunting
- www.coxandkings.co.uk/tiger-safari

Tour the Australian outback
- www.outback-australia-travel-secrets.com/australian_outback.html

Tree planting
- treesforlife.org.uk
- Trekking
- www.lonelyplanet.com/travel-tips-and-articles/76228

Tubing
- www.snowtubingsource.com/top-10-largest-snow-tubing-parks
- The World
- aboardtheworld.com/our_story

Underwater accommodation
- www.atlantisthepalm.com/rooms/supersuites/underwater.aspx
- www.themantaresort.com
- www.conradmaldivesrangali.com
- www.jul.com/Jules.html
- www.poseidonresorts.com/#

Unique places
- www.palaciodesal.com.bo
- natureobservatorio.com/concepten.html
- www.jumbostay.com
- www.theboot.co.nz
- www.v8hotel.de/en/the-v8-hotel.html
- www.airbnb.co.uk/rooms/2563430

Vespa
- ww.personalguidesicily.com
- scootertourspain.com
- www.experiencetravelgroup.com/vietnam/exp/saigon-vespa-tour

Vintage cars
- www.schlossfuschlsalzburg.com/en/vintage-cars-limousines
- classictravelling.com/classic-car-tours/classic-tours

- Volcano
- www.blacktomato.com/country/iceland/the-ultimate-icelandic-volcano-adventure
- Whale watching
- www.whalewatching.com
- www.telegraph.co.uk/travel/activityandadventure/7397122/Whale-watching-10-of-the-best.html

White Desert
- www.white-desert.com
- Wine
- www.chateau-hospitalet.com/en
- chateaumusar.com
- Wisteria
- www.boredpanda.com/wisteria-flower-tunnel-kawachi-fuji-gardens-japan
- Wrestling
- www.senegal.co.uk/domaine-les-paletuviers?&back=true

Xanadu
- www.youramazingplaces.com/the-100-most-beautiful-and-breathtaking-places-in-the-world-in-pictures-part-1
- daddu.net/most-beautiful-places-in-the-world
- Yachting
- www.visit-croatia.co.uk/index.php/activities-croatia/sailing-croatia
- www.seychelles.travel/component/content/article/37-explore/special-interest/54-sailing

Yachting/sailing destinations
- www.touristmaker.com/blog/top-10-world-s-best-yachting-destinations
- miglife.net/best-yachting-destinations-around-the-world
- usatodaytravels.com/best-sailing-destinations-in-the-world.html

Best yachting towns
- www.yachtingmagazine.com/50-best-yachting-towns-3

Yak safaris
- www.travelblog.org/Asia/Pakistan/Northern-Areas/Hunza/Passu/blog-677997.html
- www.bhutantravelplan.co.uk/trekking-in-bhutan.htm

Yodelling
- www.ski-buzz.co.uk/austria/yodel-your-way-to-the-tirol-win-a-summer-trip-to-mayrhofen
- Zero gravity flights
- www.space.com/8709-hand-family-unforgettable-gravity-holiday.html

Zero G
- www.gozerog.com/index.cfm

Zip wires
- www.zip2000.com
- www.edenproject.com/visit-us/whats-here/adventure-activities/zip-wire
- ziprider.com/rides/coppercanyon
- www.gravitycanyon.co.nz/activities/fox

About The Author

A graduate of the University of Keele in Staffordshire, Carol E Wyer is a former teacher, linguist, and physical trainer.

She spent her early working life in Casablanca, Morocco, where she translated for companies and taught English as a foreign language. She then returned to work in education back in the UK and set up her own language company in the late eighties.

In her forties, Carol retrained to become a personal trainer to assist people, who, like herself, had undergone major surgery.

Having spent the last decade trying out all sorts of new challenges such as kickboxing, diving, and flying helicopters, she is now ensuring her fifties are "fab not drab". She has put her time to good use by learning to paint, attempting to teach herself Russian, and writing a series of novels and articles which take a humorous look at getting older.

Carol lives in rural Staffordshire with her own retired Grumpy. It is little wonder that she is a regular blogger and social networking addict.

Mini Skirts and Laughter Lines

Amanda Wilson can't decide between murder, insanity, or another glass of red wine. Facing fifty and all that it entails is problematic enough. What's the point in minking your eyes when your husband would rather watch Russia Today than admire you strutting in front of the television in only thigh boots and a thong?

Her son has managed to perform yet another magical disappearing act. Could he actually be buried under the mountain of festering washing strewn on his bedroom floor? He'll certainly be buried somewhere when she next gets her hands on him.

At least her mother knows how to enjoy herself. She's partying her twilight years away in Cyprus. Queen of the Twister mat, she now has a toy boy in tow.

Amanda knows she shouldn't have pressed that Send button. The past always catches up with you sooner or later. Still, her colourful past is a welcome relief to her monochrome present—especially when it comes in the shape of provocative Todd Bradshaw, her first true love.

Amanda has a difficult decision to make – one that will require more than a few glasses of Chianti.

Surfing in Stilettos

Amanda Wilson is all geared up for an exciting gap-year, travelling across Europe. She soon finds her plans thwarted when she is abandoned in France with only a cellarful of Chateau Plonk, a large, orange Space Hopper, and Old Ted, the dog, for company.

Fate has intervened to turn Amanda's life on its head. First, Bertie, the camper van, breaks down. Then her dopey son, Tom, who is staying in their house in the UK, is wrecking it, one piece at a time. Next, the jaw-dropping video Skype calls that her irrepressible mother insists on making are, by contrast, making Amanda's humdrum trip even less palatable.

Finally, she discovers that her new-found, French friend, Bibi Chevalier, had engineered a plan to ensure that her philandering husband would never stray again; unfortunately, Amanda is unwittingly drawn into the scheme, becoming a target.

Meanwhile, on a beach in Sydney, a lonely Todd Bradshaw realises that his first true love, Amanda Wilson, is definitely the only woman for him. Can he get back into her good books and hopefully back into her arms with his latest plan? Or will fate intervene yet again and turn everyone's lives upside down?

Just Add Spice

Dawn Ellis needs to escape from her painfully dull existence. Her unemployed husband spends all day complaining about life, moping around, or fixing lawnmowers on her kitchen table. The local writing class proves to be an adequate distraction with its eccentric collection of wannabe authors and, of course, the enigmatic Jason, who soon shows a romantic interest in her.

Dawn pours her inner frustrations into her first novel about the extraordinary exploits of Cinnamon Knight, an avenging angel -- a woman who doesn't believe in following the rules. Cinnamon is ruthless and wanton, inflicting suffering on any man who warrants it. Little does Dawn realise that soon the line between reality and fiction will blur. Her own life will be transformed, and those close to her will pay the price.

How Not To Murder Your Grumpy

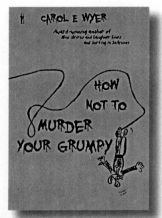

Is your Grumpy Old Man getting under your feet? Is he wrestling with retirement? Are you wondering if you should bundle him up and entrust him to basket-weaving classes? Then this book could be the answer to your prayers. This light hearted guide is packed full of lively ideas, anecdotes and quips. Not only does it set out to provide laughs, but offers over 700 ideas and ways to keep a Grumpy Old Man occupied.

From collecting airline sick bags to zorbing, you will be sure to find an absorbing pastime for your beloved curmudgeon. There are examples of those who have faced extraordinary challenges in older age, fascinating facts to interest a reluctant partner and innovative ideas drizzled, of course, with a large dollop of humour.

Written tongue-in-cheek, this book succeeds in proving that getting older doesn't mean the end of life or having fun. It provides amusing answers to the question, "How on Earth will my husband fill in his time in his retirement?" It offers suggestions on what might, or most certainly might not, amuse him. Ideal for trivia buffs, those approaching retirement, (or just at a loose end) and frustrated women who have an irritable male on their hands, this book will lighten any mood and may even prevent the odd murder.

Grumpy old Menopause

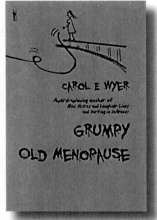

Have you started to write post-it notes with your kids' names on them? Do you need to change your underwear after every sneeze? Guess it's time to read this book then. It'll help you get through "that" time in your life with a spring in your step and a smile on your face.

With numerous suggestions, sensible advice and amusing anecdotes, Grumpy Old Menopause will help you sail through that tricky part of a woman's life with ease and humour. It should prevent you from turning into Mrs Crabby or worse still, a demonic monster.

"An excellent mix of humour and sound advice. This book is a must-read for all women ... I highly recommend Grumpy Old Menopause. It is the perfect blend of humour and excellent advice to help all women sail through the menopause." - Nicky Snazell, Fi STOP Consultant Physiotherapist in Spinal Pain, Fellow of Institute for the Study and Treatment of Pain. International Lecturer in Pain and Health

Three Little Birds

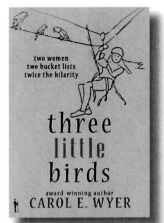

two women
two bucket lists
twice the hilarity

three
little
birds

award-winning author
CAROL E. WYER

Charlie Blundell cannot get over the tragic death of her only daughter. She drifts between her job at the Art cafe and her hospital radio show, the only things which give her life purpose.

Her best friend, the madcap Mercedes, cajoles Charlie into writing a 'carpe diem' list, but then swaps Charlie's list with her own. Now, each must complete the other's challenges, and the outcomes will astound both of them. The challenges begin as a series of relatively harmless, fun activities. Soon, though, the stakes increase when Charlie has to complete her challenges to save the hospital radio station.

As the tasks become more demanding, a handsome stranger takes an interest in her, but he is not what he seems. One challenge causes a secret buried deep within her to surface, which may prove to be her undoing.

Three Little Birds is a story of love, friendship and discovery, laced with hilarity and topped by a wickedly funny parrot called Bert.

Lightning Source UK Ltd.
Milton Keynes UK
UKOW04f1049280615

254231UK00003B/69/P